Security in a greater Europe

MANCHEstER
1824
Manchester University Press

Security in a greater Europe

The possibility of a pan-European approach

Charlotte Wagnsson

Manchester University Press
Manchester and New York
distributed exclusively in the USA by Palgrave Macmillan

The right of Charlotte Wagnsson to be identified as the author of this work has been asserted by her in accordance with the Copyright, Designs and Patents Act 1988.

Published by Manchester University Press
Oxford Road, Manchester M13 9NR, UK
and Room 400, 175 Fifth Avenue, New York, NY 10010, USA
www.manchesteruniversitypress.co.uk

Distributed in the United States exclusively by
Palgrave Macmillan, 175 Fifth Avenue,
New York, NY 10010, USA

Distributed in Canada exclusively by
UBC Press, University of British Columbia, 2029 West Mall,
Vancouver, BC, Canada V6T 1Z2

British Library Cataloguing-in-Publication Data is available

Library of Congress Cataloging-in-Publication Data is available

ISBN 978 0 7190 8671 7 paperback

First published by Manchester University Press in hardback 2008

This paperback edition first published 2012

The publisher has no responsibility for the persistence or accuracy of URLs for any external or third-party internet websites referred to in this book, and does not guarantee that any content on such websites is, or will remain, accurate or appropriate.

Printed by Lightning Source

Contents

Preface

Throughout the lengthy journey of writing this book, I have benefited from constructive comments provided by participants at the ECPR conferences in Cantebury (2001), Bordeaux (2002), The Hague (2004) and Istanbul (2006), and at the ISA conferences in Budapest (2003) and San Diego (2006). A few commentators who I have met in different forums deserve special mention: Ian Manners, Richard Bengtsson, Knud-Erik Jörgensen and Adrian Hyde-Price. Johan Eriksson provided extremely useful comments on constructivism and other theoretical issues and Arita Eriksson generously shared her expertise in European security.

I thank Bo Petersson for providing valuable and constructive comments throughout this project: his support and encouragement have been of great importance.

I want to thank Jan Hallenberg for encouraging me to join the Swedish National Defence College, and the head of department, Christina Weglert, who played a key role in creating the pleasant environment in which to work. The department held stimulating meetings and discussions during which Kjell Engelbrekt and Bertil Nygren provided useful comments. I extend my sincere thanks to Andrew Mash for supporting me with editing and proofreading the early drafts and the team at Manchester University Press for their help during the book production process. My thanks also go to Lars-Olof Allard, Bertil Nygren and Stephen Henly for help with translations and transcriptions.

Maria Hellman has played a vital role in this project. With a special eye for essential methodological and theoretical aspects, she functions as my key intellectual discussion partner. She has selflessly taken time to read and provide detailed comments on the manuscript.

Finally, I wish to thank my family: Fredrik for his encouragement, Nathan for distracting me in his own pleasant way, Louise for providing me with a lively break and Nadine for offering me yet another one. My mother Marie-Louise deserves special appreciation. I dedicate this book to her.

List of abbreviations

CIS	Commonwealth of Independent States
CFSP	Common Foreign and Security Policy
COPS	European Union Political and Security Committee
EEC	European Economic Community
ENPs	European Union Neighbourhood Policies
EPC	European Political Cooperation
ESDP	European Security and Defence Policy
ESS	European Security Strategy
EU	European Union
EUMS	European Union Military Staff
EUROPOL	European Law Enforcement Organisation
KFOR	Kosovo Force (NATO)
NATO	North Atlantic Treaty Organisation
NGO	non-governmental organisation
OSCE	Organisation for Security and Co-operation in Europe
PCA	Partnership and Cooperation Agreement
PJC	Permanent Joint Euro-Atlantic Partnership Council
PPC	Permanent Partnership Council
UN	United Nations
WTO	World Trade Organisation

1 Security in a greater Europe

Introduction

> No one calls into question the great value of Europe's relations with the United States. I am just of the opinion that Europe will reinforce its reputation as a strong and truly independent centre of world politics, soundly and for a long time, if it succeeds in bringing together its own potential and that of Russia, including its human, territorial and natural resources and its economic, cultural and defence potential. Together we have already taken the first steps in that direction. The time has now come to think about what should be done to make sure that a united and secure Europe becomes the harbinger of a united and secure world.[1]

Two weeks after the terrorist attacks of 11 September 2001, the Russian President sketched a grand vision of Russia and the European Union (EU) joining forces in world politics to develop into a 'truly independent centre of world affairs'. Was it a statement made on the spur of the moment? Or did perhaps the Russian President seize an opportunity during the turbulence of post-9/11 to push for much sought after closer EU–Russia relations? In fact, President Putin was only accentuating a decade-long foreign and security policy trend.

Since the late 1990s, Russia and the EU had gained influence in the international arena by pooling diplomatic efforts in some vital areas, such as regional conflicts in the Middle East and the need to strengthen the United Nations (UN). A joint approach could further strengthen their impact on major global issues where both want to 'make the European voice heard'. Russia, with its long experience as a highly active and experienced actor in the international arena and with a seat on the UN Security Council, could add weight to the EU's emergent global diplomacy.[2]

Together with Japan, China and the United States, Russia and the EU are the powers most commonly listed in discussions about the outlook for a potentially multipolar world in the twenty-first century.[3] A joint Moscow-Brussels approach would mean that both stand a significantly better chance of turning Europe into a major pole in world affairs and of increasing its relative strength vis-à-vis the USA. The EU cannot compete with the USA militarily in quantitative terms, but the two are clearly on an equal footing in the economic realm.[4] The EU is strong in other areas as well; in the environmental sector it has even divested the USA of its role as global leader.[5] Moreover, in the past decade the EU has challenged the USA as the world's leading 'moral' power as it has come to present a different ethics for international and security relations. Whereas the USA remains true to its longstanding ideal of the spread of freedom, the EU promotes human rights and the rule of law. If the EU and Russia can harmonise their 'ethical efforts', by pushing for a more strict application of rule of law in international relations, this might limit the USA's freedom of manoeuvre in the international arena.

Although it is highly unlikely that EU member states would give up their established partnership with the USA,[6] they could choose to pursue policies on specific global security issues that impinge on US aims – which was also done by a small number of European states during the 2003 Iraq war. If the EU becomes increasingly cohesive, and in addition allies itself more closely with Russia, such European deviations from US policy might become increasingly problematic for policy makers in Washington. The EU and Russia already jointly diverge from the USA on key issues in the security sphere. Both disapprove of the current unipolar system, with its hegemon that from time to time resorts to unilateral behaviour, preferring instead multilateralism and a multipolar world where Europe would form a significant bloc. They may also satisfy their respective needs for a stronger self-image by way of negative identification with their transatlantic 'other'.[7]

Yet, wide divisions persist within the European security sphere. During its pursuit of greater 'actorness' in security affairs, tensions between EU member states, demonstrated during the Iraq war, have continually caused friction inside the EU. Russia, in turn, diverges from Western Europe on some key issues, such as on the spread of norms in the international arena. These and other cleavages present the USA with an opportunity to play up divisions in order to prevent Europe from developing into a cohesive global actor that might become too independent from Washington.

In order to provide further insight into how and to what degree major European security actors converge and diverge, this book presents an extensive and thorough analysis of official standpoints. The focus is on the relationship between the EU and Russia, but also on bilateral relations between Russia and the major EU member states.

The term 'Europe' needs clarification. This volume distinguishes between 'EU-Europe', which includes the EU and its member states, and 'greater Europe', which envisages Russia, the EU and its member states. It would be unsatisfactory to limit the analysis to Russia and the EU. Closer cooperation between Russia and Europe in the security sphere hinges not only on relations between Russia and the EU, but to a significant degree on bilateral relations. The empirical enquiry therefore contrasts Russia's standpoints on security with those of the EU bureaucracy and with those of the three major EU member states: France, Germany and the United Kingdom.

Despite differing in various ways, ranging from culture to size and from economy to political system, France, the UK, Germany and Russia share experiences of being great powers – major European states with shared histories and memories. Yet, Russian leaders continually express doubts about whether their country is regarded as part of Europe by the remainder of the European states. This book does not aim to determine whether Russia is, or is perceived to be, a part of Europe; but it does explore in detail how some official standpoints tend to facilitate while others place barriers in the way of further cooperation between Russia and various leaderships located within 'EU-Europe'.

The possibility of a pan-European approach

During the Cold War, governments faced a wide range of potentially destabilising threats. Nevertheless their ultimate common aim was quite clear: to keep the world secure from nuclear war. Although much of the current security policy debate still revolves around how to stop the spread of weapons of mass destruction, nuclear war is not currently at the top of politicians' security policy agendas. Instead, the new, more multi-faceted post-Cold War security situation begs the question: what are the leading actors in the security sphere claiming to protect in the twenty-first century? Have Russia, the major EU member states and the EU reached a level of unanimity that will enable them to pursue a unified policy? What priority do the individual leaderships give to central 'referent-objects' of security, such as human rights, the principles of a market economy, the 'transatlantic link', democracy and international institutions; and how does each leadership differ?[8]

The aims of this book are to gauge the kind of security agendas that the major European players are pursuing, and to assess the implications these have for greater Europe's chances of emerging as a unified global diplomat. It compares the rhetoric of the EU, the United Kingdom, Germany, France and Russia in connection with three defining events in international security – the crisis in Kosovo in 1999, the terrorist attacks of 11 September 2001 and the Iraq crisis in 2003 – in order to assess whether they display a tendency to defend similar referent-objects of security. The empirical enquiry provides an indication of Europe's ability to unite, which in turn has implications for US policy.

The first case (Kosovo 1999) involved a 'wake up call' that sparked the evolution of the European Security and Defence Policy (ESDP). It was also one of the significant events that prompted a reconsideration of norms and rules for action in the international system. It was later used as both a negative and a positive example of how conflicts should be handled.

The second case (11 September 2001) serves to illuminate important dividing lines and convergences among the European actors. For many, it signified a paradigm shift after which international interaction abandoned its dominant focus on state-to-state relations. A new, diffuse and not even united actor – international terrorism – had interrupted the ordinary mechanisms of international relations. The events of 11 September 2001 prompted a reconsideration of norms and rules for action. In the USA, a number of the rules of international conduct were henceforth ignored. The US administration claimed that the USA was at war. In Europe, political leaders also had to adjust to the fact that a largely unknown enemy with an extraordinary capacity to create chaos now threatened traditional states and their citizens. The second case study focuses on how the Europeans officially interpreted 11 September 2001, and on what, in essence, was at stake in the face of this evil. Did their basic standpoints as expressed during the Kosovo conflict remain the same or were they altered by the new global security situation? Did cleavages among actors narrow or widen?

The final case study (the war in Iraq of spring 2003) also discusses a major crisis, and one that continues to affect global security dynamics. The USA invaded Iraq, using as its key argument that rogue states with links to terrorism demand forceful action. According to the 2002 version of the US National Security Strategy, the USA would defend itself not only in a reactive way, but also in a proactive way – invoking self-defence in order to act pre-emptively against terrorists.[9] Thus, disregarding the lack of a United Nations Security Council resolution, and with the support of only one of the four states studied in this volume, the USA invaded Iraq. Rules for action and norms of behaviour in international relations were clearly at stake. How did the four states and the EU respond to this challenge to habitual practice in global affairs? What did they stand up for or defend? Were the major dividing lines that had crystallised during the previous two crises exacerbated?

In order to increase our understanding of the ability of greater Europe to unite in the sphere of security, we need to gain deeper knowledge and understanding of the standpoints of individual European actors on these crises. The cases were not selected with a view to test a hypothesis, i.e. they were not selected from the exigency of a traditional positivist study. The case studies serve to identify tensions and convergences among key European actors at critical instances in the evolution of the ESDP in order to deepen our understanding of that evolution. Since the basic preferences of European leaderships are most easily revealed during times of major crisis, when rules for action and norms of behaviour in international relations are at stake, such crises were selected for analysis. The study can also demonstrate how political preferences change – or remain stable – over time.

Competing constructions of security

Some thirty years ago, security was predominantly about escaping nuclear disaster. In the contemporary globalising world, the kind of security that political leaderships pursue is far from self-evident. Politicians tend to advocate 'security' in order to protect anything from the environment to the economy or a specific national or religious identity. As a result, security agendas have come to diverge more between states, even among allies.

This calls for an analysis that can reveal the extent to which leaderships advocate rival versions of security. Such research does not make judgments about what security is in any objective sense, but instead provides an open-minded account of how leaderships strive to accomplish their favoured version of security. The ensuing empirical account of official standpoints allows each actor to 'speak for itself', and this produces a unique set of comparable 'stories on security' from the points of view of each of the key European actors.[10]

A constructivist approach to security studies suits such an ambition particularly well, since constructivism involves the conviction that the concept of security is context-bound and requires specification.[11] It is an approach less circumscribed by preconceptions about the nature of international relations, and about the standpoints that national leaderships have historically tended to take.[12]

In contrast, both liberal and neorealist scholars adopt a more narrow analytical focus. In line with a pessimistic stance on the likelihood of cooperation and of the emergence of an international society, neorealists play down the impact of norms and instead take into account capabilities and interests.[13] They gain an acute argument on the EU's weaknesses as a security actor but lose out on a much needed complex and multifaceted analysis of European security that includes norms and values. Many liberals, on the other hand, who believe and approve of the EU's normative actorness, tend to overemphasise its internal cohesion.[14] By placing similarities among member states in the foreground, such research designs cannot address the problematic issue of exactly *which* norms the individual governments promote, and the price they are prepared to pay to achieve these.

In addition to existing research, then, we need to pay attention to the way in which EU member states interpret the meaning of 'being normative', and how the EU negotiates between different versions of morality. This volume reveals serious divergences on these issues, both in core EU documents and between EU member states. Tensions between the three major member states on the nature of 'morality' are key to understanding the major challenges that lie ahead of the EU.

Furthermore, constructivism involves a reliance on the significance and power of language and it is therefore a suitable approach for mapping out cleavages and similarities in the actors' interpretations of the political world. Describing and defining the world in one way or another is essentially a power play; the power of definition affects the essence of a debate and determines which issues are included or excluded in a communication process.[15] The battle for control of a political debate is, in turn, a central battle in political reality.[16] As Murray Edelman highlights, it is:

> language about political events, not the events in any other sense, that people experience; even developments that are close by take their meaning from the language that depicts them. So political language is political reality; there is no other so far as the meaning of events to actors and spectators is concerned.[17]

Thus, if EU member states do not speak the same language, if they do not direct their attention towards the same goals, it is harder to realise common objectives in the sphere of security. Similarly, the European governments and the EU are most likely to pursue further cooperation with Russia if their basic official standpoints on and understandings of what ought to be protected do not deviate too much.

Norms and interests: the essence of security

Leaderships normally justify security strategies with reference to both interests and norms. The need to seek legitimacy is vital in modern politics, and normative considerations are as central as interests in official justifications of security policies. State representatives are obliged to present an acceptable moral basis for their politics in both the domestic and the international arena. The transformation of the global political theatre from a war between communism and capitalism to a new script makes it even more important to provide a legitimate basis for security policy.[18]

As a result, in order to obtain a full picture of how a leadership rationalises its security policy, it is not possible either to restrict the analysis to a focus on interests, as realists tend to do, or focus strictly on ideas, identities and other variables central to the constructivist research agenda.[19] It is essential to remain open to how two different main types of logic – rational calculations linked to interests, and statements linked to identities and norms – mix into political messages.[20]

The ensuing analysis reveals which European actors converge best with regard to norms and interests and, as a consequence, are most likely to cooperate. It seems likely that Europe would unite in normative and interest-based issue-areas where it disagrees with the USA. If this is the case, it is vital to be able to identify such areas in order better to understand past disputes, and foresee possible future crises, in transatlantic relations. It is useful to know precisely on which fundamental issues individual European leaderships have tended to agree and disagree in the recent past.

It might be expected that the actors will diverge on a number of important standpoints that have implications for their ability to undertake joint action. The leaderships are likely to deviate over the norms they wish to protect and promote in the international arena, the importance of the export of norms for the sake of stability, and the means they consider legitimate for the export of norms. They will differ on the role the USA should play in the world and on the actions that are legitimate in order to protect the world from terrorism. Diverging views on the role of the UN and the EU in world affairs are also examples of areas that could make concerted European action in the world more complicated. This volume sets out to discover how the leaderships differ, the potential for convergence and the implications this has for the USA.

The investigation focuses on the standpoints adopted by the leaderships during times of crisis, when they are likely to defend their most fundamental positions in the security sphere. An in-depth analysis of official reactions to events in the sphere of 'hard security' can expose the fine detail of differences of emphasis and nuance over core issues such as polarity, the nature of alliances, intervention and the role of norms in global affairs.

In line with the constructivist approach, state identities and interests are not treated as given and leaderships can change their standpoints over time due to both external and internal events and processes, for example, a change of regime in another country. The analysis focuses on processes of change and continuity, remaining open to shifts of meaning in leaderships' political messages. Notably, when referring to the 'British', 'French' or 'Russian' position, I envisage the position taken by the political regime in power at the time, and not a 'fixed' national standpoint. The three case studies can thus inform us about the durability of the actors' standpoints. If a leadership is shown to rally round a small number of favoured basic referent-objects of security when faced with a crisis, it is likely to react in a similar fashion during future crises.

How, then, do we recognise a 'norm' or an 'interest' in a political text? In line with the classical realist Hans Morgenthau, this study understands the concept of 'interests' in connection with the broad concepts of influence, power and security. Using Morgenthau's definition as a starting point, the study defines an argument as belonging to the analytical category of 'interests' if the leader rationalises an argument as being part of a strategy to counter security threats or to maximise the state's (or the EU's) political power.[21]

Norms, in turn, are defined in accordance with Peter Katzenstein, who perceives of norms as 'collective expectations for the proper behaviour of actors with a given identity'.[22] 'Norms' define what is considered to be 'standard' or 'normal' for an actor in a given social context.[23] In the framing analysis below, norms are seen as the building blocks of ideologies, religions, political systems and other collective ideational constructs. The analysis maps out statements that include references to 'democratic norms', 'liberal norms', and norms underpinning a system aimed at 'justice', 'equal treatment', and so on. If an actor refers to shared norms, ideologies or morally appropriate behaviour, this is defined as a normative message.

In many cases, norms and interests are mutually reinforcing in a line of argument. The sort of interests decision makers pursue in a particular period is related to the political and cultural restraints – linked to ideas, identities and social interaction with other actors – of their surroundings. The study of the evolution of norms is therefore important to an understanding of the evolution of interests and vice versa.[24] The point, therefore, is not to judge who defends interests and who defends norms, but what *kind* of norms and interests the various actors claim to protect. The focus on interests will reveal whether a leadership places state interests above individual security or vice versa, while the focus on norms will expose whether a leadership primarily promotes the liberal values underpinning the free market or a more equal world order.

Official standpoints: opening and closing windows for cooperation

Governments often cooperate for dissimilar reasons. Convergence of official goals is normally a sufficient basis for cooperation. The fact that Russia and the EU might defend the UN's central position in world affairs for quite different reasons does not reduce their chances of making joint efforts to strengthen the organisation's status. Similarly, even though signatory powers to the Kyoto Protocol disagree on the exact meaning and implications of the complex issue of climate change, they nevertheless signed the agreement making concrete their shared intent to address the problem of environmental security. This shows that the vital question is whether the leaderships express convergence on a standpoint, not why they do so. As a result, the analysis takes account of justifications and refrains from uncovering hidden intent, even though occasional references to historical memories and other under-lying driving forces that can provide a clue to the durability of an actor's position are mentioned.[25]

Features such as these are sought through a framing analysis, the intent of which is to unravel differences at the rhetorical level that have political effects. Politicians have to consider the words and concepts they use carefully in order to fit them into their social context, where certain shared symbols are used in order to facilitate communication.[26] Yet, leaders tend to provide shared concepts with different meanings. While one actor may associate the concept of 'multipolarity' primarily with a balance of power, another actor may link it to a just world order where no single state can impose its will on another. Such competing frames ultimately lead to policy differences.[27]

The frames that this study seeks to reveal are located in texts, and are identifiable by the appearance of certain key concepts and phrases.[28] In practice, the target of the analysis is political *rhetoric* or 'persuasive communi-cation'.[29] Such rhetoric is used to describe and justify security policy, which in Schön and Rhein's words result in so-called rhetorical frames.[30]

In this sense, the framing analysis, and the kind of constructivism that this study builds on, bear a certain resemblance to discourse analysis. However, as opposed to the framing approach, discourse analysis is often informed by an ambition to unmask dominant discourses that serve to oppress other inter-pretations of the political world.[31] Also, discourse analysis maps patterns of ideological and ideational meaning that are located in texts, whereas framing analysis, as applied in this context, aims more narrowly at certain key parts of the political message. It focuses specifically on what is at stake, how a problem is constituted, how it should be evaluated and the plausible solutions that exist in relation to it.[32] Discourse theorists distinguish themselves in other ways as well, for example, by expecting texts to be largely structured in terms of binary oppositions.[33]

The framing method was developed in social movement research and is used widely in media studies, but it has only been applied to security studies to a limited extent.[34] This volume demonstrates that framing is particularly useful in the area of security studies, in that vital components of security politics – such as how guilt and responsibility are allocated and how the salience of a problem is being judged or looked on – are also central to the framing approach.

A key aspect of framing analysis that is also vital to the political processes is *problem definition*. How a problem is defined is key to political processes since it has repercussions for both political standpoints and the solutions envisaged. Solutions may determine problem definition. Politicians are inclined to emphasise those aspects of a problem to which their favoured political solutions apply. Problem definition is closely linked to agenda setting and thus normally includes identifying both the emergence of problems and, depending on the answer, how they should be resolved.[35]

The question of guilt is normally the most prominent of all aspects of problem definition, which brings us to the issues of *causal interpretation* and *moral evaluation* – framing aspects centred on *who* or *what* is to blame.[36] The political rhetoric analysed in the three case studies is strongly coloured by different techniques for apportioning blame. This is no surprise since security politics are generally quite focused on defining an 'other' – not only to identify the nature of the problem or threat, but also to strengthen an actor's own identity.[37]

This study deals with the deliberate strategic framing used to influence a receiver, as opposed to subconscious or cognitive framing. Strategic framing aims to make certain features or interpretations of politics *salient* to the audience, that is, to make these stand out in the process of communication in order to impose a particular meaning or understanding on an audience.[38] This may be done by use of well-known concepts, by references to shared memories or by frequent repetition.

How actors make sense of a problem also depends on the *level of analysis* that they employ.[39] The analysis below asks whether actors evaluate a problem primarily from the standpoint of European or global security. It is reasonable to assume that a problem is a more salient issue if politicians link it not only to the European, but also to the global security situation. An issue linked to the global security situation is assumed to be treated as a more salient problem than one that is linked merely to the European context.

Finally, a key political battleground in the international arena during a crisis situation is the question of who, or which institutional vehicle, to appoint as 'problem solver'. This is intimately connected to identifying the cause of and the solution to the problem at hand, that is, to issues of *responsibility* and *mandate*. It raises the question of who is entitled to deal with a security problem or who according to some might have an obligation to do so: the UN, the North Atlantic Treaty Organisation (NATO), a nation state or perhaps the EU?

The analysis is conducted using all the statements made by the relevant actors – in the form of speeches, interviews and public statements – about the three particular crises. The study makes use of the customary method of analysing the politics of national security by focusing on the most senior representatives of nation states.[40] By doing so, it treats the state as a unitary actor and does not investigate internal dynamics and policy processes. Of concern are the positions the governments and the EU actually took, and the signals they sent to the external world – signals that had tangible consequences for their relations with partners in the international arena. Statements are of interest not in terms of the individual actors' opinions, but as building blocks that together make up or construct each state's official policy.

Who, then, speaks at the EU level? A small number central actors act as the primary spokespersons for the EU on matters related to the Common Foreign and Security Policy (CFSP) and the ESDP. The major focus is on the Secretary-General of the Council and High Representative for the Common Foreign and Security Policy, the Commissioner for External Relations, the

President of the Commission and the Presidency. These actors are given the task of clarifying and justifying EU policy, and may correctly be called the primary framing actors of EU security policy for the purpose of this study. The analysis remains alive to potential tensions between these actors, who may clash as a result of their different institutional memberships. A few major sources of 'EU reasoning' on security are included as well: the 2003 EU Security Strategy; Presidency conclusions from the regular summits; conclusions from the European Council, which brings together the Heads of State or Government and the President of the European Commission; joint statements emanating from EU–Russia summits; and a few additional official documents that explain EU standpoints on security issues.

'EU-Europe' as a security actor

The advent of the EU as an actor in the security sphere that takes a diplomatic line of its own means that a powerful player – and a new kind of actor – has become entrenched in the traditional struggle for power but also the common good in the European security area. What does this mean to the established European security actors? Do institutional constraints and binding agreements push the EU leadership's reasoning towards a common EU policy line?

Further EU integration in the security sphere – at least with regard to hard security – is hard to foresee if there are fundamental differences between member states, and between member states and official EU policy. The ensuing scrutiny of greater Europe's ability to unite on its attitude to global affairs therefore focuses on the policy lines of Russia, the EU bureaucracy and the three 'key member states'. The analysis explores the ways in which the three are caught up in their customary national rhetoric, while at the same time forming the constituent parts of an EU that is attempting to forge a separate and stronger identity as an actor in the security sphere. It provides an important, albeit not exhaustive, measure of the degree of consistency within the EU.[41]

In addition to being key member states, France, Germany and the UK are particularly important partners for Russia and therefore central to the potential emergence of 'greater Europe' as an actor in global affairs. Yet, the three states represent different fundamental outlooks on the world and the EU. In Germany, EU integration has traditionally been treated as an alternative to German nationalism. French leaderships have largely seen the EU as a suitable vehicle for realising their own international ambitions. The UK has regarded the EU with scepticism and has sought to ensure that the USA remains involved in European security affairs. Such differences are likely to colour the rhetoric of the national leaderships, but whether this is the case and how it is expressed are for the empirical analyses to answer.

The EU, in turn, differs from its parts. State-centric balance of power thinking characterised European security politics for centuries. The EU has forged an alternative way of operating, demonstrating that former antagonists can integrate, and that competitiveness can turn into the evolution of a 'security community'.[42]

For a long time, the EU did not display actorness in the international sphere.[43] As an actor manoeuvred by traditional member states that were far from coordinated between each other in the sphere of security, it primarily maintained regional perspective on foreign and security policy. Until 1993, its external dimension was not even officially defined as 'foreign policy'; the European Political Cooperation (EPC) was merely intended to coordinate the policies of the member states.

However, in recent years the EU has developed its capacity to act both within and beyond its borders. In the early 1990s aid programmes were launched in the countries of the former Soviet Union, followed after 1993 by more developed relations with non-European countries in Asia, South America, the Mediterranean and North America.[44] The Maastricht Treaty created the CFSP in 1993. It was revised in 1996–97 and the changes were institutionalised in the Treaty of Amsterdam of 1999. An accord between the France and the UK in St Malo in December 1998 was an important milestone in the process of reform.

At the Cologne European Council in June 1999, a decision was made to develop the ESDP and to negotiate a military dimension, aimed at developing a more autonomous defence capability. The Helsinki Headline Goal process subsequently resulted in the creation of substantially increased actorness in the sphere of security. The aim was to create an EU Military Force of 50–60,000 persons to carry out the Petersberg tasks defined in the Amsterdam Treaty, and to develop capability goals in the fields of command and control, intelligence and strategic transport. New permanent political and military bodies were also established: a Standing Political and Security Committee of national representatives at senior/ambassadorial level exercises the political control and strategic direction of operations under the authority of the Council; a Military Committee composed of the Chiefs of Defence represented by military delegates provides military advice, and a Military Staff offers military expertise and performs early-warning, situation assessment and strategic planning for the Petersberg tasks.

The concrete process of strengthening the EU's actorness has been accompanied by visionary statements portraying an actor with a truly global perspective in the sphere of security. The EU also claims to possess exceptional qualities as an actor in the security sphere. According to the European Security Strategy, dealing with new threats requires a combination of economic, humanitarian, intelligence, judicial, military and other means.[45] The EU is also said to have capacity because of its ability to keep particular structural processes in motion. Its particular form of multilevel governance gives rise to structural processes – such as aid for development, crisis prevention and stabilising non-member states and regions – that have long-term consequences. The EU diverges from the notion of 'defence policy' in the military sense by taking a broader approach to security that includes a range of areas.

In addition, Charlotte Bretherton and John Vogler argue that the EU wields influence not only when it acts, but also by its way of being a new kind of entity; it exerts influence as a model regional economic integration or as an 'island of peace'.[46] Similarly, Ian Manners argues that it wields a particular kind of power – the capacity to redefine what is considered 'normal' in international relations.[47]

Yet, the EU's security policy still evolves and changes as a result of the interplay between the standpoints of its member states. The unpredictable nature of the integration process makes it all the more fascinating to study, and all the more important to seek out variables and 'explanations' that make it less 'unpredictable'. The intriguing puzzle of how a common policy can be forged from a range of separate national positions merits special attention.

Background to EU–Russia relations

This volume does not just take the EU into account, it also asks how closely the EU is likely to cooperate with Russia in order to gain leverage in global affairs – possibly even by turning away from the USA. The analysis in Chapters 2–6 investigates obstacles at the rhetorical level that could hamper further rapprochement; do Russia and 'EU-Europe' speak the same language, defend the same norms and values, and aim to achieve the same kind of security?

The prospects for increased EU–Russia cooperation and rapprochement looked gloomy in 2007, after a period of deteriorating relations resulting from a range of disputes. The conflict over energy was the most serious source of discord. Russia was accused of using energy for blackmail after having reduced gas supplies to Georgia, the Ukraine and Belarus, an accusation that the Russian leadership strongly refuted. Potential future conflicts over energy could impede the evolution of EU–Russia cooperation. In order to grasp fully the potential for future rapprochement, however, a range of other factors have to be considered. In addition to presenting an extensive review of the speeches and statements that add up to a comprehensive account of the norms and interests that Russia and the EU promote, this volume provides a thorough account of the development of EU–Russia relations as well as background on the factors that have hampered or driven their cooperation since the break-up of the Soviet Union.

A brief background to the evolution of EU–Russia relations is useful even at this stage, before the empirical scrutiny is presented, and is therefore provided below.

The concrete basis for mutual relations between the EU and Russia, which defines the scope and shape of interaction, is the Partnership and Cooperation Agreement (PCA). The PCA expired in 2007 but is renewed automatically if a new document is not negotiated. Two summits are held each year in the framework of the PCA. In addition, monthly meetings on ESDP issues between the EU Political and Security Committee (COPS), the EU Troika (the EU Presidency, the CFSP High Representative/Council Secretariat, the future presidency and the European Commission) and the Russian Ambassador to the EU were institutionalised at the Brussels summit in October 2001. Ministers and members of the Commission convene annually in the Cooperation Council, senior officials meet more frequently in the Cooperation Committee and nine specialised subcommittees alternate their meetings between Moscow and Brussels. Moreover, members of the Russian Duma and the European Parliament meet on a regular basis in a Parliamentary Cooperation Committee. A Russian liaison officer was appointed to work with the EU Military Staff in Brussels in 2002. The Russian foreign minister discusses international developments and crisis-management issues with the EU's High Representative for the Common Foreign and Security Policy on a regular basis.

A range of motivating forces spur EU–Russia cooperation. Moscow places great weight on deepening relations with the EU, largely because of the economic incentives. Also, in contrast to NATO, the EU is not burdened by a historic legacy as Moscow's opponent. During the 1990s, the Russian leadership persistently promoted the Organisation for Security and Co-operation in Europe (OSCE) as the ideal vehicle for structuring European security.[48] The EU is Russia's most recent candidate for evading NATO-centrism in European security. Moreover, close cooperation with the EU represents an opportunity for Moscow to achieve what it has been striving for since the end of the Cold War – a clear and significant role in the European security structure.

Economics is a basic driving force behind closer cooperation and there is mutual dependence in this area. The EU is far more important to Russia as a partner in the economic sphere than the USA. The EU is Russia's main trading partner, accounting for 40 per cent of Russia's trade in the 1990s and more than 50 per cent since EU enlargement in 2004.[49] European companies are the main foreign investors in Russia's expanding economy.[50]

Energy is potentially a major source of conflict between the EU and Russia. The EU fears that Russia will increasingly use its energy resources to 'blackmail' other states, and badly needs to make itself less dependent on Russian oil and gas.

Yet, despite many problems, economic relations are likely to increase in the future.[51] Economic considerations spill over into the security arena. There is ample evidence that Russian leaders are aware of the link between a strong economy and international power and influence, and link security to the promotion of development goals.[52]

Apart from economics, Russia and the EU must collaborate in order to cope with common problems. The common pursuit of stability is a strong force for further EU–Russian rapprochement. The two parties are mutually dependent, and Russia has historically played a role in European security. For a number of reasons, Russia will not become a member of the EU in the foreseeable future. It is all the more important, therefore, that the two parties strengthen other mechanisms that can facilitate cooperation in the regional and global arena.

Javier Solana has recognised this mutual dependence in the security sphere, arguing that 'Russia is a natural security partner for Europe – our security is indivisible. We cannot have a secure Europe without a secure Russia'.[53] A strong motivation for cooperation is the EU's desire to promote stability along its borders. The EU's aims for cooperation with Russia in the security realm were codified in its Common Strategy on Russia, adopted directly after the end of the Kosovo campaign, in Cologne in June 1999. The Strategy states that lasting peace on the continent can only be achieved if Russia is democratic, stable and prosperous and firmly anchored in Europe. It reflects the logic that the development of democracy, rule of law and a market economy – and other components inherent to the Tacis Programme – both draws Russia closer to the European community of values, and favours security and stability.[54] According to the strategy, closer relations will help Russia to assert its 'European identity'. Four principal objectives are outlined that pertain to democratisation, integration of Russia in the European economic area, strengthening of security in Europe as well as globally, and cooperation against common security challenges in Europe.[55]

The Commission's country strategy paper on Russia 2002–06 states that 'soft security' threats from Russia – nuclear safety; the fight against organised crime, including drug trafficking and illegal immigration; the spread of diseases; and environmental pollution – are of serious concern to the EU.[56] The EU needs Russian collaboration not least to combat organised crime. Russia is seen as a source of criminal activity.[57]

Russia also sees benefits in cooperation in the security sphere – as long as the EU does not threaten to interfere too much in its perceived sphere of influence. The Russian leadership values cooperation against 'new threats' to security, including the threat from international terrorism.[58] The Russian Medium–Term Strategy towards the EU 2000–10 also acknowledges a mutual interdependence and emphasises how cooperation can serve to curb common threats such as damage to the environment, terrorism, illegal drug trafficking and transnational organised crime.[59] Moreover, Russia has framed the EU as a 'strategic partner'.[60] Vladimir Putin's participation in the EU summit in Stockholm in March 2001 was a milestone by virtue of its symbolically important demonstration of the will to deepen the cooperation between Russia and the EU.[61] Above all, Russia is interested in cooperation to contain terrorism, organised crime, and the proliferation of weapons of mass destruction.

Russian leaders have tended to regard a strong EU as beneficial to Russia because it disperses power in the international system. The ESDP has been interpreted as taking the world one step away from US hegemony and towards multipolarity.[62]

Thus, while Russia appreciates EU moves towards multipolarity, the EU retains its ambition of wielding influence over its neighbour on issues of global significance, the most obvious example thus far being ratification of the Kyoto Protocol.[63] EU leverage on Russia increases as cooperation deepens; the EU supported Russia's application for membership of the World Trade Organisation (WTO) and, in return, Russia finally agreed to ratify the Kyoto Protocol. Russian ratification in October 2004 was vital to the implementation of the protocol.

Security issues have been discussed on a regular basis at biannual EU–Russia summit meetings since 1999. Representatives from both sides have supported the rapprochement and described relations in terms of a 'strategic partnership'.[64] Former German Chancellor Gerhard Schröder defined Russia as central to stability in Europe and declared the EU willing to intensify cooperation.[65] The then newly appointed High Representative for the EU Common Foreign and Security Policy, Javier Solana, declared partnership with Russia to be the EU's most important task because it 'offers the greatest opportunity to affect the course of world affairs for the better and to begin the new century in a manner which will truly affect the course of history'.[66]

Cooperation against organised crime and terrorism, including control of borders and individuals, was boosted by the terrorist attacks of 11 September 2001, after which the Russian leaders increased contacts with the EU. Addressing the German Bundestag on 25 September 2001, Putin argued that Europe can function as a powerful and truly independent centre of world affairs, especially if it unites its capacities with Russia's human, natural and territorial resources and its cultural, economic and defence potential.[67] Soon afterwards, President Putin called for a common security space in Europe.[68] On 3 October 2001, Russia and the EU agreed to expand cooperation in the areas of nuclear security, space, energy and the economy and to set up a group to monitor common security issues on a monthly basis. Putin declared that the partnership between Russia and the EU was becoming ever deeper.[69] According to the Deputy Foreign Minister Aleksei Meshkov, '[the] stability of Europe and stability of Russia are synonymous' and Russia and the EU need to collaborate to contain 'new threats'.[70] Cooperation against organised crime – including money laundering and the trafficking of drugs and human beings – resulted in an action plan the following year.[71] Cooperation plans and programmes have been forged in other areas as well, for example, with regard to environmental problems and non-proliferation.

Nonetheless, despite pressing common concerns and plentiful signs of goodwill, the EU–Russia partnership has thus far produced only meagre practical results and practical cooperation has not evolved as swiftly as could be expected. Russia has only made a limited contribution to ESDP missions, by participating in the EU Police Mission in Bosnia and Herzegovina, which became operational on 1 January 2003.[72] Military-technical cooperation has also not evolved very far. Russia has provided assets – heavy-lift transport aircraft and satellite reconnaissance – in support of an EU-led crisis management operation. The two parties launched a bilateral space dialogue in 1998, but cooperation in the field of military-relevant satellite imaging has been limited. During the Afghanistan conflict in 2001, Russia offered aircraft which the EU lacked, but the two parties did not manage to agree the terms for this joint effort.[73]

At the St Petersburg summit of May 2003, Russia and the EU launched a much-needed framework intended to systematise and step up their common efforts. They agreed to focus their cooperation on four so-called common spaces: Research, Education and Culture; Economy; External security; and Freedom, Security and Justice. In practice, cooperation was to follow four 'Road Maps' based on the underlying logic that Russia would benefit as much as possible from the EU integration without enjoying membership. However, finding common objectives around which the two parties could unite within each of the spaces became a major problem. The Road Maps were not agreed until the Moscow summit in 2005.

The Economy and External Security common spaces cover cooperation against terrorism and the proliferation of weapons of mass destruction as well as joint efforts in conflict prevention, crisis management and post-conflict reconstruction, particularly with regard to 'frozen' conflicts in the so-called shared neighbourhood. However, the document suffers from a lack of suggestions for practical cooperation in crisis management or crisis prevention. The emphasis is most of all on exchanges of views and joint exercises.[74]

The Freedom, Security and Justice common space covers the areas of Justice and Home Affairs, and targets illegal activities of a cross-border nature. A central issue for the Russian leaders is the demand for visa-free travel, but they have had difficulties in achieving quick successes on this point, which they regard as a vital step towards realisation of the Russian slogan 'a Europe without dividing lines'.[75]

Both the EU and Russia have acknowledged the problems with advancing cooperation and tend to blame one another for the difficulties. The EU has complained that Russia fails to implement agreements.[76] After the Rome summit of November 2003, the then External Relations Commissioner Chris Patten acknowledged the problems, recognising the need for new, 'clear and simple guidelines for dealing with Russia', which would make cooperation run faster and smoother.[77]

The difficulties in implementing cooperative projects can partly be ascribed to bureaucratic obstacles. Russia's unreformed bureaucracy and military system have placed hurdles in the way of cooperation. In turn, Russia has had difficulties with learning to understand how to deal with the intricate structures in Brussels.

A few concrete political conflicts also contribute to hampering the practical process of rapprochement. The Kaliningrad issue and Moscow's aversion to the Shengen Visa regime, as well as Russia's critique of the situation for the Russian-speaking population in Latvia and Estonia, are examples of political controversies that have surfaced in the past decade. The EU's qualms that Russia will use energy supplies as a political lever against the EU or against states in the former Soviet Union, is another example.

Russia's sanctions against Georgia, following a conflict between the two states, became yet another cause of irritation between the two parties in 2006. EU representatives criticised Moscow for the sanctions, while emphasising that the EU did not want to harm its long-term relations with Russia.[78] Another major cause of dispute during the EU–Russia summit of November 2006 was Russia's ban on imports of agricultural products from Poland. Also in 2006, Russia still refused to ratify the EU's Energy Charter, which would end Gazprom's control over Russia's pipelines and open them up to other economic actors. These and other disagreements in the economic realm contributed to hindering progress in mutual relations. Outside the economic realm, Russia and the EU also disagreed over the issue of sanctions against Iran over its Uranium-enrichment project, and Moscow decided to receive the Palestinian Hamas leadership in Moscow while the EU refused to have official contact with the organisation.

Nonetheless, most bureaucratic problems and political conflicts can be solved. One example is the solution of a twenty-year-old conflict in November 2006, pertaining to European airlines being obliged to pay additional royalties to the Russian airline Aeroflot in order to fly over Russian territory on routes between the EU and Japan, China and South Korea. Many such problems are gradually dealt with and resolved. The rhetorical divergences, however, are often linked to fundamental issues and may therefore be more difficult to overcome.

The structure of the book

The book consists of three case study chapters, two analytical chapters that evaluate the results of the case studies – one focused on internal EU cohesion and the other on differences and convergences between the EU and Russia – and a concluding chapter.

Chapter 2 analyses verbal reactions to 'Operation Allied Force' in Kosovo, which began on 24 March 1999 and officially ended on 10 June the same year. Chapter 3 discusses the dramatic events two years later that led to major transformations in the machinery of the international system. The chapter examines the actors' framing of 11 September 2001, from the terrorist attacks to the official end of the US campaign in Afghanistan on 5 December 2001, when an agreement on the future of Afghanistan was signed in Rome. Chapter 4 scrutinises the leaders' framing of the Iraq crisis from the build-up to the war from 1 December 2002 until its official end on 1 May 2003.

Chapter 5 evaluates the EU's internal cohesion by extrapolating the findings from the case studies into three major 'gaps' in reasoning on security. The gaps revolve, to a significant extent, around the role of norms in international affairs, around the governments' favoured methods of preserving stability, and around the issue of the role of the USA in global security. The chapter extends the analysis by analysing a number of more recent EU documents. It ends by elaborating on the consequences for practical cooperation.

Chapter 6 analyses the central rhetorical divergences exposed by the case studies which seriously hamper cooperation between Russia and the EU. The divergences appear to mirror deep policy controversies that are tied to existential issues and consequently to the two parties' identities. Given the difficulties in eradicating their basic differences, the chapter suggests that pragmatism is the most plausible way for Russia and the EU to advance their integration in the sphere of security. Increased cooperation on as many issues and levels as possible might boost a kind of neo-functionalism, which might, in the long run, contribute to further rapprochement in the sphere of security.

Chapter 7 makes a case for the volume's contribution to the constructivist field of research in international relations. The main part of the chapter, however, is dedicated to further reflections on the empirical findings. Above all, it emphasises how diverging norms and bilateral disturbances complicate European actorness; but it also sheds light on the potential for closer EU–Russia co-operation in the global arena, and suggests possible consequences for the USA.

Notes

1 'Nikto ne stavit pod somnenie vysokuiu tsennost otnoshenii Evropy s Soedinennymi Shtatami. Prosto ja priderzhivaius mneniia, chto Evropa tverdo i nadolgo ukrepit svoiu reputatsiiu moshchnogo i deistvitelno samostoiatelnogo tsentra mirovoi politiki, esli ona smozhet obedinit sobstvennye vozmozhnostiami rossiiskimi – liudskimi, territorialnymi i prirodnymi resursami, s ekonomicheskim kulturnym i oboronnym potentsialom Rossii. Pervye shagi v etom napravlenii my s vami vmeste uzhe sdedali. Teper prishla pora podumat o tom, chto neobkhodimo predpriniat, chtoby edinaia i besopasnaia Evropa stala predvestnikom edinogo i bezopasnogo mira.' Putin, V., 'Address to the German Bundestag', 25 September 2001, Official translation from the home page of the Ministry of Foreign Affairs of Russia.

2 Emerson, M., *The Elephant and the Bear: The European Union, Russia and their Near Abroads* (Brussels: Centre for European Policy Studies, 2001), p. 19.

3 Krauthammer, C., 'The unipolar moment', *Foreign Affairs* 70:1 (1990/1991), p. 23; Waltz, K., 'Structural realism after the Cold War', *International Security* 25:1 (2000), p. 30; Kupchan, C., 'The rise of Europe, America's changing internationalism, and the end of US primacy', *Political Science Quarterly* 118:2 (2003), p. 213.

4 Bretherton C. and Vogler, J., *The European Union as a Global Actor* (London: Routledge, 2006), p. 88.

5 Ibid., Chapter 4.

6 Dombrowski, p. and Ross, A., 'The "new strategic triangle" and the US grand strategy debate', in J. Hallenberg and H. Karlsson (eds), *Changing Transatlantic Security Relations: Do the US, the EU and Russia Form a New Strategic Triangle?* (London: Routledge, 2006).

7 On the tendency for politicians to use negative identification in order to strengthen an actor's identity and cohesion, see Bloom, W., *Personal Identity, National Identity and International Relations* (Cambridge: Cambridge University Press, 1990), pp. 80–84.

8 'Referent objects' of security are items that are existentially threatened and have a legitimate claim to survival in the view of political leaderships. Realists have traditionally treated the state as the central referent object of security. The scholarly debate during the 1990s broadened the security agenda and questioned the realist focus on the state. A central issue was whether new referent objects, for example, individuals and the environment, should be scrutinised alongside the state. Scholars have not reached any consensus on this issue. Buzan, B., *Peoples, States and Fear: An Agenda for International Security Studies in the Post-Cold War Era* (Hertfordshire: Harvester Wheatsheaf, 1991); Krause, K., 'Critical theory and security studies: The research programme of "critical security studies"', *Cooperation and Conflict* 33 (1998), pp. 298–333; Baldwin, D., 'The concept of security', *Review of International Studies* 23 (1997).

9 National Security Strategy of the United States of America, 17 September 2002.

10 This approach sets the book apart from the many endeavours in the field that are conducted with a normative bias, with the implicit or explicit aim of promoting either EU or Russian interests.

11 Baldwin (note 8), pp. 23–26. For an introduction to constructivism see Adler, E., 'Seizing the middle ground: Constructivism in world politics', *European Journal of International Relations* 3:3 (1997).

12 It should be pointed out that the aim is not to 'test' constructivism, but to use it in order to learn as much as possible from the empirical material. In order to avoid preconceptions, and to make sense of the findings, the analysis mainly links back after the empirical analysis to previous research on historical identities and the interests of the actors.

13　For example, in his studies Adrian Hyde-Price tends to disregard central parts of the intricate pattern of convergence and divergence in European security that emerge as a result of the actors' normative preferences. Hyde-Price, A., *European Security in the Twenty-first Century: The Challenge of Multipolarity* (London: Routledge, 2007).

14　Ian Manners provides a detailed and solid account of the EU's normative basis according to the body of EU laws and policies, but does not address divergences among EU states. Manners, I., 'Normative power Europe: A contradiction in terms?', *Journal of Common Market Studies* 40:2 (2002); Manners, I., 'The constitutive nature of values, images and principles in the European Union', in S. Lucarelli and I. Manners (eds), *Values and Principles in European Union Foreign Policy* (London: Routledge, 2006). Lisbeth Aggestam provides valuable background on how it was possible to overcome internal differences and deviating role-conceptions to negotiate agreement on the CFSP. Aggestam concludes that the 'three greats' have gradually converged on the role of Europe as an ethical power, but provides little data to support this thesis. Aggestam, L., *A European Foreign Policy? Role Conceptions and the Politics of Identity in Britain, France and Germany* (Stockholm: Stockholm University Department of Political Science, 2004), p. 243.

15　Entman, R., 'Framing: Towards clarification of a fractured paradigm', *Journal of Communication* 43:4 (1993), p. 55.

16　Many scholars acknowledge that the use of language affects practical political action. K. M. Fierke illustrates the point that language is coloured by pressure to adapt to a community discourse by suggesting that NATO expanded to the east initially against its will. When the applicant states used their dialogue with NATO to recall the organisation's past ideals and responsibilities, NATO was pressured to go along with the enlargement. In Fierke's words, actors become 'entangled in their language' and are thus restricted because others might hold them accountable for any inconsistency between stated intentions and subsequent actions. Fierke, K. M. and Wiener, A., 'Constructing institutional interests: EU and NATO enlargement', *Journal of European Public Policy* 6:5 (1999), p. 31. Johan Matz demonstrates how Russian leaders in the early 1990s became tied to a specific way of treating certain security issues: they became 'caught in their own rhetoric'. Matz, J., *Constructing a Post-Soviet International Political Reality* (Uppsala: ACTA Universitatis Upsaliensis, Statsvetenskapliga Föreningen, 2000), pp. 250–251.

17　Edelman, M., Constructing the Political Spectacle (Chicago: University of Chicago Press, 1988), p. 104.

18　Helene Sjursen argues that the main challenge to Western Europe's security and defence policies and its perceptions of security has been directed towards the framework on which European security policy was developed. Sjursen, H., 'Security and defence', *Arena Working Paper* 10:3 (2003), pp. 57–58.

19　Many constructivist stress the importance of norms in international relations. Adler (note 11); Katzenstein, P. (ed.), *The Culture of National Security: Norms and Identity in World Politics* (New York: Columbia University Press, 1996); Finnemore, M., 'Constructing norms of humanitarian intervention', in ibid., Chapter 1, but this study is true to constructivism in the sense that it remains open to how language constructs meaning, without predefining the kinds of meaning that can be constructed.

20　For a good example of such an approach see Tonra B. and Christiansen, T. (eds), *Rethinking European Union Foreign Policy* (Manchester: Manchester University Press, 2004), which argues that the EU's foreign policy is an ideal empirical testing ground for a constructivist approach that takes account of both interests and ideas, and values and identities.

21 Hans Morgenthau defines the national interest in terms of power. According to Morgenthau, an actor can only advance its favoured interests if it is able to make use of its power: 'International politics, like all other politics, is a struggle for power. Whatever the ultimate aim of international politics, power is always the immediate aim.' Morgenthau, H., *Politics Among Nations: The Stuggle for Power and Peace*, revised by Keeth W. Thompson (Boston: McGrawHill, 1993/1948).

22 Katzenstein (note 19).

23 In McSweeney's definition, norms are 'the stuff of social action, furnishing the standards and norms which legitimize it as conforming or breaking with a notion of the routine, the normal, or the stable'. McSweeney, B., *Security, Identity and Interests: A Sociology of International Relations* (Cambridge: Cambridge University Press, 1999), p. 212.

24 Finnemore (note 19), pp. 157–158.

25 Justifications are not the same as underlying motives. Fierke and Wiener (note 16), pp. 721–742.

26 Burns, T., 'Rhetoric as a framework for analyzing cultural constraint and change', *Current Perspectives in Social Theory* 19 (1999), p. 168.

27 Donald Schön and Martin Rein argue that policy positions stem from frames, that is, 'underlying structures of belief, perception and appreciation'. A frame conflict often concerns the definition of a situation that has implications for both what is at stake and what should be done. Schön, D. and Rein, M., *Frame Reflection: Towards the Resolution of Intractable Policy Controversies* (New York: Basic Books, 1994), pp. 23, 29.

28 Frames are essentially 'underlying structures' and it is a natural consequence of their nature that they are mostly tacit. In order to analyse and discuss frames in a conscious manner, they must first be identified by reconstructing them from texts or political practice. Schön and Rein (note 27), p. 34.

29 Perelman, C., *The Realm of Rhetoric* (Notre Dame: University of Notre Dame Press, 1982).

30 Schön and Rein distinguish between 'action frames', which inform policy practice, and 'rhetorical frames', which underpin the use of argument in policy debate. Schön and Rein (note 27), p. 32.

31 Milliken, J., 'The study of discourse in international relations: A critique of research and methods', *European Journal of International Relations* 5:2 (1999).

32 Entman (note 15), p. 52.

33 Milliken (note 31); and Herring, E., 'Military security', in A. Collins (ed.), *Contemporary Security Studies* (Oxford: Oxford University Press, 2007) elaborate on differences between constructivism and discourse theory in greater detail.

34 Snow, D. and Benford, R., 'Master frames and cycles of protest', in A. Morris and C. McClurg Mueller (eds), *Frontiers in Social Movement Theory* (New Haven, Conn.: Yale University Press, 1992) (social movement research); Bynander, F., *The Rise and Fall of the Submarine Threat: Threat Politics and Submarine Intrusions in Sweden 1980–2002* (Uppsala: Acta Universitatis Upsaliensis, 2003); Eriksson, J., *Threat Politics: New Perspectives on Security, Risk and Crisis Management* (Aldershot: Ashgate, 2001) (security studies).

35 Rochefort, D. and Cobb R. (eds), The Politics of Problem Definition: Shaping the Policy Agenda (Lawrence: University Press of Kansas, 1994), pp. 3–4, 24–25.

36 Ibid., p. 15.

37 So-called negative identification denotes a process of strengthening a group's identity by setting itself apart from a less perfect, negative, 'other'. Contrasting the 'self' with a morally or otherwise inferior 'other' may serve to strengthen a specific identity and, in many cases, functions as an important part of the process of identification.

Hedetoft, U., 'National identity and mentalities of war in three EC countries', *Journal of Peace Research* 30:3 (1993), p. 241; Bloom, W., *Personal Identity, National Identity and International Relations* (Cambridge: Cambridge University Press, 1990), p. 80.

38 Entman, R., 'Framing: Towards clarification of a fractured paradigm', *Journal of Communication* 43:4 (1993), p. 53.

39 Rochefort and Cobb (note 35), p. 12.

40 The texts consist of statements and declarations by national foreign ministers, prime ministers and presidents, and by EU officials responsible for foreign and security policy.

41 Consistency is the 'extent to which the bilateral policies of Member States are consistent with each other, and complementary to those of the EU'. Bretherton and Vogler (note 4), p. 31.

42 Deutsch, K., Political Community and the North Atlantic Area : International Organization in the Light of Historical Experience (Princeton, NJ: University of Princeton Press, 1957), p. 5.

43 Bretherton and Vogler propose five requirements for actorness in the international sphere. Bretherton and Vogler (note 4), p. 38.

44 White, B., *Understanding European Foreign Policy* (Basingstoke: Palgrave, 2001), pp. 2–3.

45 Council of the European Union, 'A secure Europe in a better world: The European security strategy', 12 December 2003.

46 Bretherton and Vogler (note 4), p. 33.

47 Manners (note 14), pp. 240–241, 252–253.

48 Wagnsson, C., *Russian Political Language and Public Opinion on the West, NATO and Chechnya: Securitisation Theory Reconsidered* (Stockholm: Statsvetenskapliga Institutionen, 2000), chapter 4.

49 'Russia's trade with the EU'.

50 Barysh, K. and Kekic, L., 'Putin should tilt toward the EU: Russia at a crossroads', *International Herald Tribune* (17 July 2003).

51 Russian discontent is largely focused on the trade imbalance. Russia mainly supplies raw materials rather than manufactured goods to the EU. From the EU perspective, the Russian investment climate needs to improve, which can be achieved with a range of measures. European Commission, Official home page of the European Commission's delegation to Russia.

52 Putin, V., 'Annual address by President of the Russian Federation to the Federal Assembly of the Russian Federation', Moscow, 18 April 2002; 'Annual address by the President of the Russian Federation to the Federal Assembly of the Russian Federation', Moscow, 16 May 2003; 'National Security Concept of the Russian Federation', 10 January 2000, paragraph 2.

53 Council of the European Union, 'Common Strategy of the European Union of 4 June 1999 on Russia'.

54 The Tacis Programme was launched by the European Community in 1991, and provides grant-financed assistance to twelve countries of Eastern Europe and Central Asia (Armenia, Azerbaijan, Belarus, Georgia, Kazakhstan, Kyrgyzstan, Moldova, Russia, Tajikistan, Turkmenistan, Ukraine and Uzbekistan). Its main aim is to enhance the transition process in these countries.

55 Emphasis is placed on cooperation in the areas of conflict prevention, crisis management, arms control, prevention of the proliferation of weapons of mass destruction, and nuclear disarmament. The strategy considers facilitating Russian participation in missions within the range of the Petersberg tasks. The document also places emphasis on nuclear safety, environmental concerns, energy policies, and new common threats

such as illegal immigration, organised crime, money laundering, illegal trafficking in human beings and drug trafficking.

56 European Commission, 'Russia: Country strategy paper, 2002–2006'.

57 Smith, M., *Europe's Foreign and Security Policy: The Institutionalization of Cooperation* (Cambridge: Cambridge University Press, 2004), pp. 188–189.

58 'Russia's Medium-Term Strategy Towards the EU, 2000–2010'.

59 It is suggested that Russia could contribute to solving problems facing the EU, and to strengthening Europe's position in the world. Russia could increase its military and technical cooperation with the EU to strengthen a European 'defence identity'. The strategy calls for cooperation intended to prevent or end local conflicts and to combat organised crime. Ibid..

60 Putin, V., 'Annual address by the President of the Russian Federation to the Federal Assembly of the Russian Federation', Moscow, 16 May 2003.

61 Council of the European Union, 'Presidency Conclusions, Stockholm European Council meeting, 23–24 March 2001'

62 Russian thinking in terms of multipolarity was most energetically outlined by Yevgeny Primakov, the Russian Foreign Minister and Prime Minister in 1996–98. Vladimir Putin has been more cautious about using the concept of multipolarity, but it is still applied in Russian descriptions of its preferred world order. For example, Russia's Medium-Term Strategy stems from 'the objective need to establish a multi-polar world'. 'Russia's Medium-Term Strategy Towards the EU, 2000–2010'.

63 The Kyoto Protocol is the international agreement that seeks to reduce emissions of greenhouse gases that contribute to global warming.

64 European Commission, 'Common Strategy of the European Union of 4 June 1999 on Russia', 1999/414/CFSP; EU-Russia summit, 'Joint statement', Paris, 30 October 2000; Council of the European Union, 'Presidency conclusions, Stockholm European Council meeting, 23–24 March 2001'.

65 Schröder, G., 'Address to the European Parliament in Strasbourg', 14 April 1999.

66 Solana, J., 'The EU-Russia strategic partnership', Speech in Stockholm, 13 October 1999.

67 Putin, V., 'Address to the German Bundestag', 25 September 2001.

68 Radio Free Europe/Radio Liberty, Newsline, 3 October 2001.

69 Radio Free Europe/Radio Liberty, Newsline, 4 January 2001.

70 Meshkov, A., 'Russia and the European security architecture', *International Affairs* 48 (2002).

71 Council of the European Union, 'European Union Action Plan on Common Action for the Russian Federation on Combating Organised Crime'.

72 The European Union Police Mission in Bosnia Herzegovina.

73 Lynch, D., 'Russia faces Europe', *Chaillot Papers 60* (European Union Institute for Security Studies, 2003), p. 70.

74 European Commission. 'Road map for the Common Space of Freedom, Security and Justice'.

75 Ivanov, I., 'Remarks before representatives of the sociopolitical and business circles of the FRG on the Theme "Russia–European Union: The state of, and prospects for partnership",' Munich, 10 December 2003; Putin, V., 'Joint press conference following the EU-Russia summit', London, 5 October 2005.

76 Vahl, M., 'A privileged partnership: EU-Russian relations in a comparative perspective', *DIIS Working Paper* 3 (2006).

77 Radio Free Europe/Radio Liberty, Weekday Magazine, 18 November 2003.

78 Radio Free Europe/Radio Liberty, Newsline, 18 October 2006.

2   Kosovo: a precedent?

Introduction: Europe faces a crisis

In May 1998, the North Atlantic Treaty Organisation (NATO) pressured Serbian President Slobodan Milosevic to enhance self-determination for repressed ethnic Albanians in Kosovo. When peace talks in Rambouillet broke down early in 1999, NATO chose to carry out air strikes.

The vast majority of the EU member states supported NATO's actions, justifying them as a matter of the protection of human rights and democracy in Europe. Only a few states seriously questioned the campaign. Among the NATO members, the United Kingdom, France and Germany acted most forcefully in defence of the air campaign. The British government and the major political parties, as well as the majority of British public opinion, supported 'Operation Allied Force', which began on 24 March and was officially suspended on 10 June 1999. Disagreements arose mostly over the means used rather than the operation itself. The debate centred on issues such as the use of cluster bombs and whether or when to deploy ground troops.[1]

In France, the legitimacy of Operation Allied Force was questioned by sections of the political establishment, the media and public opinion.[2] Officially, however, France supported the campaign and actively engaged in the negotiation of the international peace plan for Kosovo. Germany, which held the Presidency of the European Union at the time, played a vital role in the negotiations. Foreign Minister Joschka Fischer launched a peace plan and the idea of a Stability Pact for South Eastern Europe in April 1999.[3]

In contrast, Russia employed a whole arsenal of symbolic actions to protest against the decision to use military means. Russia immediately froze formal cooperation with NATO.[4] Prime Minister Yevgeny Primakov was heading for the USA on 23 March when, after a telephone conversation with the US Vice President, Al Gore, he ordered his plane to return to Moscow. Russia also recalled its chief military envoy to NATO, pulled out of the

Partnership for Peace and military cooperation programmes, and ordered the closure of its offices at NATO headquarters.[5]

The analysis below compares the official standpoints of the EU, Russia and three major EU states – Germany, France and the United Kingdom – during the Kosovo crisis. The analysis distils the norms and interests which the EU and the four states endorsed during Operation Allied Force.

As is explained in Chapter 1, the analysis is structured around the issues that are central to framing analysis, that is, *problem definition, moral evaluation, causal interpretation* and *salience*, as well as the actors' *levels of analysis* of and *envisaged solutions* for the Kosovo crisis.

Defining problems and apportioning blame

It is apparent that, although the three member states converged with the EU at the most basic level with regard to problem definition and moral evaluation, they diverged from one another in a number of important ways. They diverged over what kind of norms – universal or European – ought to be defended; they differed with regard to how the notion of 'Europe' played into the conflict – as a 'good' and united entity, or as an entity of secondary importance; and they also diverged on whether most emphasis should be placed on 'restoring order' and eliminating something evil, or on depicting the EU as a positive and attractive example to follow. Finally, as is demonstrated further below, they diverged on the significance and the role of NATO.

The EU, France and Germany: a problem for the 'good union'

Although the EU was a central *referent-object* in the rhetoric on the Kosovo crisis, particularly in the German and French version, as is demonstrated below, it was almost invisible as a *framing actor* during the Kosovo crisis. The EU kept a low profile throughout the crisis, mainly because the official rationales for NATO intervention in Kosovo presented by the major EU members states diverged and it was therefore safer to leave them to work out and defend their own positions, rather than articulate a controversial 'EU position' on the crisis. More bluntly, the only viable way forward was for the EU to present only general arguments that were uncontroversial for most member states.

Another explanation for the EU's weakness as an actor is that it had yet to develop a common foreign and security policy or any military capabilities. Nor had it appointed a High Representative for the Common Foreign and Security Policy (CFSP), and there was no single Commissioner responsible for the CFSP. Moreover, the Commission, led by its President Jacques Santer, was particularly weak at the time because of a report on the mismanagement of fraud, which led to the resignation of the entire commission only one week before the start of the NATO air campaign.

That said, a small number of 'EU statements' reveal a rudimentary, but still distinguishable, 'EU logic' on Kosovo. EU officials conceptualised the crisis as a project to humanise, or 'civilise', a European subregion. The salience of the crisis was indicated by the use of strong language – the problem was described as connected to the organisation's self-perception as a defender of 'civil values' such as democracy and peace. The crisis in Kosovo was in essence defined as pertaining to the EU's self-image. At stake was the EU's credibility as a defender of 'positive' norms. The German EU Presidency stressed that the EU had a moral obligation to end the violence against Kosovo's civilians.[6] Jacques Santer described the military action as connected to the principles and norms that are Europe's 'raison d'être':[7] 'The ongoing military action underlines by force the principles and values which are the raison d'être for Europe. Not to act is to accept. Europe and its partners do not accept murders, do not accept deportations, do not accept dread and hate between peoples'.[8]

In addition to linking the problem definition to the EU's self-image, and to basic EU norms, both the President of the European Council, Dieter Kastrup, and Jacques Santer justified the military campaign in Kosovo with reference to peace and stability.[9] Santer argued that the EU must make an effort to ensure stability on the European continent.[10] The European Commission emphasised practical problems such as refugees and the need for economic assistance.

The crisis was also used to boost the EU's identity and 'actorness'. It was defined as a new starting point for the EU as an actor in the security sphere. Santer discussed the long-term consequences of the EU's stance on the conflict, arguing that the events in Kosovo could be the birth of a 'true European foreign policy'.[12]

The French, German and British leaderships went along with the EU's general definition of the crisis as pertaining to 'peace', but the governments diverged from each other when elaborating on the referent object of security, on the 'enemy', on the nature of the solution, and when choosing the level of analysis.

As is demonstrated below, the British expended time and energy condemning disorder and evil, while the French and the German leaderships focused more on describing the EU as a normatively good and positive magnet that could transform its surroundings by setting a good example. They also started from the EU's *common* resolve – the common stance was portrayed as something normatively good in its own right.

The French leaders highlighted the separate value of sticking together.[13] They recalled Europe's gloomy, barbarous past and described the removal of Milosevic as a precondition for building a democratic and prosperous

Europe.[14] Greater unity in Europe would be achieved by pacifying and civilising the 'anomaly' of Serbia and by Europeanising the Balkan region.[15]
Jospin argued that they could not allow European norms to be violated 'on
the doorstep of the EU'.[16] A 'certain conception of Europe' was being put at
risk.[17]

> For decades, Europe, anyway our Europe, has been founded on peace and
> respect for human rights. To accept that these standards can be derided at the
> gateway of the European Union would have been to betray ourselves. At issue
> in today's conflict is a certain comprehension of Europe. Do we accept the
> return of barbarism to our continent or do we stand up against it? For us, the
> choice is clear.

The French government projected the message that the people of the
Balkans had to be converted into honourable Europeans, transforming from
'the other' into 'one of us', and becoming one of many members in a normatively good community. The aim was to 'Europeanise' the peoples of the
Balkan States.[19]

The German leadership also used the image of an attractive, modern EU
that could stimulate good behaviour at its periphery, and gradually incorporate the better-behaved states into its confines. The post-Cold War German
tradition of 'peace politics' was clearly present in the framing. Discussing the
Kosovo problem, Fischer described the success of the European integration
project as an issue of 'war or peace'.[20] Serbia had to transform in order to be
accepted as a part of modern Europe.[21] What was at stake was 'the European
model of civilisation'.[22] The history of oppression and genocide must never
be repeated, and Milosevic had declared war on European civilisation.[23]

In the German framing, 'community' was a notion with highly positive
normative appeal. In the view of the German Chancellor, Gerhard Schröder,
the Europeans should be proud that 'Europe speaks with one voice, even in
the face of the difficult mission in Kosovo'.[24] The German leadership emphasised that Milosevic faced not a range of states, but a single, united, and
therefore strong, opponent. 'Milosevic turns Kosovo into the slaughterhouse
of Europe in broad daylight. In doing so, he has declared war against
European civilization.'[25] Furthermore, 'The European value community
would become hollow words if we Europeans permitted only one hour away
by air, in the middle of our continent, the fundamental principles on which
the European Union is established to be trampled on – democracy, legal
rights, freedom and solidarity with the weaker'.[26]

The German leaders also emphasised European unity by making a
particular effort to sustain fragile EU cooperation with Russia throughout
the crisis.[27] The German leadership returned to the necessity of 'getting
the Russians on board' again and again when searching for a solution to the
crisis.[28]

The United Kingdom: issues of global order and universal norms

While the German and French governments systematically referred to community and to the European nature of the norms abused in Kosovo, the British Prime Minister, Tony Blair, defined the war in terms of British and universal values, those of 'tolerance', 'decency', 'civilisation', 'justice' and 'freedom'.[29] He sometimes referred to the EU, but more typically elevated the issue to a global level of analysis.[30] Blair portrayed the norms at stake by use of drastic wording, as if the British were the prime, or even solitary, defenders of a revered set of universal values, and as if the entire world depended on the UK's righteous engagement.[31]

> And, as we fight injustice and intolerance in Britain, so in Kosovo today we also fight ethnic cleansing and racial genocide. The values we are fighting for are the same values: the right to live in freedom from fear, whatever your race or religion. When defenceless people are butchered by Milosevic in Kosovo, young men murdered, women violated, it is an outrage against the very values of humanity which are the world's only salvation. We must act to stop it; we must continue the action in the Balkans until those people driven from their homes are allowed to return in peace and security to their homeland. Then let any other dictator who tries to suppress a people on the grounds of their race or religion know that when NATO takes a stand, it will not yield until the battle is won. Every day, every night our armed forces are risking their lives in defence of our values. They have our full support.[32]

The British leadership also differed from the French and German governments with regard to their inclination to engage in more intensive blaming, for example, by labelling Milosevic 'an immense and great evil'.[33] Foreign Secretary Robin Cook argued that Serbia could not be embraced by modern Europe as long as Belgrade maintained the doctrine of ethnic superiority that 'the rest of Europe rejected half a century ago'.[34] Blair applied an uncompromising attitude by recalling the experiences of the twentieth century and concluding that appeasement does not work in the face of a dictator.[35]

All three states echoed the EU's 'regional peace and stability' argument. The actors justified an active stance in Kosovo on 'good egoistic grounds' – the crisis concerned their own peace and security, and their strategic and national interests.[36] Yet, the British focused more than the others on restoring order on the European continent. Blair added salience to the issue by way of historical analogy. He highlighted previous examples of chaos spreading from the Balkans by recalling that the First World War began in Sarajevo.[37] According to the British logic, instability in one part of the Balkans might easily spill over into other parts, creating chaos and affecting the whole of Europe.[38]

The British also emphasised deterrence. According to British logic,

NATO's active stance on the Kosovo problem would deter dictators in the future.[39]

> Many of our problems have been caused by two dangerous and ruthless men –
> Saddam Hussein and Slobodan Milosevic. One of the reasons why it is now so
> important to win the conflict is to ensure that others do not make the same
> mistake in the future. That in itself will be a major step to ensuring that the next
> decade and the next century will not be as difficult as the past. If NATO fails in
> Kosovo, the next dictator to be threatened with military force may well not
> believe our resolve to carry the threat through.[40]

Finally, the British leaders applied a strategic argument in favour of military action in Kosovo that the others did not use: the necessity of preserving NATO's credibility. Since NATO had promised the Kosovar people that it would not tolerate further repression, inaction would harm the credibility of the organisation.[41] NATO's legitimacy and credibility depended on a successful mission in the Balkans.[42]

Russia: target the real problem

While significant differences between the EU member states' views of the Kosovo conflict have been highlighted above, those between Russia and the other actors in the Kosovo crisis were even more apparent. A clear difference had already become obvious at the level of problem definition. The European states set the agenda, effectively delineating the boundaries of discourse on Kosovo.

The Russian leaders argued that NATO's campaign failed to target the real source of the problems in Kosovo, which, by their interpretation, was international terrorism – Ivanov even accused NATO of supporting Islamic terrorism. The leaders condemned the Kosovo Liberation Army and called for a joint struggle against separatism and terrorism in areas such as Kosovo and Chechnya.[43] After the end of the military operation, they urged other states to support Russia in its struggle against international terrorism, a problem 'stretching from the Philippines to Kosovo'.[44]

The Russians used partly the same shared imagery of Kosovo as the three EU states. They called for the preservation of stability and emphasised the importance of the avoidance of spillover and destabilisation. However, they turned the argument around: it was the actions of NATO rather than those of Milosevic that put European stability at risk. If NATO aggression continued, a larger war in the Balkans might occur, the consequences of which were 'well known from history'.[45] In a televised appeal on 24 March, the Russian President, Boris Yeltsin, addressed 'the whole world', urging the US President to refrain from bombing, since an attack would signify 'a tragic step' and put European security at risk.[46] In the Russian interpretation, NATO's actions jeopardised European and global stability.[47]

Russians had advocated the idea of multipolarity persistently since 1996. In view of the Kosovo bombings, it referred to multipolarity both in normative terms and as corresponding to Russian interests. The normative argument held that multipolarity was desirable to all 'civilized' states, since it is the basis for a democratic and just world order. The Russian leaders defined the conflict as an immoral endeavour by contrasting NATO actions with widely shared and universal norms such as democracy, international cooperation and international law based on the United Nations system.[48] The leaders made use of norms that few state leaders would openly contest, thus attempting to convey a positive image of their state – an image of a nation carrying out a worthy mission.

In addition, the Russian leaders argued that unipolarity would disrupt the global order, resulting in anarchy and chaos. The rationale behind NATO's behaviour was obvious – to enforce US political, military and economic dictates, and to strengthen a unipolar world in which Washington would control the fate of all.[49] The United States was envisaged as the 'main initiator of aggression'. Ivanov accused NATO of 'neo-colonialism' or 'Nato-colonialism'.[50] According to the foreign minister, NATO aimed to 'return to the era of colonialism, dividing European states into some kind of protectorates'.[51] Yeltsin argued that attempts to organise European security according to a 'NATO-centric model' ignored Russia's interests, and threatened European and global stability.[52]

The Russian leaders also emphasised that if Serbian territorial integrity was violated without a mandate from the UN Security Council, Russian territory – or at least its sphere of interest – could also be violated in the same manner. Yeltsin argued that it would be intolerable if NATO's 'open aggression against a sovereign country' were to be taken as and consolidated as a precedent.[53] Ivanov accused the Western states of taking on the role of a 'globocop'.[54] He asked: 'Yesterday it was Iraq: today Yugoslavia – where is next?'[55]

Aspects of reality in focus: salience and the level of analysis

France and Germany: overlapping national and European perspectives

All the actors mentioned above differed by placing the crisis at varying *levels of analysis*. The German and French leaders primarily used a European prism when framing the conflict, but they also applied a national prism. The German leadership argued that Germany had to be on 'the right side' in the war in order to expand its role in Europe.[56] The leaders recalled their national experience, arguing that what happened at Auschwitz should never happen again.[57] The French, in turn, stated that France had played a key role in attempts to persuade Milosevic to comply, pursuing a 'particularly active and intelligent diplomacy'.[58]

That said, France and Germany applied national perspectives in addition to, rather than in place of, a European outlook on the problem. The regional 'EU perspective' was the primary dimension in the French discourse. By demonstrating that Europe could act – the leaders stressed that the EU states had the initiative in Kosovo, not the United States – they hoped to gain support for the creation of a European Security and Defence Policy (ESDP).[59] Lionel Jospin argued that in Kosovo, Europe had demonstrated its character as an 'area of civilization', but added that such an area had to possess capabilities and to be able to obtain respect on the international stage.[60] The German leadership supported the idea of a security dimension to the EU, although for the foreseeable future the Europeans would only be able to deal with low-level crises (that is, lower than the level of crisis in Kosovo).[61]

Russia and the United Kingdom: a global perspective

The British perspective was wholly global in scope. The leadership concluded that the EU had to strengthen its ability to act on its own, but argued that the ESDP should be developed 'in a way fully compatible with NATO being the basis of our collective security'.[62]

The pursuit of stability was a key theme in the British framing, as is observed above. Blair talked a lot about the globalisation of threats. He argued that many domestic problems are caused on 'the other side of the world', for example, when conflicts cause refugees.[63] He stated that intervention is sometimes necessary to stop actors such as Saddam Hussein and Milosevic who 'have the power to destabilize the world':

> I am saying that we shouldn't interfere in every conflict and the principle of non-interference in the affairs of another state is a very sound principle. But I am saying there are circumstances – racial genocide, where our strategic interests are dramatically engaged, circumstances where we have exhausted every diplo-matic solution, circumstances where we have the capability to act – that we do have to think of what I call a doctrine of international community where we are prepared to act, where we are prepared to take a lead.[64]

The Russian leaders also applied a global perspective to the crisis. They defined the NATO intervention in Kosovo as central to the future of global security dynamics.

Solution

For the EU, as well as for the European 'big three', the solution to the crisis was clearly to oust Milosevic from office, thereby relieving Europe of an unwanted element. In addition, the British defined the campaign as a means of deterring other dictators from engaging in improper behaviour.

Differences within the EU with regard to solutions mainly arose over the proper vehicle for taking on the task of getting rid of Milosevic.

The British solution: spread the right norms and sustain NATO

The United Kingdom fully endorsed NATO as the organisation to protect and implement its favoured norms. The Kosovo campaign was conceptualised as a model for future international operations in the security sphere. The British used the Kosovo conflict as an example when outlining new guidelines for solving international problems, thus taking the conflict a step beyond Europe and the EU. The new rules placed humanitarian intervention above the principle of sovereignty. Blair stated that this would 'become the basis for an approach to future conflict'.[65] He wished to qualify the principle of non-interference, since acts of genocide 'can never be a purely internal matter'.[66]

Blair traced the UK's emerging political rhetoric to ideas developing in the USA and in the world in general. He argued that the UK was following certain emerging globalised ideas and solutions – some 'key ideas and principles' involving the spread of liberty, the rule of law, human rights and an open society. Blair defined these norms as being part of a 'Third Way' coloured by internationalism rather than isolationism.[67] Future European policy on globalisation would be informed by the will to spread key norms of freedom, solidarity and democracy. Rather than beginning with theory about structures, the EU should focus on these basic objectives and then find the means of fulfilling them.[68]

The Russian solution: Strengthen international law and the UN

In contrast, the Russians condemned NATO's actions and contested the idea that Kosovo set a precedent for the future handling of international relations. The leaders situated 'the good UN' in opposition to 'the evil NATO'. They continuously referred to the primacy of the UN in solving the conflict, arguing that the central role of the UN must be guaranteed in order to prevent anarchy and chaos in international relations.[69] They did their best to blame NATO, describing the Kosovo campaign as immoral. Ivanov argued that NATO (and the USA) 'destroys cities and villages, bombs schools and hospitals, killing peaceful human beings'. He said that NATO's actions in Kosovo could qualify as crimes against international humanitarian law.[70] Yeltsin stated that international conflicts should be resolved by 'the right of law' enshrined by the UN and the OSCE – not by a primitive 'right of force'.[71] In the Russian view, NATO's actions constituted a 'barbarian aggression against a sovereign state'.[72]

The French and German solution: use NATO, but no precedent

Unfortunately, from the point of view of unity within the EU, the French and German governments essentially sided with the Russian leadership on the mandate issue – arguing that Kosovo could not be regarded as having set a precedent. The two continental states stressed the need to contain NATO's power and influence, although Fischer did endorse the idea that NATO should maintain a continuing presence in European security in order to keep the USA engaged in European security.[73] However, he also argued, with strong domestic support, that the war in Kosovo should not be regarded as a precedent that allowed NATO to intervene in future conflicts, but as a 'very, very large exception'.[74]

The French expressed concern that the UN Security Council would lose influence, and questioned NATO's right to intervene in future conflicts.[75] They portrayed the US role in the Kosovo conflict and NATO's mandate problem as closely connected to the perceived threat of unilateralism. Jacques Chirac echoed the Russian standpoint that NATO should not be given UN authority to intervene around the world because such a development could dismantle the post-World War II international order. Moreover, the French leaders referred to the need to offer an alternative to the unipolar world. Like the Russians, Chirac protested against the idea that NATO could act in place of the UN Security Council. Other organisations could try to do the same on questionable grounds, he argued, hence imposing 'the law of the strongest' on international relations.[76]

> The evolution towards a multipolar world, which seems to us ineluctable, demands, if we want it to develop in harmony and in peace, respect for international law, a law worked out democratically by a community of nations, which is represented by the Organisation of the United Nations and by its Security Council. Some of our allies, and notably our friends the Americans, think that NATO, because it is an organization composed of democracies, the objectives of which would because of this fact be legitimate by nature, can free itself from this authority of the United Nations. France is opposed to this, because the approval of an such infringement by NATO would lead to acceptance of other infringements in the future, for this or that other country or international organization, the objectives of which could, in any case from our point of view, might be arguable and, gradually, therefore, it would be a question of accepting, or of imposing, the law of the strongest.[77]

Although both the British and French governments agreed that the EU had to improve its capacity to act in the international security sphere, they justified this stance in quite different ways. While the French called for independence from the USA, the British argued that the EU must shoulder a larger responsibility to ensure that the USA would be willing to engage in European security in the future. Blair generally described the USA and the unipolar global system in a positive manner. He depicted the USA as a peaceful, non-expansionist actor, which did not engage in world conquest or colonialism but was instead ready to shoulder the responsibilities and burdens 'that come with its superpower status'.[78] More generally, Blair referred to the USA and its engagement in a positive tone and argued that the EU should be thankful for the active US role in the Kosovo conflict.[79] The British leadership thus expressed appreciation of the workings of the US-led unipolar world order, while the French clearly did not.

Clashing norms and interests: the implications

The analytical framework of this volume, which applies framing as the basic analytical tool, leads to a focus on the diverging ways of defining the problem; on the issue of blaming, which also clearly separates the actors; and on how the crisis should be resolved, including on who had a mandate to deal with the problem. This approach reveals that the actors gave quite different meanings to the security situation that prevailed at that time. The focus on the actors' levels of analysis was also valuable because it revealed crucial differences between the 'global players' – the United Kingdom and Russia – and the more Eurocentric actors – France and Germany.

The framing analysis provides examples of converging and competing framing. Although all the leaders used the concepts and phrasing that were central to the European community of discourse, they partly endowed these with different meanings, which resulted in diverging logics.

Major differences were revealed, both among the EU member states and between Russia and the other states. The leaderships endorsed a range of norms and a number of institutions. The Russian, French and German leaderships prioritised the EU and the UN, while the British government stood up for the USA, NATO and an emerging global security order. The French and German leaders applied a European – and partly a national – level of analysis. The British leadership clearly prioritised the global dimension of the crisis, taking global norms and interests as its rationale for transforming the rules for intervention in the sovereign affairs of states. Russia also applied a global perspective, but in a reverse sense, referring to universal norms to highlight the need to protect sovereignty and traditional rules of behaviour in international affairs.

Before taking the analysis further, it should be noted that the leaders sometimes treated interests and norms as two sides of the same coin. Fischer described Europe as a community of material interests and of common norms, and argued that there should be no distinction between *Staatsräson* and moral claims.[80] An even more obvious example is Blair's linkage of violations of human rights with strategic interests. In essence, Blair linked what he perceived as normative behaviour with interests, arguing that it is not possible to ignore conflicts and human rights violations in other countries and to remain secure at home. Blair explicitly defined the spread of liberty, human rights and the rule of law as part of the national interest because 'the spread of our values makes us safer'.[81] According to the British leader, this was a new phase in international relations: the existence of states is no longer threatened but they face other kinds of threats, and this leads to a merging of norms and interests.[82]

For most of the time it is still possible to classify the statements made by the various leaderships as linked to either norms or interests, but the implications of the linkages and relationships between the two logics are examined in the final analysis below.

Rival interests: different world views

What does the framing analysis disclose about the characteristics of the favoured interests of the actors? There is no doubt that the definitions of the crisis given by the actors contained strong elements of reasoning that were linked to strategic interests. The actors used notions related to interests that were well known in the European community of discourse, such as 'spillover' and 'national interest'. In essence, the three EU member states defined the crisis as threatening because it could destabilise the security situation. All four leaderships argued their adherence to the general aims of peace and stability. However, the meaning of these concepts, and their scope, differed – and the actors envisaged different methods for their realisation.

Clearly, the Kosovo campaign put the EU's credibility as an actor in European and international affairs at stake. Once again, the USA, through NATO, took the role of the central actor in matters of European security. Yet, the consequences of a successful mission in Kosovo – although NATO-led – could clearly be positive for the EU's potential future as a strategic actor in the security sphere. The EU had an interest in making use of the crisis, taking it as evidence of the need to develop a capacity to act forcefully in the realm of security.

The British deviated somewhat from the official EU line on this issue, and also from the stance adopted by the French and German governments. The latter clearly developed a secondary but parallel aim for the campaign – an interest in strengthening the EU as an independent actor in the security sphere. The British conveyed that, while the EU ought to evolve as an actor in the security sphere, it should not become *independent*. British interests would best be served if the EU evolved just enough to enable it to share the burden of maintaining European security with NATO and the USA to a reasonable degree. The main issue was not the strengthening of the EU, but to ensure that the USA remained engaged in Europe.

Another discrepancy between the three EU states sprung from their outlook on the problem. All three states framed Serbia in a way that clearly mirrors what Zolo describes as a Western view of the Balkans, that is, as 'domestic aliens' in Europe – being 'Europeans, but not in the full sense of the term'.[83] However, the British focused less than the other two on the aspect of integration, and more on demonising and exclusion. In the light of events in Kosovo, the British built up their argument around the notion of a status quo that was under attack. The message was clear: it was central to British interests that order was restored.

In contrast, instead of placing the emphasis on stability and order, the German and French leaders highlighted the EU, both as an actor in the security sphere and as a referent-object of security. The EU and its institutions were under attack and had to respond. The German government often articulated the European common responsibility to restore peace on the continent. It placed a heavy responsibility on the EU and on the common resolve of the European states.

While the French and German leaderships mainly stuck to a national and regional, that is, European frame, the British leaders started from a global level of analysis. When the British placed the conflict in a global perspective, they came to far-reaching conclusions about how to strengthen their interests. They argued for the cause of global stability at the cost of national sovereignty. They placed salience on the risk of 'global spillover'. They argued in favour of creating new principles for intervention, deterring future dictators and creating a new international security order.

Another central tenet of British interests in the light of the Kosovo crisis was to sustain NATO's credibility. The French and German governments focused more on limiting NATO's mandate, while at the same time strengthening the UN's power and influence. While the French in essence portrayed NATO and the EU as two – not opposing but often contradictory – forces, the Germans instead described them as complementary European security agencies. Both, however, agreed that NATO's power and mandate had to be circumscribed – that Kosovo should not set a 'precedent'. The French even elaborated on the need to avert a unipolar world, while the British described the present unipolar system in a favourable manner.

The Russians went further, essentially reversing the British arguments. The Russians criticised a campaign that in their view undermined European security, strengthened unipolarity, threatened the UN security system and weakened the principle of territorial integrity. A review of the official discourse suggests that favoured Russian interests were portrayed as linked to a solid respect for sovereignty, territorial integrity and the UN global order. The Russians protested about an 'unequal balance of power', and about chaos and anarchy in European and global security relations. The Russian leadership's colourful rhetoric should be understood in the context of domestic opposition to the bombings.[84] A few powers in the international arena – most importantly China and India – supported Russia's interpretation that NATO's actions constituted a break with the UN charter.[85]

Even though the Russian leadership took every opportunity to condemn NATO's actions, they soon became engaged in the peace negotiations. Former Prime Minister Viktor Chernomyrdin, appointed as Russia's presidential envoy to Yugoslavia on 14 April, played an important role. The peace plan – proposed by negotiators Chernomyrdin, Ahtisaari and Talbot and accepted by the Yugoslav Parliament on 3 June – contained some elements of success for Russia. Most importantly, it provided the UN with a role in the conflict as a source of mandate authority for NATO's operation, and it stated that Kosovo would remain within Yugoslavia. On 18 June, the Russian and US Defence Ministers also reached agreement on the structure of the Kosovo peacekeeping force (KFOR). Russia would participate in a unified KFOR command, but the Russian government would retain full control over its contingent.[86]

Apart from French support for multipolarity, the Russian way of defining the conflict did not gain any resonance among the European 'big three'. There was no room for international terrorism in the boundaries of the mainstream European discourse on Kosovo. Nor were Russian criticisms of the USA and their warnings of an 'immoral world order' accepted by the European big three, thereby excluding Russia – as well as a number of other European critics – from the European community of discourse.

In sum, three distinct 'stories on security' based on rival interests have been identified among the four states. The Russian leaders followed their own logic, which contrasted most clearly with that of the British. The EU states agreed among themselves that the campaign aimed to avoid destabilisation, but they diverged on its wider implications. One major difference was that the French and German leaderships described Kosovo as an exception rather than a precedent, while the UK drew on the crisis to promote a new global method of working that would allow for violations of sovereignty under certain preconditions. They favoured intervention to counter threats in an age of the globalisation of threats. NATO would be the central institutional vehicle in this new order, and the USA would remain the central actor. French and German interests focused more on strengthening the EU and limiting NATO's room for manoeuvre. The French converged with the Russians in advocating multipolarity as opposed to US unipolarity.

Rival norms: different institutions at stake

Although the EU did not present any detailed view, a rudimentary EU normative standpoint can be identified. The logic was that European ethics had to be safeguarded through the 'civilisation' of Serbia. EU statements focused on the humanitarian dimension and situated the problem in a strictly

European context. The 'EU position' reflected the focus of the Amsterdam Treaty on liberty, democracy, respect for human rights and fundamental freedoms, and the rule of law.[87]

Among the governments, three different lines of argument can be distinguished – two that were starkly different and one 'in the middle'. At a basic level, the major EU member states conformed to the EU's normative message. The leaderships appealed for 'peace', 'democracy' and 'human rights' – notions central to the EU's basic normative framework.[88]

However, one central difference was that the French and German governments generally defined the norms at stake as 'European'. The British deviated by using an additional set of concepts and phrases that fit into an 'Anglo-Saxon' normative framework. Their normative correctness focused on the righteousness of the US unipolar world order, and on the need to protect universal norms. The UK portrayed the USA as the guarantor of a moral world order. Moreover, the British took Kosovo as an example of how crises should be managed in the future, that is, through a new, normatively good, world order where military force could be used to protect liberty, the rule of law and human rights. The rhetoric corresponded with the 'ethical' message of the 'New Labour' mission statement as well as a number of key speeches made by Labour government representatives on coming to power in the summer of 1997.[89]

In contrast, to be normatively correct in the French and German version meant to act in a multilateral manner in accordance with common rules. To the French and German leaders, the crisis in Kosovo was an issue of future European, or EU, unity and an example of multilateralism being the best method to solve security problems. Germany translated 'unity' into 'strength', thus logically continuing the German post-Cold War tradition of multilateralism. The German emphasis on the EU's special responsibility to Kosovo also corresponds well with the German 'Verantwortungspolitik' policy of responsibility, initiated by the former Foreign Minister, Hans-Dietrich Genscher. In essence, this policy denoted a German rejection of power politics in favour of multilateral methods based on dialogue, compromise and other cooperative and moderate ways of addressing problems in the security sphere.[90]

In addition, in a truly multilateral manner, both the French and German leaderships made an effort to keep their Cold War adversary, Russia, 'on board' in seeking a solution to the crisis. They also emphasised the importance of the UN.

The Russians in turn discussed normative correctness from a global level of analysis, in line with the British, but centred on the UN and multipolarity, on the norms of territorial integrity and international law and order, on the evils of terrorism and on the immorality of NATO's actions. The Russian rhetoric essentially ignored the humanitarian dimension in the region. The

Russian leadership summarised the roots of the problems in Kosovo, and on the world at large, as being linked to terrorism, separatism, unipolarity and an immoral global order. The language used by the Russian leadership about Kosovo bore a strong resemblance to the rhetoric applied to the war in Chechnya in 1994–96; in both instances, the leadership used images of an 'other' in the shape of 'terrorists', 'separatists' and 'Islamic extremists'.[91] Ivanov repeatedly accused NATO of supporting Islamic terrorism.[92]

The Russian leaders also described NATO's campaign as an attempt to realise a new international order based on unipolarity. This scenario was portrayed as a threat to one of Russia's most significant great power attributes, its veto in the UN Security Council. Appealing to shared norms of democracy, the rule of law and international cooperation, Russia promoted rules of behaviour that it wished to elevate to the status of broader principles around which European or global security should be ordered. Appropriate behaviour, according to such logic, would be directed against terrorism, unipolarity and the erosion of the moral global order sustained by the UN Security Council. The French supported the Russian normative standpoint to some extent, while the German government remained almost silent with regard to the global dimension.

Consequences for the EU

The contrasting ways of framing the conflict, particularly with regard to the global level of analysis, reveal underlying policy controversies between the UK, on the one hand, and France and Germany, on the other.

Rather than trying to form a united and fully elaborated EU position on the crisis, the EU remained fairly passive. This turned out to be to its advantage in the longer run because, rather than permitting the Kosovo crisis to transform into an 'EU crisis', the leading member states used it to strengthen and reform the EU. The crisis assisted the development of the EU as a global actor in the security sphere.

At the Cologne European Council in June 1999, a decision was taken to develop a military dimension, the ESDP, in order to develop a more autonomous defence capability. The Helsinki Headline Goal process subsequently resulted in the creation of a substantially increased role for the EU in the security sphere. The aim was to create an EU Military Force of 50–60,000 personnel to carry out the Petersberg tasks, defined in the Maastricht Treaty, and to develop capability goals in the fields of command and control, intelligence and strategic transport. New permanent political and military bodies were also established: a Standing Political and Security Committee (PSC) of senior- and Ambassadorial-level national representatives exercises political control over the strategic direction of operations under the authority of the Council of the European Union; a Military

Committee composed of the Chiefs of Defence or their delegated military representatives provides military advice; and a Military Staff offers military expertise and undertakes early warning, situation assessment and strategic planning tasks in connection with the Petersberg tasks.

This process was already under way before the Kosovo crisis. Blair had launched the idea of a European defence at the Pörtschach summit in October 1998, and the ideas were developed further at the Franco–British summit in St Malo in December the same year. However, Javier Solana later defined the Kosovo crisis as a 'wake-up call', which clearly revealed the short-comings of European national and collective military capabilities. This insight spurred the decision to create a EU force, which would 'contribute more effectively to international peace and security', and 'play a more committed, more responsible role'.[93]

In the longer term, however, it is evident that the divergences signified only the beginning of a rift between the UK, on the one hand, and France and Germany, one the other. The actors clashed most seriously with regard to the issue of intervention in the face of a loss of national sovereignty. Germany was hesitant about, and France totally opposed to, the British vision that allowed intervention when necessary in order to protect human rights and democracy.

The most serious cleavages between France and Germany, and the UK were the differing views held by the two camps about: (a) the kind of norms that should be focused on in the security sphere, and what weight should be placed on defending these norms; (b) the institutional vehicle that should take primary place in the sphere of international security, and what mandate it should be given; (c) the role that the USA should play in the international arena; (d) the rules that should apply in the security sphere; and (e) whether the world should to be arranged in a multipolar or in a unipolar pattern. These differences caused substantial problems for EU unity in the years that followed the Kosovo crisis.

Consequences for EU–Russia relations

The Russian framing diverged substantially from that of the EU and of its member states. Above all, Russia differed with regard to its views on human-itarian norms and on the issue of intervention in sovereign states. The competing – and often mutually exclusive – ways of framing the crisis under-lined, as the literature suggests, that underlying policy controversies have tangible consequences.[94]

Russia's keenness to convey its belief that crucial norms were being sacri-ficed over Kosovo bears witness to a determination to place its politics not simply within a logic of its national interest, but also in a normative framework. The framing actors demonised international terrorism and unipolarity, but their attempts to portray themselves as normative, and the NATO campaign as immoral, were almost completely unsuccessful at the time. Russia was effectively excluded from the discourse on Kosovo – as a rule, France, Germany and the UK did not respond directly to its line of reasoning and the Russian leadership was met with silence. Russia was ignored by NATO and the Western community did not take the arguments made by the Russian leadership seriously. The EU and the European states – particularly the UK – had successfully defined the conflict in a different way. The Kosovo campaign was legitimised with reference to humanitarian motives and the need to avoid the destabilisation of the Balkans and Europe as a whole.

That said, it was evident from the Kosovo case that Russia could come close to the French and German position in future, should similar events occur. The French framing of actors was close to the Russian position on the precedent issue and on unipolarity. During the Kosovo crisis, however, the French leaders were more focused than the Russians on the regional dimension, and they therefore did not attach much weight to the Russian argument. With regard to Germany, it is notable that, although firmly committed to the values of human rights and justice, it did not join the British call for a new global humanitarian interventionism. In the German logic, it seemed that no new grand strategy could be forged, but every situation must be evaluated on its own merits – the NATO campaign should not set a precedent.

Surprising as it may seem, the Kosovo crisis still turned out positively for EU–Russian cooperation. This may to a large degree be explained by the strategies of the EU and the major member states during and after the crisis. The EU did not appear as an important actor during the Kosovo crisis – it did not even outline its stance on the issue properly. Disagreements among the member states, a weak Commission and an undeveloped foreign and security policy explain its low profile. Two rival normative ideals were identified inside the EU, largely converging in order to defend EU norms, while diverging on which actions were permissible in order to safeguard these norms, who is allowed to carry these actions out and which norms should be elevated to the status of broader European or global principles. Since the EU as such did not outline its stance on the Kosovo campaign, none of the states was explicitly inappropriate by EU standards, and their differences were also more about the global than the regional dimension.

To Russia, the Kosovo crisis became bitter evidence of its weakness in international relations. However, the ensuing strengthening of the EU as an actor in the security sphere seemed favourable to Russia. The EU had taken no direct part in the Kosovo campaign and was therefore not subject to Russian criticism. While Russia froze relations with NATO as a consequence of the campaign, it intensified its relations with the EU. Even though the EU was not the ideal vehicle for an all-European security system in the eyes of the Russian leaders, it was still better than NATO.

The Russian leaders gradually paid increased attention to the EU and took a more positive stance on the EU taking a larger share of responsibility for the security sphere. The ESDP was even interpreted as taking the world one step away from US hegemony and towards multipolarity.[95] President Putin described Europe as one of the most important poles in the emerging multipolar world.[96] Putin's participation in the EU summit in Stockholm, in March 2001, was a symbolically important demonstration of his willingness to deepen cooperation.

In conclusion, the Kosovo crisis functioned as a 'wake-up call' for the EU and led it to reform its institutions. In spite of severe differences, most notably between Russia and the UK, the conflict in Kosovo also moved EU–Russian relations forward. Above all, the subsequent strengthening of the EU's actorness favoured a gradual rapprochement. However, in a longer perspective, the crisis highlighted the potential for future controversies between Russia and the EU, and the EU and its member states.

Notes

1 Clarke, M., 'British perceptions', in M. Buckley and S. Cummings (eds), *Kosovo Perceptions of War and its Aftermath* (London: Continuum, 2001), pp. 84–86; Duke, S., et al., 'The major European allies: France, Germany and the United Kingdom', in A. Schnabel and R. Thakur (eds), *Kosovo and the Challenge of Humanitarian Intervention: Selective Indignation, Collective Action, and International Citizenship* (Tokyo: United Nations University Press, 2000), pp. 137–138.

2 Duke et al (note 1), p. 132.

3 Friis, L. and Murphy, A., '"Turbo-charged negotiations:" the EU and the Stability Pact for south-eastern Europe', *Journal of European Public Policy* 7:5 (2000), pp. 767–786.

4 Yeltsin, B., 'Statement on Russian Television', 24 March 1999, in *Diplomaticheskii Vestnik* 4 (1999).

5 Radio Free Europe/Radio Liberty, Newsline, 25 March 1999.

6 Kastrup, D., 'Presidency conclusions', Berlin European Council, 24–25 March 1999.

7 Santer, J., 'Speech to the European Parliament on the situation in Kosovo', 14 April 1999.

8 'L'action militaire en cours doit permettre de faire respecter par la force des principes et des valeurs qui sont la raison d'être de l'Europe. Ne pas agir, c'est accepter. L'Europe et ses partenaires n'acceptent pas les meurtres, n'acceptent pas les déportations, n'acceptent pas la terreur et la haine entre les peuples.' Ibid.

9 Kastrup (note 6); Santer, J., 'Speech to the European Parliament on the situation in Kosovo', 14 April 1999.

10 Santer, J., 'Press conference', 1 June 1999.

11 Santer, J., 'Speech to the European Parliament on the situation in Kosovo', 14 April 1999.; Santer, J., 'Press conference', 1 June 1999.

12 'Ce qui se passe au Kosovo est peut-être la naissance véritable d'une vraie politique étrangère européenne. Ce qui a été dit en matière de défense et la nomination de M.

PESC, M. Solana, en sont des témoignages concrets et visibles.' Santer, J., 'Press conference', 4 June 1999.

13 Richard, A., 'Interview with France-2', 25 March 1999; Chirac, J., 'Speech at the reception in honour of Corps Prefectoral', 26 March 1999; Jospin, L., 'Address to the National Assembly', 26 March 1999, 6 April 1999.

14 Jospin, L., 'Address to the National Assembly', 31 March 1999, 'Address to the National Assembly', 6 April 1999; Chirac, J., 'Address on French National Radio on the situation in Kosovo', 21 April 1999.

15 Jospin, L., 'Address to the National Assembly', 26 March 1999, 'Intervention in the Senate', 15 April 1999; Vedrine, H., 'Interview with Le Figaro', 21 April 1999, 'Interview with France-2', 29 April 1999, 'Inteview with *Sud-Ouest Dimanche*', 9 May 1999, 'Interview with *La Croix*', 21 May 1999; Richard, A., 'Interview with France-2', 25 March 1999.

16 Jospin, L., 'Address to the National Assembly', 26 March 1999.

17 Jospin, L., 'Address to the National Assembly', 26 March 1999; Chirac, J., 'Speech at the reception in honour of Corps Prefectoral', 26 March 1999.

18 'Depuis des décennies, l'Europe, en tout cas notre Europe, s'est refondée sur la paix et le respect des droits de la personne humaine. Accepter que ces valeurs soient bafouées aux portes de l'Union européenne, c'eût été nous trahir. Ce qui est en cause dans le conflit d'aujourd'hui, c'est une certaine conception de l'Europe. Est-ce que nous acceptons sur notre continent le retour de la barbarie ou est-ce que nous nous dressons contre elle? Pour nous, le choix est clair'. Jospin, L., 'Address to the National Assembly', 26 March 1999.

19 Védrine, H., 'Inteview with *Sud-Ouest Dimanche*', 9 May 1999, 'Interview with *La Croix*', 21 May 1999, 'Interview with France-2', 29 April 1999.

20 Fischer, J., 'Interview with SWR', 23 April 1999, 'Interview with *Tagesspiegel*', 23 May 1999.

21 Fischer, J., 'Address to the German Bundestag', 26 March 1999, 'Statement in the *Leipziger Volkszeitung*', 10 April 1999, Statement in *Deutschlandfunk*, 11 April 1999, 'Interview with *Die Zeit*', 15 April 1999, 'Interview with *Tagesspiegel*', 23 May 1999.

22 Schröder, G., 'Address to the European Parliament in Strasbourg', 14 April 1999.

23 Fischer, J., 'Address to the German Bundestag', 26 March 1999, 'Statement in the *Leipziger Volkszeitung*', 10 April 1999; Schröder, G., 'Statement regarding the situation in Kosovo', 24 March 1999, 'Address to the German Bundestag', 26 March 1999.

24 Schröder, G., 'Address to the German Bundestag', 26 March 1999.

25 'Milosevic macht den Kosovo am lichten Tag zum Schlachthaus Europas. Damit hat er der europäischen Zivilisation den Krieg erklärt.' Fischer, J., 'Statement in the *Leipziger Volkszeitung*', 10 April 1999.

26 'Die europäische Wertegemeinschaft würde zum hohlen Wort, wenn wir Europäer zuließen, daß nur eine Flugstunde von hier entfernt, mitten auf unserem Kontinent, die Grundsätze mit Füßen getreten werden, auf denen die Europäische Union errichtet ist: Demokratie, Recht und Gesetz, Freiheit und Solidarität mit den Schwächeren.' Schröder, G., 'Address to the European Parliament in Strasbourg', 14 April 1999.

27 Schröder, G., 'Address to the European Parliament in Strasbourg', 14 April 1999.

28 Ischinger, W., 'Statement', 13 April 1999, in *Deutschlandfunk*, 'Statement', 7 May 1999, in *Deutschlandfunk*, 'Statement', 17 May 1999, in ZDF-Morgenmagazin; Volmer, L., 'Statement', 14 April 1999, in *Deutschlandfunk*, 'Statement', 23 April 1999, in *ZDF Morgenmagazin*, 'Statement', 7 June 1999, in *Deutschlandfunk*; Verheugen, G., 'Statement on SWR', 23 April 1999; Fischer, J., 'Statement in ZDF', 7 June 1999,

'Statement in *Tagesthemen*', 9 June 1999; Schröder, G., 'Address to the European Parliament in Strasbourg', 14 April 1999.

29 Blair, T., 'Doctrine of the international community', Speech at the Economic Club, Chicago, 23 April 1999, 'Speech to the Romanian Parliament', 4 May 1999, 'Speech at the 300th anniversary of the founding of the Khalsa', 5 May 1999.

30 Blair, T., 'Door step interview at the Blace border crossing in Macedonia', 3 May 1999.

31 Blair, T., 'Door step interview at the Blace border crossing in Macedonia', 3 May 1999, 'Speech to the Romanian Parliament', 4 May 1999.

32 Blair, T., 'Speech at the 300th anniversary of the founding of the Khalsa', 5 May 1999.

33 Cook, R., 'Statement in the House of Commons', Hansard Debates, 10 May 1999.

34 Cook, R., 'Statement in the House of Commons', Hansard Debates, 19 April 1999.

35 Blair, T., 'Doctrine of the international community', Speech at the Economic Club, Chicago, 23 April 1999.

36 Fischer, J., 'Interview with *Tagesspiegel*', 23 May 1999, 'Statement in the *Leipziger Volkszeitung*', 10 April 1999, Statement in *Deutschlandfunk*, 11 April 1999, 'Interview with *Der Spiegel*' 'Interview with *Die Zeit*', 15 April 1999; Chirac, J., 'Speech at the reception in honour of Corps Prefectoral', 25 March 1999, 'Address on French National Radio on the Situation in Kosovo', 12 April 1999; Védrine, H., 'Interview in *Le Journal du Dimanche*', 28 March 1999; Blair, T., 'Statement in House of Commons', Hansard Debates, 23 March 1999, 'Broadcast to the nation on Kosovo', 26 March 1999, 'Doctrine of the international community', Speech at the Economic Club, Chicago, 23 April 1999, 'Speech to the Romanian Parliament', 4 May 1999; Cook, R., 'Statement in the House of Commons', Hansard Debates, 25 March 1999.

37 Blair, T., 'Broadcast to the nation on Kosovo', 26 March 1999.

38 Blair, T., 'Statement in House of Commons', Hansard Debates, 23 March 1999.

39 Blair, T., 'Doctrine of the international community', Speech at the Economic Club, Chicago, 23 April 1999, 'Speech to the Romanian Parliament', 4 May 1999.

40 Blair, T., 'Doctrine of the international community', Speech at the Economic Club, Chicago, 23 April 1999.

41 Blair, T., 'Statement in House of Commons', Hansard Debates, 23 March 1999.

42 Cook, R., 'Statement in the House of Commons', Hansard Debates, 25 March 1999; Blair, T., 'Statement in House of Commons', Hansard Debates, 23 March 1999, 'Doctrine of the international community', Speech at the Economic Club, Chicago, 23 April 1999.

43 Ivanov, I., 'Press conference', 29 March 1999, in Diplomaticheskii Vestnik 4 (1999).

44 Ivanov, I., 'Press conference', 13 June 2000, in Diplomaticheskii Vestnik 8 (2000); Putin, V., 'Interview with CBS, CTV and RTR', 13 December 2000, in *Diplomaticheskii Vestnik* 1 (2001).

45 Ivanov, I., 'Press conference', 25 March 1999, in *Diplomaticheskii Vestnik* 4 (1999).

46 Yeltsin, B., 'Address to the Russian Federal Assembly', 30 March 1999, in *Diplomaticheskii Vestnik* 4 (1999).

47 Yeltsin, B., 'Interview with *Der Spiegel*', 28 June 1999, in *Diplomaticheskii Vestnik* 7 (1999).

48 Yeltsin, B., 'Interview with *Der Spiegel*', 28 June 1999, in *Diplomaticheskii Vestnik* 7 (1999); Igor Ivanov, 21 June 1999.

49 Ivanov, I., 'Press conference', 25 March 1999, in *Diplomaticheskii Vestnik* 4 (1999).

50 Ivanov, I., 'Press Conference', 29 March 1999, in *Diplomaticheskii Vestnik* 4 (1999).

51 Ivanov, I., 'Press Conference', 29 March 1999, in *Diplomaticheskii Vestnik* 4 (1999), 'Address to the Russian Duma', 27 March 2003, in *Diplomaticheskii Vestnik* 4 (2003).

52 Yeltsin, B., 'Interview with *Der Spiegel*', 28 June 1999, in *Diplomaticheskii Vestnik* 7 (1999).
53 Yeltsin, B., 'Interview with Der Spiegel', 28 June 1999, in *Diplomaticheskii Vestnik* 7 (1999).
54 Ivanov, I., 'Press conference', 25 March 1999, in *Diplomaticheskii Vestnik* 4 (1999)..
55 Ivanov, I., 'Press conference', 25 March 1999, in *Diplomaticheskii Vestnik* 4 (1999)..
56 Fischer, J., 'Interview with *Tagesspiegel*', 23 May 1999.
57 Fischer, J., 'Interview with *Die Zeit*', 15 April 1999.
58 Jospin, L., 'Address to the National Assembly', 26 March 1999, 'Address to the National Assembly', 8 June 1999.
59 Richard, A., 'Statement in the National Assembly', 24 March 1999, 'Interview with *Le Figaro*', 27 March 1999, 'Interview with France-2', 12 April 1999; Jospin, L., 'Interview with France-2', 8 April 1999, 'Interview with Europe-1', 4 June 1999, 'Address to the National Assembly', 8 June 1999,.
60 Jospin, L., 'Address to the National Assembly', 8 June 1999.
61 Verheugen, G., 'Statement on N-TV', 5 June 1999.
62 Blair, T., 'Interview with the *Washington Post*', 21 April 1999.
63 Blair, T., 'Doctrine of the international community', Speech at the Economic Club, Chicago, 23 April 1999.
64 Blair, T., 'Speech to the Romanian Parliament', 4 May 1999.
65 Cook, R., 'Statement in the House of Commons', Hansard Debates, 20 April 1999.
66 Blair, T., 'Doctrine of the international community', Speech at the Economic Club, Chicago, 23 April 1999.
67 Blair, T., 'Doctrine of the international community', Speech at the Economic Club, Chicago, 23 April 1999.
68 Blair, T., 'Speech: The new challenge for Europe', 20 May 1999.
69 Ivanov, I., 'Joint press conference with Madeleine Albright', 26 January 1999, in *Diplomaticheskii Vestnik* 2 (1999), 'Press Conference', 29 March 1999, in *Diplomaticheskii Vestnik* 4 (1999), 'Address to the participants at the first Russian global conference of the Russian media,' 21 June 1999, in *Diplomaticheskii Vestnik* 7 (1999), 'Address to the Participants at the global conference for former foreign ministers,' 7 July 1999, in *Diplomaticheskii Vestnik* 8 (1999); Yeltsin, B., 'Address to the Russian Federal Assembly', 30 March 1999, in *Diplomaticheskii Vestnik* 4 (1999), 'Interview with *Der Spiegel*', 28 June 1999, in *Diplomaticheskii Vestnik* 7 (1999), 'Statement in the Kremlin', 31 August 1999, in *Diplomaticheskii Vestnik* 9 (1999).
70 Ivanov, I., 'Press conference', 29 March 1999, in *Diplomaticheskii Vestnik* 4 (1999).
71 Yeltsin, B., 'Interview with *Der Spiegel,*' 28 June 1999, in *Diplomaticheskii Vestnik* 7 (1999).
72 Sergeev, I., 'Press conference', 31 March 1999, in *Diplomaticheskii Vestnik* 4 (1999).
73 Fischer, J., 'Statement in *Deutschlandfunk*', 11 April 1999, 'Interview with *Der Spiegel*', 19 April 1999.
74 Fischer, J., 'Interview with *Die Zeit*', 15 April 1999.
75 Védrine, H., 'Interview with Europe-1', 27 April 1999.
76 Chirac, J., 'Press conference at NATO summit', 24 April 1999.
77 'L'évolution vers un monde multipolaire, qui nous paraît inéluctable, exige, si l'on veut qu'il se développe dans l'harmonie et dans la paix, le respect d'un Etat de droit international, un Etat de droit démocratiquement élaboré par la communauté des nations, qui elle-même est incarnée par l'Organisation des Nations Unies et par son Conseil de sécurité. Certains de nos alliés, et notamment nos amis américains – estimaient que l'OTAN parce qu'il s'agit d'une organisation composée de démocraties dont les objectifs seraient de ce fait légitimes par nature, pouvait s'affranchir de

cette autorité de l'Organisation des Nations unies. La France s'y est opposée, car l'acceptation d'une telle dérogation pour l'OTAN conduirait à admettre d'autres dérogations, demain, pour tels ou tels autres pays ou organisation internationale, dont les objectifs pourraient, en tous les cas de notre point de vue, être contestables et, de proche en proche, il s'agirait donc d'accepter ou d'imposer la loi du plus fort.' Chirac, J., 'Press conference at NATO summit', 24 April 1999.

78 Blair, T., 24 March 1999.

79 Blair, T., 'Speech at NATO's 50th Anniversary conference', 8 March 1999, 'Interview with the *Washington Post*', 'Doctrine of the international community', Speech at the Economic Club, Chicago, 23 April 1999, 'Speech to the Romanian Parliament', 4 May 1999.

80 Fischer, J., 'Statement in *Deutschlandfunk*', 11 April 1999, 'Interview with *Die Zeit*', 15 April 1999.

81 Blair, T., 'Doctrine of the international community', Speech at the Economic Club, Chicago, 23 April 1999.

82 Blair, T., 'Doctrine of the international community', Speech at the Economic Club, Chicago, 23 April 1999.

83 Zolo, D., *Invoking Humanity: War, Law and Global Order* (London: Continuum, 2002), pp. 7–11.

84 Buckley, M., 'Russian perceptions', in M. Buckley and S. Cummings, *Kosovo Perceptions of War and its Aftermath* (London: Continuum, 2001), p. 156.

85 Averre, D., 'Russia and the European Union: Convergence or divergence?', *European Security* 14:2 (2005), p. 18.

86 Radio Free Europe/Radio Liberty, Newsline, 21 June 1999.

87 Treaty of Amsterdam, Article F, Paragraph 1, www.europarl.europa.eu/topics/treaty/pdf/amst-en.pdf.

88 Kuusisto, R., *Western Definitions of War in the Gulf and in Bosnia*, Commentationes Scientiarum Socialum 54 (Helsinki: Finska Vetenskaps-Societeten, 1999).

89 Cook. R., 'Speech on the government's ethical foreign policy', 12 May 1997, 'Human rights into a new century', Speech in the Locarno Suite, British Foreign and Commonwealth Office, London, 17 July 1997.

90 L. Aggestam, *A European Foreign Policy? Role Conceptions and the Politics of Identity in Britain, France and Germany* (Stockholm: Stockholm University Department of Political Science, 2004), pp. 205, 226.

91 Wagnsson, C., *Russian Political Language and Public Opinion on the West, NATO and Chechnya: Securitisation Theory Reconsidered* (Stockholm: Statsvetenskapliga Institutionen, 2000), pp. 84–87.

92 Ivanov, I., 'Press conference', 29 March 1999, in *Diplomaticheskii Vestnik* 4 (1999).

93 Solana, J., 'Decision to ensure a more responsible Europe', *International Herald Tribune*, 14 January 2000.

94 Schön, D. and Rein, M., *Frame Reflection: Towards the Resolution of Intractable Policy Controversies* (New York: Basic Books, 1994), pp. 23, 29.

95 Putin, V., 'Interview with CBS, CTV and RTR', 13 December 2000, in *Diplomaticheskii Vestnik* 1 (2001).

96 Putin, V., 'Interview with the German newspaper *Welt am Sonntag*', 11 July 2000, in *Diplomaticheskii Vestnik* 7 (2000).

3   11 September 2001: a new perspective unfolds

Introduction: new perspectives on international security

The catastrophe of 11 September 2001 provided a new perspective on international relations for Western political leaders and added a new dimension to EU–Russia relations. However, the points of departure of the European leaderships diverged considerably. The EU and its member states portrayed the terrorist attacks as an extraordinary event and as a new experience, while Russia described it as nothing more than a recurrence of an all too familiar problem. The Russian President, Vladimir Putin, whose country had repeatedly been the target of terrorist acts, argued that the United States had failed to predict the attacks because of its unwillingness to recognise that the world had changed since the Cold War.[1] The Russian leaders seized the opportunity finally to gain an audience for their analysis of the global security situation.

All leaderships declared their moral aim to be to protect the whole of civilised mankind – or the 'principles of humanity' – against the evil of terrorism.[2] They emphasised that terrorism emanated from particular geographical areas located beyond their own borders, although they refused to link terrorism to any religion or nationality.[3] The notion of a 'clash of civilisations' between Christianity and Islam was unanimously rejected.[4] The Russians, together with the French, made a particular effort to explain the necessity of avoiding such a clash between the Western and Muslim/Arab world.[5]

Apart from these basic similarities, however, it became apparent that each actor would treat the problem in its own way. What did the governments primarily aim to protect in view of 11 September 2001, and how did they differ? What are the implications for the long-term process of rapprochement? The analysis below provides a basis for further discussion of these questions. As was explained in Chapter 1, the scrutiny is structured around the issues central to framing analysis, that is, the *problem definition, moral evaluation, causal interpretation, salience* and *level of analysis of*, as well as the *proposed solutions to*, terrorism.

Defining problems, apportioning blame, moral evaluation and causal interpretation

France, Germany and the EU: the foundations of the EU under attack

EU officials generally defined the events of 11 September 2001 as a threat to the civilised world, and to the norms of liberty, freedom and democracy.[6] However, they placed the EU project at the centre by designating 'EU norms' as a referent-object in view of the terrorist threat.[7] The European Council reacted by elevating the fight against terrorism to the level of a priority objective of the EU.[8]

In discussions with the EU, the leaders of France and Germany indicated that the problem was a European one. They were defending universal values but, in addition, they alluded to the 'European' character of the norms that were at stake.[9] Moreover, France and Germany argued that it was not enough to endorse or spread the 'right' European norms. They went a step further by calling for a reformed and just world order. The German Foreign Minister, Joschka Fischer, argued that Europe now had a chance to promote a preventive, non-military policy that would promote peace and solve many problems in the Third World.[10] Chirac argued that Europeans had to act together in order to defend European values and to achieve a more just and more secure world.[11] 'The mission of our country, and of Europe, is to act so that these humanitarian values advance. That is what we must continue to do together. Then, we shall advance towards a more united, more just and therefore secure world'.[12]

The United Kingdom: universal norms under attack

In contrast, the British leadership did not place the EU at the centre of attention, but focused most intensively on 'universal norms' that it regarded as common to the entire civilised world: norms of reason, democracy and tolerance.[13] The British Prime Minister, Tony Blair, zealously argued for the need to focus on basic, decent and universal norms, and to protect these from attack by international terrorists.[14] Addressing Muslim leaders and communities, he argued that the norms at stake were common to both Muslims and Christians. Speaking to a US audience, he emphasised the democratic element of these norms. Irrespective of the audience, the importance of basic norms was central to his message: 'I thought it particularly important in view of the fact that these attacks were not just attacks upon people and buildings; nor even merely upon the USA; these were attacks on the basic democratic values in which we all believe so passionately and on the civilised world.'[15] Moreover, 'This is not a fight that Britain could stay out of, even if we wanted to. It involves all of us and all people who believe in the same values of freedom and tolerance and respect for other people and the peace-ful way of life, for all those reasons it is important that we are involved.'[16]

Russia: Putting terrorism in context

In common with the other actors, the Russian leaders defined international terrorism as a challenge to the whole of civilised mankind, but their framing of the problem was much more comprehensive.[17] They defined the terrorist acts not as a unique event, but as an example of a phenomenon that had plagued the world for some time, and as something already familiar to the Russian people. The Russian leaders placed 11 September 2001 in a larger context, defining it as belonging to a group of 'new threats' that had endangered the world since the end of the Cold War.[18] They interpreted these new threats as interrelated, and argued that they had not been contained successfully because of the absence of an international mechanism to combat them.[19]

In essence, the Russian leaders came to portray their state as something of a 'winner' of a discursive struggle. On the day of the terrorist attacks, Putin argued that they provided proof of the relevance of Russia's call on the international community to unite in the struggle against terrorism – the 'plague of the 21st century'.[20] The leaders reminded the world that Russia had repeatedly urged the international community to join its long-term efforts in fighting international terrorism.[21] They gave the impression that 11 September had forced Western politicians to realise that the Russian warnings were not empty words. The leaders concluded that, after 11 September, the international community had (finally) come to share its approach and join its struggle.[22]

Aspects of reality in focus: salience and the level of analysis

A global or a regional focus?

A finding that is shared with the Kosovo case study is that the actors diverged with regard to their level of analysis. The British government focused primarily on the national and global levels of analysis. The key role of the USA in world affairs constituted a central part of their outlook on the terrorist problem. The ardent focus on demonising, on capturing the guilty, and on maintaining the status quo chimed well with the US message.

Nor did the British leadership promote Europe with the same zeal as the other two.[23] Unlike France and Germany, the British did not link the new EU tasks in combating of terrorism to its growth as an actor in the security sphere, and they certainly did not describe the EU's role in terms of multi-polarity. Blair's solution was not an EU working independently of the USA. The UK ought to be 'fully engaged in a united Europe, working with an internationalist USA'.[24] The UK was portrayed as a bridge between Europe and the USA.[25]

The EU, France and Germany concentrated on the need for a UN-centred, multilateral approach to the global terrorist threat.[26] Above all, they applied a significantly more regional focus than that of the UK, placing emphasis on the EU's potential. The EU officials made a special effort to designate the EU – with its 'unique toolkit' – as a central part of the answer to the terrorist threat. They elaborated in detail on the EU's role as an 'exporter' of stability.[27] The EU was portrayed as the most appropriate organisation to provide a global response to the fight against international terrorism.[28]

> The European Union is in a unique position to address this issue. We are the world's largest provider of development assistance. We are active in almost every part of the globe. We provide resources to help tackle the unimaginable poverty which is such a blight on the face of the world. We also bring pressure and influence to bear so that basic human rights are respected, governments are held accountable for their actions, and the rule of law is respected. Violence is frequently born out of frustration. Those who have nothing, risk nothing by taking up arms. This is not a justification for conflict, even less for the terrible terrorist attacks of last month. But it is a recognition that poverty and deprivation provide the breeding ground for discontent and anger, where ethnic and religious issues are easily exploited and magnified. The EU is not only providing extensive assistance to others, it is also itself a powerful witness of the success of a regional approach to conflict prevention.[29]

The Russian leadership also elaborated on the potential of Europe, emphasising the need for deeper cooperation between Russia and the EU in the aftermath of 11 September.[30] Putin argued that Europe would reinforce its reputation as a strong and truly independent focus of world politics only if it succeeded in merging its potential with that of Russia.[31]

For the most part, however, Russian leaders discussed terrorism from a global perspective that was combined with a national outlook on the problem. They clearly used 11 September to draw attention to, and gain acceptance for, their own domestic security agenda. They attempted to gain acceptance for their definition of terrorism as a widespread phenomenon with roots in several locations, including Chechnya.[32] They compared terrorists operating in Chechnya with Osama Bin Laden, and concluded that, while it was important to capture Bin Laden, other terrorists had to be taken care of too.[33]

Solutions

The EU, France and Germany: taking a 'root cause approach'

The EU was keen to focus on the 'root causes' of terrorism. Its spokespeople elaborated on 'the seedbed of terrorism' – regional conflicts, poverty and underdevelopment.[34] It wished to reduce the breeding ground for terrorism by tackling destitution in the poorest countries, and promoting prosperity, security, democracy and the rule of law through development.[35]

EU officials linked the root causes approach to the problems of globalisation.[36] The EU was portrayed as 'a power seeking to set globalisation within a moral framework'.[37] The EU Commissioner for External Affairs, Chris Patten, associated terrorism with 'the dark side of globalisation'.[38] The EU's policy was summarised as 'multilateralism and solidarity'.[39] The leadership called for the promotion of a fair international system based on security, prosperity, democracy and development.[40] Globalisation had to be harnessed in order to make it work for the good of the poor. This required a focus on policies tackling poverty, the size of the income gap between the richest and the poorest, and other social and economic imbalances.[41] Such tactics were portrayed as a method of self-preservation for the EU.[42]

In line with the EU, the French emphasised the links between globalisation, poverty and terrorism. Chirac stated that while globalisation brought many advantages, it also carried dangers with it, and therefore had to be managed and 'humanised'.[43] He concluded that the world would be more secure if it became more just.[44] The French leaders elaborated extensively on the underlying causes of terrorism.[45] The French Foreign Minister, Hubert Védrine, argued that, after the end of the Cold War, many in the West had made the mistake of thinking that everyone agreed on the spread of democracy and the Western market economy.[46] France, however, had not delayed in addressing the injustices and inequalities that nurtured terrorist acts – the injustices dividing the North from the South.[47]

The German leadership also put terrorism in a larger context, arguing for a new and more humane world order.[48] For moral reasons, the industrial countries could not remain unmoved by conflicts in the South, and the events of 11 September 2001 had provided new incentives for international cooperation to address poverty.[49]

The United Kingdom: sustaining the status quo and exporting democracy

The UK did not elaborate on how to make globalisation more 'moral', on the North–South divide, or on the need for reform of the global system to the same degree as France and Germany. It generally went along with the EU's politics of prevention, but the British message focused much more on sustaining the status quo in the face of international terrorism than on reforming the international system.

The British leaders explained that engagement was necessary in order to protect the UK's prosperity, its standard of living and its way of life from the consequences of terrorism.[50] 'So this military action we are undertaking is not for a just cause alone, though this cause is just. It is to protect our country, our people, our economy, our way of life'.[51] In Blair's view, the attacks of 11 September 2001 targeted British lives and prosperity, its standard of living and livelihood, and global economic confidence:[52]

> It was also an attack [indistinct] just on lives but on livelihoods. We can see since the 11 September how economic confidence has suffered with all that means for British jobs and British industry. Our prosperity and standard of living, therefore, require us to deal with this terrorist threat … We will act because, for the protection of our people and our way of life, including confidence in our economy, we need to eliminate the threat Bin Laden and his terrorism represents.[53]

Rather than focusing on far-reaching transformations of the international economic or security system, Blair mainly focused on maintaining the status quo by dealing with the 'chaos and strife' originating in certain specific regions and hot spots, and supporting the Middle East peace process.[54]

As a natural element of this concentration on the defence of the status quo, British officials focused considerably more on the perpetrators of 11 September than did the EU, Germany and France.[55] They kept returning to the theme of the punishment of completely immoral terrorists and argued that the UK, firmly united with the USA, would not rest until the evil of terrorism was driven from the world.[56] The leaders discussed at length the terrorists' 'wickedness', 'fanaticism' and lack of humanity, mercy and justice.[57] In order to provide an underpinning for the active British support of the US-led campaign in Afghanistan – which the UK joined on 7 October together with Australia, Canada, France and Germany – Blair spoke at length about Bin Laden, his background and his connections to the Taliban.[58]

It would be unfair to conclude that the British focused exclusively on controlling and capturing terrorists. The export of endangered 'British norms' was portrayed as of key importance to the solution of the problem of international terrorism. Spread of democracy to all regions of the world was the best prescription for avoiding further outbreaks of terrorism:

> We know a good deal about many of these terror groups. But as a world we have not been effective at dealing with them. And of course it is difficult. We are democratic. They are not. We have respect for human life. They do not. We hold essentially liberal values. They do not. As we look into these issues it is important that we never lose sight of our basic values.[59]

> Let us be clear – the way that the world embraces and supports the new Afghanistan will be the clearest possible indication that the dreadful events of 11 September have resulted in a triumph for the international community acting together as a force for good, and in the defeat of the evil that is international

terrorism. I think that we all know now that a safer world is built, ultimately, out of secure countries representing all their people living in peace with their neighbours. That is how terrorism will eventually be defeated, and that, step by step, must be the new international order that emerges from the worst terrorist outrage in our history.[60]

While the British focused more on the spread of democracy, the Germans and the French concentrated on human rights in the fight against terrorism.[61]

At the beginning of this new century Germany stands on the right side – we are almost tempted to say 'at last' – on the side of the inalienable rights of all people. These human rights are the main achievement and the heritage of the European Enlightenment. These values of human dignity, liberal democracy and tolerance are our big strengths in the fight against terrorism.[62]

France, Germany and Russia: endorsing multilateralism and non-military means

A key difference between the UK, on the one hand, and the EU, France and Germany, on the other, is that the latter three placed more emphasis on multilateralism and on other – not least preventive – measures, and used less energy demonising Bin Laden and explaining why it was necessary to find and punish those responsible for the attacks of 11 September. France and Germany were quicker to adopt a broader perspective on the terrorist threat, while the UK was more occupied with energetically supporting the USA in its so-called war on terror during the autumn of 2001.

The EU's main argument was that terrorism had to be countered through multilateral efforts.[63] Together with French and German leaders, EU officials placed particular emphasis on the central role of the UN in this endeavour.[64]

In addition to the UN, Germany focused on the EU as particularly suited to addressing the terrorist problem.[65] Gerhard Schröder portrayed European cooperation as the best way to forge a new politics in response to globalisation and argued that Europe must speak with one voice on the issue of international terrorism.[66] The terrorist attacks had demonstrated that security was indivisible.[67]

The French leadership argued that a cooperative and multilateral/multipolar approach was necessary in order to tackle global problems,[68] and emphasised the importance of united EU action against terrorism.[69] They framed their response to 11 September as an opportunity to boost EU 'actorness'.[70] Lionel Jospin argued that Europe had to act as an 'organiser of multipolarity'.[71] Hubert Védrine stated that 11 September had demonstrated the impossibility of US isolationism and unilateralism.[72]

France and Germany did not rule out military action. Both states regarded armed action as justified, with reference to UN Security Council resolution 1368.[73] The German leadership described Germany as a 'reliable partner' that had broken with the 'taboo of militarisation'.[74]

Yet, France and Germany focused more on prevention and less on military action than the UK. Peaceful means and institutionalism were the answer to terrorism, according to the German leadership.[75] Early on, Schröder highlighted that it was not enough to rely on military means, but called for multilateral efforts that exploited preventive and other non-military methods:[76] 'However, a fixation on exclusively military measures would be unfortunate. We must and we want to develop a comprehensive plan for how to fight terrorism in order to prevent and overcome crises. This plan must be founded on political, economic and cultural cooperation as well as cooperation in security matters.'[77]

The Russian leaders, in turn, suggested that all means had to be used in the fight against terrorism.[78] They argued in favour of early warning and the prevention of emerging threats, but also supported firm reaction to the emergence of such threats.[79] They argued the necessity of addressing problems with similar, and sometimes identical, channels of financing to terrorism, such as drug trafficking, the illegal proliferation of weapons and illegal migration.[80] This broad approach corresponds to the Russian framing of threats since the early 1990s – an all-encompassing policy directed at all kinds of threats, ranging from separatism and ideological tensions to ethnic conflicts.[81]

Even though the Russian leaders firmly supported the US handling of the aftermath of 11 September 2001,[82] they used the occasion to emphasise the need for multilateralism.[83] They argued that the old security structures were unable to cope with new threats, and also complained that such security structures did not offer Russia any real opportunity to participate in drafting and taking decisions:

> Today we must say once and for all: the Cold War is done with! We have entered a new stage of development. We understand that without a modern, sound and sustainable security architecture we will never be able to create an atmosphere of trust on the continent, and without that atmosphere of trust there can be no united Greater Europe! Today we must say that we renounce our stereotypes and ambitions and from now on will jointly work for the security of the people of Europe and the world as a whole.[84]

The Russian leadership therefore used the opportunity, once again, to try to escape Cold War thinking and bring about a new world order in which Russia was 'treated as an equal'.[85] It even suggested that a state's prestige among other states should be measured not by its military or economic might, but by its ability to fulfil its international obligations.[86]

The Russian leaders called for long-term cooperation instead of single acts of retribution, and for a global system to counteract new challenges and threats.[87] Above all, the Russian leaders called for an international legal framework – supported by the UN – to sustain the battle against terrorism, including a clear definition of the problem.[88]

In line with the EU, France and Germany, the Russian leaders also focused on linkages between terrorism, the North–South divide and processes of globalisation.[89] They stated that the UN must increase its efforts to improve socio-economic conditions.[90] They argued for stronger control over the processes of globalisation, and that the UN should coordinate efforts to achieve just and fair resolutions to key global problems.[91]

Clashing norms and interests, and their implications

The events of 11 September 2001 stirred up fundamental reactions. The attacks seemed to provoke a need, on the part of both the EU and its individual member state governments, to project themselves as honourable and significant members of the international community. Each actor claimed to have the right answer, and to be able to make the right contribution, to the fight against terrorism – to the benefit of the rest of the international community. The attacks became a window of opportunity for boosting the actors' self-esteem as worthy members of the 'civilised world'. While the atrocities of 11 September evoked a need to unite in the face of an evil 'other', they also provided an opportunity for the separate governments – and for the EU – to strengthen individual identities.

In a sense, the actors began to compete to appear 'the best member of the class' in the fight against terror. This, in turn, seemed to spring from a need to strengthen the actors' respective identities and self-image. The actors' self-assured rhetoric might also have served to boost confidence, and consequently to nurture a sense of security and safety that was badly needed after the traumatic events of 11 September had generated unexpected chaos in world affairs.

The attacks certainly provided the EU with an opportunity to confirm its identity. EU officials conveyed the message that the terrorist acts concerned the EU at its very core, since terrorism endangered precisely those norms that it was founded on. The EU defined its Charter of Fundamental Rights as a referent-object to be safeguarded in view of the evil of terrorism. EU officials referred to the necessity of protecting the norms of democracy, human dignity, human rights and civil liberties.

To Russia, 11 September 2001 was a chance to confirm its identity as a reliable and morally righteous part of the Western community – a goal that it had striven towards for more than a decade. The German leaders also appeared to link 11 September to issues of identity. Given Germany's Cold War legacy of not participating in military conflicts, the German leaders were careful to justify their active engagement. Germany had already participated in peacekeeping in Kosovo and East Timor, but German forces were now to participate in combat for the first time since World War II. The leadership proclaimed its willingness to break with the taboo of militarisation and take on a greater international responsibility. Active engagement would confirm Germany as a reliable and responsible, transatlantic and European partner.

The way in which the actors' different starting points connected and the salience of 11 September to issues of identity, exemplified above, provide a useful background, which allows the diverging norms and interests that were uncovered in the framing analysis to be elaborated and interpreted further below.

Interests: defend the status quo or launch reforms

Framing analysis provides first-hand evidence that the British government came to the conclusion that British economic prosperity and the Western way of life had to be protected from the terrorist threat. The leaders focused on protecting what the British had in terms of material wealth and a relatively safe location in a stable international system.

In interpreting 11 September the British broadly resorted to a defence of the world 'as it had been'. They portrayed the terrorist events as something new, which had disrupted a relatively stable order and threatened the British way of life. As a consequence of this defensive stance, the leadership focused narrowly on demonising and capturing those responsible. Basically, they suggested that by acting determinedly the global community could strike back and eliminate the threat – changing things back to normal and re-establishing the status quo.

While British interests may be labelled 'conservative', the interests of other actors were definitively more progressive, although not 'revolutionary'. Germany, France and the EU promoted interests that focused less on preserving the current security system and more on transforming it in order to undermine the breeding ground for terrorism. All the actors shared the same goal of accomplishing a stable world order. The main difference was that, while the British started from a determination to preserve a favourable world order, if necessary by way of certain reforms, the other actors inferred that the world order had failed and must therefore be thoroughly recreated in an improved form.

Although the French and German governments proclaimed their solidarity with the USA, they focused less than the UK on blaming, capturing the perpetrators of 11 September and protecting the status quo. Instead, there was much discussion of necessary transformation, delineating the changes required to undermine the sources of terrorism, and refining the tools to be used in order to prevent new terrorist acts.

The indivisible nature of security remained a central feature of EU, German, French and Russian interests. This led to the conclusion that a secure world could only be achieved through multilateralism. The four leaderships framed 11 September as a potential new start for global cooperation. In their view, the terrorist attacks could contribute to an increased awareness among state leaders of the need to transform the international system from unilateralism to multi-lateralism.

The British regime also emphasised the global coalition against terrorism. However, it did not sign up to the campaign to promote joint action aimed at strengthening multilateralism as *the* new working method in the security sphere. Instead, in the British approach the means appeared to be of secondary importance. The British leaders focused on immediate and efficient problem solving, not on constructing new institutional structures and working methods. What mattered was to defend effectively a world order under attack, above all by directly targeting those responsible for those attacks. The UK firmly supported US actions following the terrorist acts and, more than any other actors, it approved of US unilateralism.

In direct contrast, France linked its call for unity to the issue of polarity. It took 11 September as evidence of the ineffectiveness of US isolationism and unilateralism. A multipolar system was clearly in the French national interest and the French leaders described Europe as a potential organiser of multipolarity. Germany also argued in favour of multilateralism, arguing that unilateralism could not solve modern problems. The German leaders emphasised Europe's potential, portraying it as a central and capable actor in world politics.

The EU promoted multilateralism as the only viable method of tackling terrorism. EU officials portrayed the UN as the natural leader of the multilateral endeavour. The EU itself would also play a key role. That the EU should become a vital part of the solution to the terrorist problem was central to its interest in the security sphere.

EU officials also heavily emphasised prevention. Last but not the least, they attempted to establish the EU as a good example for the rest of the world – primarily by conveying the image of a regional success story in conflict prevention. France and Germany, and also Russia, endorsed the idea of the EU taking on a larger role in the sphere of global security.

In contrast to the other actors, and in particular contrast to the UK, Russia defined terrorism in a more comprehensive way. According to the Russian national interest, all kinds of terrorism had to be dealt with. The world community had to target not just al-Qaida and the perpetrators of 11 September, but all terrorists operating in the different regions of the world. Moreover, the world had to be protected from new threats, of which terrorism was only one – albeit the most serious. It was not a 'terrorist shield' that was needed, but an entire system of defence against a range of new threats.

This way of defining the problem should be understood in the light of Russia's security agenda since the end of the Cold War, an agenda that had targeted all kinds of new threats and insecurities, problems which would not easily go away. As a consequence of this long-term and comprehensive view of the problem, the Russians did not argue – as the British did, in some ways – that terrorism could be extinguished. It was characterised as more of a permanent nuisance.

Because Russia argued that the risk from large-scale terrorist acts had not started on 11 September 2001– but could be traced back to the end of the Cold War, when a new era in international security relations had begun – the Russian analysis was not bound to a specific area or time period, but was of a more all-embracing character. This approach stands in contrast to that of the British, who framed terrorism as something much more specific. The British focused on terrorism in the shape it had revealed itself on 11 September.

The Russian leadership linked their comprehensive view of terrorism to a call for major global transformations. First, in order to satisfy Russian interests, a system to counteract new challenges and threats had to be realised.

Second, they conveyed a vision of a multipolar world that would be less vulnerable to new threats. Europe was envisaged as a key actor in the multipolar order. The UN, in turn, would be the centre of a new global system. The new security structure would provide Russia with better opportunities to participate in taking central decisions in the realm of international security.

Third, Russia demonstrated an awareness that brute force was not enough and called for stable development all over the world in order to reduce the inequalities in socio-economic development which nurtured terrorist movements. Globalisation had to become 'manageable' and the UN had a key role in this as a coordinating centre that could solve central problems.

In sum, the UK identified no immediate need to change the security system after 11 September, but primarily set out to preserve the status quo. The other actors took 11 September as a serious reminder of certain deficiencies in the global system that could no longer be ignored. Although all actors acknowledged the need for reforms that could serve to prevent the future growth of terrorism, France, Germany and the EU focused more on the need for a wide range of measures that could result in a far-reaching transformation of the global system.

Normative standpoints: defending norms or normative behaviour?

The most evident difference with regard to the normative dimension of the justifications of policies was that the British leadership focused intensively on the defence of and further spread of norms, while the other actors placed relatively more emphasis on normatively correct behaviour, in terms of an ardent commitment to multilateralism, and on reforming the global system.

In analysing the events of 11 September 2001, France and Germany focused primarily on what had gone wrong with the processes of globalisation and the moral lessons that could be derived from these mistakes, while the British focused on how to ensure that Western norms and its way of life continued to thrive – for the good of the world.

France and Germany elaborated less on exporting the 'right norms' as a solution to problems, and more on the need for better institutional structures, and for multilateral action as the best way to counter the new threats. In the French and German interpretation, it was normatively correct to unite and use multilateral methods of action with the aim of achieving a just world. The leaders focused on the victims of globalisation and on the gaps between rich and poor, and also on what the rich world could do to help. The appropriate way of dealing with terrorism would entail not only targeting the perpetrators and eliminating the direct menace, but also treating the problem in a more comprehensive fashion and dealing with it as an issue of global inequality and injustice for which, implicitly, both the perpetrators and the rich world were to blame.

While the British also referred to the need for reforms, they did not do so with the same zeal and to the same extent as the other actors. Instead, they focused on the need to protect Western norms from a serious challenge. The British perception was that the terrorist attacks emanated from the Third World and challenged the Western world order. The terrorist acts, in a sense, constituted an attack on the process of globalisation, which, in British eyes, was a positive process because it symbolised human progress through the spread of material well-being and Western norms such as liberty, democracy and stability.

The UK was not wholly uncommitted to an 'ethical' foreign policy. Ever since the British Foreign Secretary, Robin Cook, had held his famous press conference in May 1997 to launch New Labour's 'ethical dimension to foreign policy', the Labour leadership had been committed to reform of the international system, for example, by pushing for policies to reduce poverty in the South.[92] However, in comparison with the other actors included in this study, the British government does not stand out as progressive. It focused more on capturing those responsible for the attacks, and on defending and spreading positive norms, than on reforms to alter the character of the international system to make it more morally just.

The EU and its member states did not hesitate to ascribe themselves a missionary role. Their task was to stabilise the world – in the British case primarily by way of exporting democracy, and in the French and German case by means of the multilateral politics of prevention aimed at 'just' reforms. The British maintained the strongest focus on the export of norms. The

French and the Germans focused less on norms by themselves, but instead maintained a focus on creating a multilateral, cooperative and all-inclusive world order.

The Russian leaders portrayed Russia as a state *acting* in a normatively correct way not by diffusing norms, but by standing up decisively against an evil – and by doing so in accordance with international law. Russia's aim was not to protect a set of revered norms from terrorism, but to manage the terrorist threat by strengthening universal codes of conduct. In the official Russian interpretation, stable development in all the regions of the world was required in order to undermine the breeding ground for terrorism, and the UN had a central role to play in achieving this. Law and order would thus be strengthened, resulting in a more secure international system.

Russian officials argued that the global community had to agree a common outlook on terrorism. By proclaiming a willingness to act through multilateral efforts and to adhere to common visions, all based on international law, it conveyed an image of itself as a state conforming to the most appropriate form of behaviour in the face of terrorism.

In essence, Russia called on the West to accept the Russian normative interpretation. The other major players had become trapped in an old system of norms because of their unwillingness to change their way of thinking and their reluctance to form new bonds of trust. Their interpretations of the world therefore relied on stereotypes stemming from the Cold War. According to Russia, these norms originated from an outdated security structure, which could not cope with new threats and new challenges.

The Russian leaders started from a normative framework according to which terrorism was best defeated by the establishment of a joint combat system based on a world order founded on law and justice, and run according to the statutes of the UN. This legalistic approach was perhaps the most striking part of the Russian normative argument.

The consequences of 11 September for the EU

All actors framed the events of 11 September 2001 in terms of both norms and interests. However, these norms and interests differed considerably.

Although the actors did not always use the concept 'globalisation', much of the framing focused on how to relate to a globalised world. According to the British normative standpoint, the globalisation processes that were diffusing the Western way of life and norms had to be defended from attacks from outsiders such as terrorist movements.

The EU, as well as France, Russia and Germany, took a normative stance by which globalisation had to be 'managed' or 'harnessed' in order to achieve a more just and stable world. In essence, they professed a willingness to incorporate more and more actors into the civilised world, actors that could function according to the same normative rules of behaviour as the Western states.

Despite all the internal differences, 11 September provided the EU project with a new impetus. The EU defined the struggle against terrorism as one of its key objectives and set out to implement a whole range of new measures in the security sphere. EU officials highlighted several consequences of the terrorist attacks for the EU as an organisation. The EU was given an opportunity to highlight its capacity as a multifaceted actor with a range of tools available that were well suited to addressing the threat of terrorism.

On 21 September 2001 a range of measures to combat terrorism was adopted, including a European arrest warrant allowing suspects to be handed over directly from one judicial authority to another, and the identification of presumed terrorists, and of the organisations supporting them, in Europe in order to draw up a common list of terrorist organisations.[93] The EU called for enhanced joint efforts with regard to non-proliferation and enhanced export controls on arms and other items capable of being used for terrorist purposes.[94]

The leaders of the EU member states, above all the French leadership, took the chance to promote Europe as a significant power in world affairs. It was the official view of the French leaders that the European Security and Defence Policy (ESDP) could transform Europe into a major player in world affairs. In this way, France, as one of the leading EU member states, could also attain a more authoritative position in the international arena.

However, from the longer-term perspective, the basic differences outlined above highlighted the obstacles to the development of the EU as an actor in the security sphere. While the UK zealously allied itself with the USA's fervent determination to quell further outbreaks of terrorism, the other actors took the opportunity to call for new methods in the security sphere and for reform of the international security structure.

Such diverging analyses of how to act in the face of the 'new' global situation had serious repercussions during the build up to the Iraq war one year later. Against the backdrop of how the actors' framed 11 September, their reaction to the Iraq war was quite easy to predict. The EU, French, Russian and German leaderships resorted to a fervent defence of the role of the UN and of multilateralism. The French and Russian governments interpreted the world in terms of polarity. The UK demonstrated an ardent commitment to basic and universal norms. By targeting those directly responsible for terrorism, including a 'clean up' of rogue states, it also demonstrated its solidarity with the USA.

The consequences of 11 September for Russian relations with the EU

At the end of the Cold War, the US political establishment re-conceptualised the world according to a new logic, which the administration of President George H. W. Bush called a 'new world order'. This new order was to be secured by the USA as the global hegemon, and the instability and chaos represented by rogue states and other unreliable actors were characterised as antagonistic to it. On 29 January 1991, Bush used the new world order to justify the upcoming first Gulf War against Saddam Hussein: 'What is at stake is more than one small country; it is a big idea: a new world order, where diverse nations are drawn together in common cause to achieve the universal aspirations of mankind – peace and security, freedom, and the rule of law.'[95]

The leaders of the newly established Russian Federation immediately joined with the US framing of this new world order, under which Russia and the USA were no longer enemies, but partners and friends, and the enemies were of a new character.[96] However, with the passing of time, the Russian leaders began to accuse the West of retaining the old interpretation of the world as divided into two camps – the East and the West. It was not until after the terrorist attacks of 11 September that Russia was reassured that the EU and its member states had turned their full attention to a new kind of 'other' in the shape of rogue states and terrorist networks such as al-Qaida.

Reactions to the events of 11 September 2001 furthered Russian political ends in many respects. Although welcoming the support provided by some European states during the military campaign in Afghanistan, the USA demonstrated that it could manage without the backing of the North Atlantic Treaty Organisation (NATO). The US administration allocated unprecedented resources to combating terrorism. The terrorist attacks therefore led to a weakening of the Western security structure, which had traditionally been based on NATO. In this sense, developments after the terrorist attacks helped to modify the traditional, fairly NATO-centric, understanding of the transatlantic security structure. Henceforth, the USA began to rely more on ad hoc 'coalitions-of-the-willing', rather than routinely turning to NATO and its traditional partners.

Such a security system, based on a more 'open' interplay between states, during which coalitions can switch, suited Russia better than a NATO-based Western bloc that, even if not hostile, was rather 'closed'. The new system provided Russia with enhanced opportunities to forge temporary coalitions with Western states, which it took during the Iraq war.

Moreover, while the Western security community was somewhat diluted, Russia improved relations with both the EU and the USA after 11 September. Russia had frozen its formal relations with NATO as a consequence of the bombing of Belgrade in 1999, although it had taken up its place in the Permanent Joint Euro-Atlantic Partnership Council (PJC) in

May 2000.[97] Relations with NATO and the USA, however, remained fairly cool until the summit meeting in Ljubljana, Slovenia, between President Putin and President George W. Bush in June 2001. The summit started a process of rapprochement, during which Russia agreed to withdraw its military bases from Cuba and Vietnam and implicitly accepted NATO enlargement and the US withdrawal from the ABM Treaty.[98] After the terrorist attacks of 11 September, Putin was the first foreign leader to express his sympathies to the US President over the telephone. Putin also decided to commemorate the victims of the terrorist attacks with a minute's silence in Russia on 13 September. On 8 October he agreed to the military operation in Afghanistan.[99]

Russia's support for the USA following the terrorist attacks both strengthened its position in the international arena and ameliorated its relations with the USA and NATO. Domestically, the most controversial step was probably when Putin gave his consent to a US military presence in Central Asia and Georgia, without extracting any immediate concessions of his own. In addition, Russia accepted both the decision to enlarge NATO, and a new arms control agreement at a summit meeting between Putin and Bush in Crawford, Texas, in November 2001.[100] In return, Moscow gained increased acceptance for its conduct in Chechnya by emphasising the links between the Chechen separatists, the attacks of 11 September 2001 and terrorists based in Afghanistan.[101] At the end of September 2001, Putin expressed satisfaction about the fact that Washington had changed its tone on the conflict in Chechnya.[102] In 2002, Russia was allowed extended participation in NATO decision making, in particular with regard to the fight against terrorism, regional emergencies and arms control. In December 2002 the NATO Secretary General, George Robertson, designated Russia NATO's 'first partner' in the fight against international terrorism.[103] The Russian Foreign Minister, Igor Ivanov, concluded that Russia had returned to the international arena as a key player in 2001. In Ivanov's view, relations with NATO and the USA had radically improved as a consequence of Russian support for the anti-terrorism coalition, the growth of the Russian economy and Putin's foreign policy.[104]

Russia also set out to advance cooperation with the EU following the events of 11 September 2001. Collaboration in the fight against terrorism accelerated during that autumn. The joint statement at the EU–Russia summit in October 2001 declared that the two parties would step up their cooperation to combat international terrorism, and also work to address the underlying causes of the phenomenon. Russia and the EU agreed to expand cooperation in the areas of nuclear security, space, energy and the economy, and to set up a group to monitor common security issues on a monthly basis. The two parties would fight money laundering, synchronise national legislation, and develop a mutually acceptable definition of terrorism. The search for a common definition was clearly in line with Russian demands for common legal ground on the issue. Most notably, the two parties claimed to be stepping up cooperation in the issue area 'with due regard for international law and the United Nations Charter'.[105] Such phrasing was in accordance with the Russian framing of 11 September, but also with the framing of the French and German leaderships.

The determination to cooperate against terrorism seemed to spill over into other areas in the security sphere. The two parties reiterated their commitment to unite their efforts at their summit in Brussels on 11 November 2002. They particularly mentioned three tasks: (a) finalising the agreement between EUROPOL (the European Law Enforcement Organisation) and Russia on the exchange of technical and strategic information, in order to be able to sign it as soon as possible; (b) exploring ways to strengthen judicial cooperation in response to terrorism and organised crime; and (c) intensifying their work under the auspices of the UN.[106]

President Putin called for a common security space in Europe.[107] Blair stressed the opportunity to forge new relationships because of the interests Russia shared with the West in the light of the evil of terrorism.[108]

The collaboration in the fight against terrorism that evolved in the years that followed bears witness to the fact that Russia can make a contribution to European and global security. It has experience and knowledge in areas where European states are relatively weak, including many aspects of the war against terrorism, fighting organised crime and enforcing non-proliferation. According to a joint declaration from the EU–Russia summit in November 2003, 'the fight against terrorism and our commitment to prevent proliferation of weapons of mass destruction are cornerstones of our cooperation in the field of security'.[109] Moreover, the Russian leaders agreed with the French, German and EU vision of strengthening the EU as an actor in international affairs to enable it to be recognised as a significant pole in a multipolar system.

While the terrorist attacks on the USA boosted EU–Russian cooperation, by far the greatest change took place at the discursive level – from 11 September on, Russia entered the European discursive space. During the Kosovo crisis Russia had been effectively excluded from the discourse, but they now came to occupy a fairly central place in the discursive realm. The Russian leaders had for a long time emphasised the primacy of the terrorist threat on the international security agenda, but without gaining much recognition from the international community. This shows the extent to which Russia had been dependent on others – primarily the USA – with regard to setting the agenda. Russia could not set the international security agenda because it had not succeeded in securitising the terrorist threat in an international setting. The terrorist attacks on the USA opened a welcome 'window of opportunity' to allow Russia to gain attention for its claims. It also gave Russia new hope that its voice would be better heard in international affairs in general.

Most importantly, the Russian government converged with the French and German leaderships on the need to use normatively correct methods to address terrorism and, above all, to use multilateral endeavours. The Russian leadership even called for a normative yardstick, by which a state's global status could be measured not by its power, but by its ability to fulfil its obligations in the international system, that is, to act appropriately according to common rules of conduct. Transplanting this logic to the European arena, the Russian leaders called for 'increased community' by condemning Cold War thinking, which reproduced old stereotypes and hindered the development of trust among actors. They conveyed a vision of a multipolar world where the EU, further strengthened by the added power of Russia, would be able to function as a powerful centre. Germany, France and the EU also emphasised the efficiency of multilateralism and cooperation in the light of the terrorist threat. The French joined the Russian call for multipolarity. France, Germany, the EU and Russia also highlighted the EU's potential as a powerful and capable actor in the security sphere. Finally, all four actors called for reforms that could undermine the breeding grounds for terrorism.

A central aspect of the preferred Russian multilateral global system would be a common legal framework that could facilitate the struggle against new threats, including a common definition of the problem. It is likely that the Russian leaders also calculated that such a common definition would facilitate international acceptance of Russia's handling of the Chechen problem. If they could succeed in getting Chechen resistance officially classified as terrorism, it would be more difficult for the international community to criticise the methods used by Russia to subdue the Chechen rebellion. However, on this point, they did not achieve their aims. The EU and its member states did not give their official backing to Russia's handling of Chechnya. They did not accept the Russian framing of Chechnya as nothing more than another case of terrorism, which ought to have the same consequences as 11 September. The Chechen problem remained a substantial obstacle to the development of closer relations between Russia and the EU.

In conclusion, Russia's relations with the EU evolved after 11 September, and it managed to confirm its role as a more important partner for the EU and the USA in the security sphere than had previously been the case. The most significant changes took place at the ideational level. Most importantly, Germany and France came closer to Russia's official interpretation of world affairs. The three actors shared a central analysis of world events and this contributed to the formulation of their views in the build up to the Iraqi conflict in 2002–03, where the central point at issue was, once again, the role of institutions and multilateralism in world affairs as opposed to righteous causes that require the protection of hegemonic norms.

Even though it did not manage to securitise the Chechen problem in the way it wished, Russia was finally given the opportunity to seek support for its discourse on international terrorism as a chief evil in the modern world. Terrorism was finally securitised at the international level. After 11 September, Igor Ivanov argued that the EU's and Russia's standpoints on terrorism were identical, and that the two would continue to coordinate their efforts against terrorism.[110] The finding of common discursive ground with the EU was a success for the Russian campaign to forge ever closer bonds with actors in the Western community, and to become a full member of that community.[111]

Notes

1   Radio Free Europe/Radio Liberty, Newsline, 17 September 2001.
2   EU–Russia summit, 'Joint statement', Brussels, 3 October 2001.
3   EU–Russia summit, 'Joint statement', Brussels, 3 October 2001; Prodi, R., 'Address to the European Parliament', 24 October 2001; Putin, V., 'Speech at a meeting of the Russian Security Council', 28 September 2001; Jospin, L., 'Interview with France-2', 12 September 2001; Blair, T., 'Statement to the House of Commons', 14 September 2001; Straw, J., 'Statement in House of Commons', Hansard Debates, 14 September 2001; Schröder, G., 'Address to the German Bundestag', 19 September 2001.
4   Schröder, G., 'Address to the German Bundestag', 19 September 2001; Blair, T., 'Joint press conference between Tony Blair and President Mubarak', 11 October 2001; Chirac, J., 'Interview with CNN', 13 September 2001; Council of the European Union, 'Conclusion and Plan of Action of the Extraordinary European Council meeting on 21 September 2001'; Council of the European Union, 'Declaration by the Heads of State or Government of the EU and the President of the Commission: Follow-up to the September 11 attacks and the fight against terrorism', 19 October 2001; Prodi, R., 'Address to Asian Ambassadors meeting', Brussels, 24 September 2001, 'Speech to the European Trade Union Confederation', Brussels, 11 October 2001.
5   Chirac, J., 'Interview with CNN', 13 September 2001; Putin, V., 'Speech at a meeting of the Russian Security Council', 28 September 2001, 'Joint statement with George Bush', 13 November 2001, 'Interview with Greek TV channels NET-TV and Mega', 5 December 2001.
6   Council of the European Union, 'Conclusion and Plan of Action of the Extraordinary European Council meeting on 21 September 2001'; Solana, J., 'A broad consensus against terrorism', *Financial Times*, 13 September 2001.
7   Prodi, R., 'Speech at Jawarlal Nehru University', New Delhi, 23 November 2001.
8   Council of the European Union, 'Conclusion and Plan of Action of the Extraordinary European Council meeting on 21 September 2001'.
9   Jospin, L., 'Address to the National Assembly', 3 October 2001; Chirac, J., 'Speech on the radio/television', 16 November 2001; Schröder, G., 'Address to the German Bundestag', 19 September 2001.
10 Fischer, J., 'Address to the German Bundestag', 8 November 2001; 'Address to UN General Assembly', 12 November 2001.
11 Chirac, J., 'Speech on the radio/television', 16 November 2001.

12 'La vocation de notre pays, et de l'Europe, est d'agir pour que ces valeurs de l'humanisme progressent. C'est ce que nous devons continuer de faire ensemble. Alors, nous serons sur la voie d'un monde plus juste, plus solidaire et donc plus sûr.' Chirac, J., 'Speech on the radio/television', 16 November 2001.

13 Tony Blair described the 'civilised world' as being founded on the norms of reason, democracy and tolerance. Blair, T., 'Statement to the House of Commons',14 September 2001.

14 Blair, T., 'Statement to the House of Commons',14 September 2001, 'Statement to the House of Commons', 8 October 2001, 'Interview with Al-Jazeera', 9 October 2001, 'Joint press conference between Tony Blair and President Mubarak', 11 October 2001,, 'Interview with CNN', 6 November 2001.

15 Blair, T., 'Statement to the House of Commons',14 September 2001.

16 Blair, T., 'Interview with CNN', 6 November 2001

17 Putin, V., 'Statement on the terrorist acts in the US', 11 September 2001, 'Interview with ARD', 19 September 2001, 'Joint statement with George Bush', 13 November 2001.

18 Ivanov, I., 'Address to the UN', 24 September 2001.

19 Ivanov, I., 'Interview with CNN', 12 September 2001, 'Address to the UN', 24 September 2001.

20 Putin, V., 'Statement on the terrorist acts in the US', 11 September 2001.

21 Putin, V., 'Statement in Moscow', 24 September 2001; Ivanov, I., 'Press Conference in Moscow', 13 September 2001.

22 Ivanov, I., 'Interview in ORT', 21 September 2001.

23 Blair, T., 'Joint press conference with President Arafat in Gaza', 2 November 2001, 'Statement to Parliament', 4 October 2001, 'Speech to the European Research Institute', 23 November 2001.

24 Blair, T., 'Speech to the European Research Institute', 23 November 2001.

25 Blair, T., 'Speech to the European Research Institute', 23 November 2001.

26 Prodi, R., Address to the European Parliament', 12 September 2001; Patten, C., 'Speech in Stockholm', 4 December 2001; Solana, J., 'Intervention at the conference "The Fire and the Crystal"', Rimini, 21 October 2001.

27 Prodi, R., 'Address to the European Parliament', 13 November 2001.

28 Solana, J., 'Intervention at the conference "The Fire and the Crystal"', Rimini, 21 October 2001.

29 Ibid.

30 Putin, V., 'Interview with Greek TV channels NET-TV and Mega', 5 December 2001.

31 Putin, V., 'Address to the German Bundestag', 25 September 2001.

32 Putin, V., 'Statement in Moscow', 24 September 2001, 'Press Conference in Brussels', 2 October 2001.

33 Ivanov, I., 'Interview in RTR', 27 October 2001.

34 Council of the European Union, 'Presidency Conclusions, Laeken European Council Meeting, 14–15 December 2001'.

35 De Ruyt, J., 'Measures to eliminate international terrorism', Statement by Jean De Ruyt, Permanent Representative of Belgium to the United Nations, on behalf of the European Union and the countries of Central and Eastern Europe associated with the European Union, to the United Nations General Assembly Plenary, 1 October 2001; Prodi, R., 'Speech to the European Trade Union Confederation', Brussels, 11 October, 2001; Council of the European Union, 'Declaration by the Heads of State or Government of the EU and the President of the Commission: Follow-up to the

September 11 attacks and the fight against terrorism', 19 October 2001; Council of the European Union, 'Conclusion and Plan of Action of the Extraordinary European Council meeting on 21 September 2001'.

36 Council of the European Union, 'Conclusion and Plan of Action of the Extraordinary European Council meeting on 21 September 2001'.

37 Council of the European Union, 'Presidency Conclusions, Laeken European Council meeting, 14–15 December 2001'.

38 Patten, C., 'Speech in Stockholm', 4 December 2001.

39 Prodi, R., 'Speech to the European Trade Union Confederation', Brussels, 11 October, 2001.

40 Council of the European Union, 'Declaration by the Heads of State or Government of the EU and the President of the Commission: Follow-up to the September 11 attacks and the fight against terrorism', 19 October 2001.

41 Prodi, R., 'Address to the European Parliament', 24 October 2001.

42 Patten, C., 'Speech in Stockholm', 4 December 2001.

43 Chirac, J., 'Statement at the Regional Forum on Europe's future', 4 October 2001.

44 Chirac, J., 'Interview with the Italian Journal *La Stampa*', 27 November 2001.

45 Jospin, L., 'Interview with Ouest-France', 26 September 2001, 'Address to the National Assembly', 3 October 2001.

46 Védrine, H., 'Address to the UN General Assembly', 28 November 2001.

47 Védrine, H., 'Interview with Canal Plus', 18 November 2001.

48 Fischer, J., 'Address to the German Bundestag', 11 October 2001'; 'Address to UN General Assembly', 12 November 2001

49 Volmer, L., 'Address to the Ruhr Political Forum', 12 November 2001.

50 Blair, T., 'Statement to Parliament', 4 October 2001, 'Statement', 7 October 2001, 'Statement to the House of Commons', 8 October 2001; Straw, J., 'Statement in House of Commons', Hansard Debates, 4 October 2001.

51 Blair, T., 'Statement to the House of Commons', 8 October 2001.

52 Blair, T., 'Statement', 7 October 2001', 'Interview with Al-Jazeera', 9 October 2001

53 Blair, T., 'Statement to Parliament', 4 October 2001.

54 Blair, T., 'Speech by the Prime Minister at the Lord Mayor's Banquet: 12 November 2001', 12 November 2001

55 Blair, T., 'Statement in response to terrorist attacks in the United States', 11 September 2001, 'Statement including question and answer session', 12 September 2001.

56 Blair, T., 'Statement in response to terrorist attacks in the United States', 11 September 2001.

57 Blair, T., 'Statement including question and answer session', 12 September 2001, 'Statement to the House of Commons',14 September 2001, 'Interview with CNN', 16 September 2001, 'Interview with CNN', 6 November 2001.

58 Blair, T., 'Statement to Parliament', 4 October 2001, 'Press conference with Arab journalists', 19 October 2001, 'Interview with CNN', 6 November 2001.

59 Blair, T., 'Statement to the House of Commons',14 September 2001.

60 Blair, T., 'Statement to Parliament on the war on terror', 14 November 2001.

61 Fischer, J., 'Address to the German Bundestag', 26 September 2001; Chirac, J., 'Joint press conference with George Bush', 18 September 2001; Jospin, L., 'Address at opening of yearly session of the National Defence College', 24 September 2001.

62 'Zu Beginn dieses neuen Jahrhunderts steht Deutschland auf der richtigen Seite – fast ist man versucht zu sagen: endlich – , auf der Seite der unveräußerlichen Rechte aller Menschen. Diese Menschenrechte sind die große Errungenschaft und das Erbe der europäischen Aufklärung. Diese Werte der Menschenwürde, der freiheitlichen

Demokratie und der Toleranz sind unsere große Stärke im Kampf gegen den Terrorismus.' Schröder, G., 'Address to the German Bundestag', 19 September 2001.

63 Patten, C., 'Speech in Stockholm', 4 December 2001; Louis Michel, President-in-Office of the Council of the European Union, 2 October 2001; Prodi, R., 'Address to Asian Ambassadors meeting', Brussels, 24 September 2001; Council of the European Union, 'Conclusion and Plan of Action of the Extraordinary European Council meeting on 21 September 2001'.

64 European Union Council 12 September 2001; Council of the European Union, 'Conclusion and Plan of Action of the Extraordinary European Council Meeting on 21 September 2001; EU General Affairs Council, 8 October 2001, De Ruyt 1 October 2001; Solana, J., 'Intervention at the conference "The Fire and the Crystal"', Rimini, 21 October 2001; Chirac, J., 'Statement at the Regional Forum on Europe's future', 4 October 2001; Fischer, J., 'Address to the German Bundestag', 8 November 2001.

65 Fischer, J., 'Address to the German Bundestag', 8 November 2001, 'Address to the French National Assembly', 30 October 2001.

66 Schröder, G., 'Address to the German Bundestag', 19 September 2001.

67 Schröder, G., 'Address to the German Bundestag', 12 September 2001.

68 Védrine, H., 'Address to UN National Assembly', 10 November 2001'Press conference', 14 November 2001, 'Interview with Canal Plus', 18 November 2001.

69 Jospin, L., 'Address to the National Assembly', 3 October 2001; Chirac, J., 'Speech on the radio/television', 16 November 2001.

70 Jospin, L., 'Address to the National Assembly', 3 October 2001.

71 Jospin, L., 'Declaration of the government in parliament on the situation in Afghanistan', 21 November 2001.

72 Védrine, H., 'Interview with *Le Monde*', 22 September 2001. In November, however, Védrine concluded that he did not think that the US had turned 'multilateralist' after 11 September. Védrine, H., 'Interview with *Le Monde*', 'Press conference', 2 November 2001.

73 Schröder, G., 'Address to the German Bundestag', 19 September 2001; Védrine, H., 'Press conference', 25 October 2001, 'Press Conference', 2 November 2001.

74 Schröder, G., 'Address to the German Bundestag', 11 October 2001, 'Interview with *Zeit*', 18 October 2001; Fischer, J., 'Address to the German Bundestag', 8 November 2001.

75 Volmer, L., 'Address to the Ruhr Political Forum', 12 November 2001.

76 Schröder, G., 'Address to the German Bundestag', 19 September 2001.

77 'Allerdings: Eine Fixierung auf ausschließlich militärische Maßnahmen wäre fatal. Wir müssen und wollen ein umfassendes Konzept zur Bekämpfung des Terrorismus, zur Prävention und zur Bewältigung von Krisen entwickeln. Dieses Konzept muss auf politische, wirtschaftliche und kulturelle Zusammenarbeit sowie auf Zusammenarbeit in Fragen der Sicherheit gegründet sein.' Schröder, G., 'Address to the German Bundestag', 19 September 2001.

78 Ivanov, I., 'Press conference in Moscow', 13 September 2001, 'Address to the UN', 16 November 2001; Putin, V., 'Interview with ARD', 19 September 2001; Jospin, L., 'Interview with France-2', 5 December 2001.

79 Ivanov, I., 'Address to the UN', 24 September 2001.

80 Vladimir Putin, V., 'Speech at the CEAP summit', 19 October 2001; Ivanov, I., 'Address to the UN', 16 November 2001.

81 Wagnsson, C., *Russian Political Language and Public Opinion on the West, NATO and Chechnya: Securitisation Theory Reconsidered* (Stockholm: Statsvetenskapliga Institutionen, 2000).

82 Ivanov, I., 'Address to the UN', 24 September 2001.

83 Ivanov, I., 'Interview with CNN', 12 September 2001, 'Press conference in Moscow', 13 September 2001.

84 'Segodnia my dolzhni raz i navsegda zaiavit: s "kholodnoi voinoi" pokoncheno! My nakhodimsia na novom etape razvitiia. My ponimaem – bez sovremennoi, prochnoi i ustoichivoi arkhitektory bezopasnosti nam nikogda ne sozdat na kontinente atmosferu doveriia. A bez atmosfery doveriia ne mozhet byt edinoi Bolshoi Evropy! Segodnia my obiazany skazat, chto my otkazyvaemsia ot nashikh stereotipov i ambitsii i otnyne budem sovmestno obespechivat bezopasnost naseleniia Evropy i mira v tselom.' Putin, V., 'Address to the German Bundestag', 25 September 2001.

85 Ivanov, I., 'Interview with Romanian media in Bukarest', 4 December 2001.

86 Ivanov, I., 'Address to the UN', 24 September 2001.

87 Ivanov, I., 'Interview with CNN', 12 September 2001.

88 Ivanov, I., 'Interview in ORT', 21 September 2001, 'Address to the UN', 24 September 2001; Putin, V., 'Address to the participants of the 24th conference of European ministers of justice', 4 October 2001, 'Joint statement with George Bush', 13 November 2001, 'Interview with Greek TV channels NET-TV and Mega', 5 December 2001.

89 Ivanov, I., 'Address to the UN', 24 September 2001, 'Address to the UN', 16 November 2001.

90 Ivanov, I., 'Press conference in Shanghai', 16 October 2001, 'Address to the UN', 16 November 2001; Putin, V., 'Speech at the CEAP summit', 19 October 2001.

91 Ivanov, I., 'Address to the UN', 24 September 2001.

92 Cook, R., 'Speech on the government's ethical foreign policy', 12 May 1997.

93 Council of the European Union, 'Conclusion and Plan of Action of the Extraordinary European Council meeting on 21 September 2001'.

94 Council of the European Union, 'Declaration by the Heads of State or Government of the EU and the President of the Commission: Follow-up to the September 11 attacks and the fight against terrorism', 19 October 2001.

95 Bush, G. H. W., 'Address before a joint session of the Congress on the state of the union', 29 January 1991.

96 Wagnsson (note 81), Chapter 4.

97 The PJC was created by a Founding Act on Mutual Relations, Coopeartion and Security between NATO and the Russian Federation, signed on 27 May 1997, and was intended to develop common approaches to European security and to political problems.

98 Putin, V., 'Joint statement with George Bush', 13 November 2001; Fedorov, Y., 'Strategic thinking in Putin's Russia', in Y. Fedorov and B. Nygren (eds) *Russian Military Reform and Russia's New Security Environment* (Stockholm: Swedish National Defence College, 2003), p. 163.

99 Radio Free Europe/Radio Liberty, Newsline, 9 October 2001.

100 Bush–Putin summit, 13–15 November 2001.

101 Radio Free Europe/Radio Liberty, Newsline, 18 September, 19 September, 25 September 2003.

102 Radio Free Europe/Radio Liberty, Newsline, 1 October 2001.

103 Radio Free Europe/Radio Liberty, Newsline, 9 December 2002, 25 September 2003.

104 Radio Free Europe/Radio Liberty, Newsline, 3 January 2002; see also Skak, M., 'Russian security policy after 9/11', Paper prepared for the Joint International Convention of Central Eastern European International Studies Association and International Studies Association, Budapest, 26–28 June 2003, pp. 6–7.

105 EU–Russia summit, 'Joint statement', Brussels, 3 October 2001.
106 EU–Russia summit, 'Joint statement', Brussels, 3 October 2001.
107 Radio Free Europe/Radio Liberty, Newsline, 3 October 2001.
108 Blair, T., 'Joint press conference with Vladimir Putin', 5 October 2001.
109 EU–Russia summit, 'Joint statement', Rome, 6 November 2003.
110 Ivanov, I., 'Statement at press conference in Moscow', 2 November 2001.

4 Iraq reshuffles Europe

Background: a war approaching

The US-led coalition waged its 'official' war against Iraq from 19 March to 1 May 2003.[1] The Bush Administration had been building up to the armed intervention throughout 2002 by defining three countries thought to possess or have the potential to develop weapons of mass destruction – Iran, Iraq and North Korea – as an 'axis of evil', and by adopting a National Security Strategy allowing for first strikes.[2] In Jan Hallenberg's analysis, the decision to get rid of Saddam Hussein's regime had already been taken in principle in the United States at the presidential level in the autumn of 2001.[3] On 28 January 2003 US President George W. Bush announced what he had already indicated in September 2002 – a readiness to attack Iraq even without a United Nations (UN) mandate.

UN Security Council resolution 1441, which was passed on 8 November 2002, became central to the debate leading up to the war. The resolution forced new arms inspections on Iraq and threatened 'serious consequences' if disarmament was not documented. However, it did not define exactly what would happen if Iraq violated the resolution. The actors interpreted the resolution in a variety of ways. The analysis in this chapter scrutinises the leaders' rhetoric during the build-up to the war from 1 December 2002 until the end of hostilities on 1 May 2003. This section gives a general picture of the divisions and coalitions in Europe at the time.

Two camps, for and against an armed intervention, crystallised in early 2003. On 30 January, eight North Atlantic Treaty Organisation (NATO) members, the British, Spanish, Portuguese, Italian, Czech, Hungarian, Polish and Danish state leaders, declared their support for the USA in an open letter.[4] In addition, ten central and eastern European states, the 'Vilnius Ten', issued an open letter in support of the USA.[5]

Russia, France and Germany united against the USA in a kind of alliance, which US Secretary of Defense Donald Rumsfeld called 'Old Europe'. Russia had taken its stand against a military intervention in Iraq long before it became an issue for international debate. Even during the immediate aftermath of 11 September 2001, it was clear that Russia's support for the US struggle against terrorism was neither limitless nor unreserved. Three weeks after the attacks on the USA, the Russian Ambassador to Iraq, Aleksandr Shein, said that if Western states attacked Iraq as a part of the 'revenge' for 11 September, Russia would respond in a sharply negative way.[6]

After a meeting in Versailles on 22 January 2003, France and Germany also stated that war must be avoided.[7] To France, a foreign policy independent of the USA but in line with Europe is more of a rule than an exception. The German Chancellor, Gerhard Schröder, had proclaimed during his election campaign the preceding summer that Germany would take no part in a war against Iraq.[8]

In early February the USA and the United Kingdom pressed for a new UN resolution legitimising an armed intervention in Iraq. Germany, France and Russia opposed the new resolution, repeating that the inspectors should be given more time, and on 10 March they threatened to veto the resolution in the Security Council. In the end, on 17 March, the USA and the UK withdrew the resolution and prepared for war. The decision was far from uncontroversial in the UK. Several ministers resigned in protest, among them Robin Cook, the former Foreign Secretary, who had zealously promoted the Kosovo campaign.[9]

In the official British interpretation, the Iraq regime stood in 'material breach' of several UN resolutions, including resolution 1441, which signified that an armed intervention was legitimate.[10]

The analysis below reveals what the governments primarily aimed to protect in view of the Iraq crisis and how they differed. It is structured, as is explained in Chapter 1, on issues central to framing analysis, on *problem definition, moral evaluation, causal interpretation, salience, level of analysis* and *solutions* to the Iraqi crisis.

Defining problems and apportioning blame

Saddam Hussein to blame

The EU framing of the Iraq crisis centred on Saddam Hussein as a major threat to the region and the entire world.[11] The EU Commissioner for External Relations, Chris Patten, indicated that an armed intervention might become necessary:

> It would be good for the UN if we could accomplish this task without casualty or collateral damage or without the daunting consequence of military intervention. It would also be good for Iraq, good for the region and good for the world. But that does assume that Saddam Hussein will now work with the inspectors.

Unfortunately, we have little evidence even now that he has yet learned that he cannot go on defying world opinion forever. I have always believed that the terms of the UN resolution obliged us to face two realities. First, we should make a serious effort to disarm through the inspectors. But second, if the inspectors make it clear that this is mission impossible we cannot avoid the consequences. The alternative would be the sort of humiliation that would make it more difficult to assert the authority of the UN in future cases.[12]

The three major EU member states converged with the EU in holding Saddam Hussein responsible for the escalating Iraq crisis.[13] Vladimir Putin also placed a significant part of the responsibility on Iraq.[14] All the actors thus generally agreed on the definition of the problem – they described Iraq as a problem that had to be attended to – but the detailed problem definition and the suggested remedies varied considerably.

Britain: outlining the al-Qaida, weapons of mass destruction, Iraq problem

The British leadership's framing of the crisis marks it out as a typical problem solver. The leaders made a great effort to explain why Iraq was an existential problem, and then focused on how to solve it as quickly as possible.[15]

The proliferation of weapons of mass destruction was called the greatest threat to British national security and to the peace of the world.[16] Iraq's possession of weapons of mass destruction was defined as a particularly severe menace because Saddam Hussein could proliferate the weapons to other dangerous actors such as terrorist groups.[17] The leaders labelled terrorism and possession of weapons of mass destruction by 'rogue' states as closely linked 'twin threats'.[18] Terrorism and unstable rogue states seeking to acquire weapons of mass destruction threatened to generate chaos in international affairs (thereby undermining the stable world that the British promoted).[19]

> The Cold War is over. Europe is at peace, if not always diplomatically. But the world is ever more interdependent. Stock markets and economies rise and fall together. Confidence is the key to prosperity. Insecurity spreads like contagion. So people crave stability and order. The threat is chaos. And there are two begetters of chaos. Tyrannical regimes with WMD and extreme terrorist groups who profess a perverted and false view of Islam.[20]

The British problem definition centred ever more closely on Saddam Hussein himself. On 25 February, Tony Blair hinted that the end of the Iraqi regime would benefit the Iraqi people.[21] On 20 March, he argued that Saddam Hussein should be removed because it was the only way to disarm Iraq.[22] In the immediate wake of the intervention, the British openly defined the problem as pertaining to Saddam Hussein himself, concluding that he had to go.[23] The leadership had been building up to this move by demonising the Iraqi leader, using descriptions such as 'tyrant', 'murderous, barbaric regime' and 'psychopatic killer'.[24]

Continentals with a view of a broader context

Instead of describing Iraq in terms of a perpetual and exceptional threat to global security, the German, French and Russian leaders defined it as a problem strictly related to the potential existence of weapons of mass destruction on Iraqi soil. They interpreted the UN resolution as aiming to do nothing more than verify that Iraq did not have and could not develop weapons of mass destruction: a change of regime, for example, was not justified.[25] The Russian leaders argued that if the inspectors did not find proof of the existence of weapons of mass destruction not only should there be no armed intervention, but the sanctions on Iraq should also to be lifted.[26]

The three leaderships questioned the connection between international terrorism, 11 September 2001, al-Qaida and Iraq.[27] The Russians directly challenged the definition of Iraq as a military threat.[28]

> You know, Iraq is said to pose a threat. Meanwhile, neighbouring nations say that there are no threats coming from the territory of Iraq. Iraq is said to threaten US security. But we don't see any serious, substantive arguments in favour of Iraq posing a real threat to the USA today. That is why at this point we cannot say with confidence that Iraq is presenting a threat to regional or international security.[29]

Russia, Germany and France placed a high value on cohesion and community among the Western states. They essentially reversed the British line of reasoning, arguing that an intervention would destabilise the global situation since it would increase the risk of terrorist and extremist activities all over the world and weaken the anti-terrorist coalition.[30]

The German leaders questioned not only the problem definition, but also the placement of Iraq at the top of the international agenda. They put the issue in a broader context and structured their arguments along a series of lines. First, Green Party Foreign Minister Joschka Fischer argued that the main priority for the international community ought to be the fight against terrorism – not Iraq.[31] Second, finding solutions to regional crises all over the world should be a priority task in the struggle against terrorism.[32] An intervention was counterproductive, since it would make it harder for the international community to unite to solve regional conflicts.[33] Third, Fischer argued that Iraq ought not to have been put at the top of the 'regional crisis agenda', since there were more urgent issues to solve – primarily the Israeli-Palestinian conflict.[34] An intervention would produce fatal consequences for regional stability.[35]

The German and Russian leaders also complained that those who argued in favour of intervention had constantly changed their line of argument.[36] The Germans argued that, first, the intervention had been explained as a consequence of 11 September 2001 but, later, it had been rationalised as a way to stand up to the threat of nuclear rearmament. Later still it had been defended with reference to the existence of biological and chemical weapons in Iraq, and finally the aim of an intervention had been defined as removing a dictator.[37] The Russians concluded that those in favour of an armed intervention had attempted to find a reason to justify its launch at any cost.[38] The Russian Foreign Minister, Igor Ivanov, argued that the failure to catch bin Laden should not be compensated for by exposing Iraq as 'the chief evil on the planet'.[39]

Moral evaluation and causal interpretation

Britain as liberators of the Iraqi people ...

An obvious frame conflict also surfaced between the UK and the other actors with regard to the *moral framing* of the crisis. The British leadership portrayed the goals of their campaign as just and humanitarian, since it would liberate the oppressed Iraqi people.[40] It would be a war not of conquest but of liberation.[41] An intervention would serve the innocent victims of Saddam Hussein's regime, who were enduring everything from malnutrition to threats from weapons of mass destruction.[42] According to this logic, the right principles – justice and order – would increase the well-being of the Iraqi people. The British moral definition was largely based on its vision of a world characterised by freedom, democracy and justice – conveying that, in order to bring about such a world, hard choices and sacrifices had sometimes to be made.[43] Another significant British line of argument with a moral flavour held that the Westernised world order had to be safeguarded from chaos generated by terrorists and rogue states.[44]

... The Continentals: institutions will stabilise

The other leaderships focused less on problem solving and more on endorsing action that followed commonly accepted international rules of behaviour, and which would serve to preserve the global structure and boost multilateralism in world affairs.

The EU's moral discussion of the crisis centred on how to avoid unilateralism and rivalries rooted in balance-of-power thinking. The officials focused on the task of accomplishing a system of global governance that could deal with serious crises like Iraq. A necessary dimension of such a system would be to strengthen the UN, while another would be to make EU foreign policy more efficient.

> I think we face a very clear choice in the coming months. Are we to go back to the way the world was run in the 19th century, a world of rival national sovereignties and balances of power, or do we try to rebuild the institutions and habits of global governance which have been so painfully constructed in the last half century?[45]

The French leadership described the crisis in a clearly moral way. Like the EU leaders, they focused on how to create a global structure that could handle crises. The first principle adopted by the French leader centred around an active policy of collective security. The second involved respect for law and morality, signifying that international action would be the only legitimate route. Solidarity and justice were the building blocks of the third principle, entailing a moral and political responsibility with regard to the negative aspects of globalisation.[46]

Overall, the French leaders placed great emphasis on the moral dimension, characterising their standpoint as 'the primacy of law and morality over force'. Moral behaviour was defined as behaviour relying on respect for the principles of action in the international community.[47] Dominique de Villepin warned against unilateralism and the use of force, instead calling for respect for law and international morality, and collective, legitimate action.[48] Echoing the Russian rhetoric during the Kosovo crisis in 1999, de Villepin argued that unilateral military action was a victory of the 'law of the strongest' against the primacy of international law and international morality.[49]

Russian moral arguments resembled the French in their focus on the need for a just world order.[50] Russia's persistent determination to act on the basis of international law was to strengthen its image in international relations.[51] The leaders recycled the arguments from the Kosovo crisis, arguing that a new and just world ought to be constructed not on the 'right of force', but on the 'force of right', that is, by political means and in accordance with UN resolutions.[52]

In addition, the Russians emphasised the right to self-determination for all people, including the Iraqi people.[53] They defined interference in the internal affairs of sovereign nations such as Iraq as contrary to the principles and norms of international law and the UN Charter.[54] The Russians strongly questioned the efficiency of imposing democratic norms on nations by force, not least attempts to 'export democracy' to the Islamic world.[55] They compared such attempts to export capitalist democratic revolution with Che Guevara's and the Soviet Union's deplorable record of attempting to export socialist revolutions.[56]

The German leadership's moral argument was characterised by a pragmatic rather than a principled approach. According to the German cost-benefit analysis, an intervention was not worth its price. Saddam Hussein was in the wrong but an intervention was not rational, since it would bring about too much suffering. The leaders focused strongly on the humanitarian consequences of a potential war.[57] They also drew attention to the risks faced by soldiers on such missions.[58] Schröder described Germany's position as springing from morality, law and political order.[59] However, in contrast to the French and Russians whose line of reasoning can be characterised as a 'missionary' stance, he emphasised that Germany did not wish to criticise other states on moral grounds.[60]

Aspects of reality in focus, salience and level of analysis

The leaderships targeted the Iraqi crisis from both regional and global aspects of reality. At the European level, it was a highly salient issue for the EU – and for its member states – in large part because of the severe problems it caused its evolving 'actorness' in the security sphere. At the Middle East regional level, Germany, France and Russia cautioned that an intervention would be destabilising, while the UK argued the opposite. From a global perspective, all actors defined the crisis as affecting the evolving world order.

All actors officially pledged a will to preserve functional relations with the USA. The British argued the necessity of preserving good relations between the USA and Europe, ensuring that the democratic world stood together.[61] The Germans also argued the necessity of preserving good relations with the USA.[62] The French stated that the Iraq crisis did not endanger their relations with the USA, which had been forged by a common history and a cultural heritage.[63]

The EU: yet another 'wake-up call'

The EU spokesmen had a difficult task. External Relations Commissioner Chris Patten described it as 'a very bad passage' for the Common Foreign and Security Policy (CFSP) and for the EU as a whole.[64] Patten argued that the CFSP had suffered a severe setback because member states took 'firm national policy positions as if they spoke for the European Union as a whole'.[65] He noted that 'our ability to work together in Europe is also clearly on the line'.[66]

EU officials nonetheless portrayed the crisis as something positive for the EU. Patten highlighted what the CFSP had achieved in the past in the Balkans and in Afghanistan and underlined that the EU must build on what the member states shared in their approach to the Iraqi conflict as well.[67] Looking ahead, Javier Solana argued that in the same way as the Balkan wars had served as a wake-up call for the EU, the Iraq crisis would have a similar effect.[68] Romano Prodi defined the situation as a 'moment of truth' for Europe's foreign and defence policy, which would determine whether Europe would be left out of the management of world affairs.[69]

The officials argued that the EU had to learn to take greater responsibility in world politics.[70] The experience of the Iraq crisis had led to a conviction that a European strategic concept similar to US strategic defence policies had to be forged.[71] The conceptual framework ought to explain the positions of the EU.[72]

The German and French leaders adhered to the EU's logic.[73] Fischer argued that the EU had to make its voice better heard.[74] In his view, the world needed more of Europe.[75] The French leaders linked the arguments they had used both in Kosovo and following 11 September 2001. They described Europe – with its values, identity and principles – as a necessary component in a multipolar world order.[76] The transformation of the EU was portrayed as a necessary step towards a safer world.[77] The French President, Jacques Chirac, argued that the strengthening of Europe, including of its military element, was essential to the global balance.[78]

Adopting a global perspective, the EU focused on its ability to contribute to a safer world, and on the UN's central role. EU officials argued that the UN and the multilateral system, which had been put at risk during the Iraq crisis, had to be strengthened.[79] The Greek Presidency portrayed the EU as 'the most important opportunity of avoiding a unipolar world in which a superpower has sole responsibility for world society'.[80] The Presidency also described the EU, as a union based on shared values, as particularly apt for dealing with countries that possess weapons of mass destruction.[81]

> Europe is a community of values; it has experience in incorporating into itself countries that have been under dictatorship and autocratic regimes; it has shown that it can integrate countries into a new reality of democracy and freedom and contribute to peace in the wider region of the European continent. This invaluable experience is, I think, a guide and important basis for confronting new problems in all regions of the globe. I believe that this experience is not a weakness, as is often said regarding Europe, but a very important strength, and we must use this very important strength, I think, to formulate a unified and powerful international voice.[82]

Germany, France, Russia: cohesion and multilateralism

The German, French and Russian leaders placed a lot of emphasis on the global level when targeting the effects of an intervention. The actors focused on cohesion, describing any intervention as a threat to the unity of the international community since it would harm the international coalition against terrorism and undermine progress towards a better world order.[83]

The French argued that an intervention would be a threat to global stability for two reasons. First, use of force could increase tensions and hatred, serving the cause of Islamic terrorist groups.[84] Second, the removal of Saddam Hussein would signify a change in the rules of conduct in international relations, which would result in a situation of great instability.[85] According to this logic, if a dictator like Saddam Hussein was removed from power, a number of other dictators ought to be ousted as well for the sake of coherence, for example, the dictatorship in North Korea. No one would know where to start or end such a process.[86] This line of argument was very similar to the Russian critique of the NATO bombing of Kosovo in 1999.

The Russian President, Vladimir Putin, also recycled the argument used during the Kosovo crisis, warning that an intervention risked setting a precedent.[87]

While the French used *multipolarity* as a key concept, as is discussed above, the Germans favoured a different concept that did not focus as directly on balancing – a world order based on *multilateralism*, a notion that signals the need for cooperation and institutions and, more precisely, cooperation within the framework of the UN.[88] The UN's central role as a guardian of peace had to be preserved in order to achieve international security and the envisaged world order.[89] The Germans focused on effectiveness, arguing that an efficient disarmament regime coordinated by the UN was also the best way to halt, and even reverse, the proliferation of weapons of mass destruction.[90]

Britain: action necessary to deter dictators

The British presented the issue in a very different way. They warned that if the international community failed to act determinedly on Iraq, it would soon be challenged by other actors pursuing or possessing weapons of mass destruction:[91] 'Since 1991, Saddam Hussein has ignored repeated UN resolutions calling for Iraq's disarmament. If he continues to get away with it, other would-be proliferators will take heart and the world will become a far more dangerous place.'[92]

In response to critics who argued that any regime or state that did not achieve Western standards could be targeted in the future, the British argued that Saddam Hussein was uniquely dangerous because of his 'deadly combination of capability and intent'.[93] He differed from other would-be proliferators by virtue of his appetite for weapons of mass destruction, his aggression and his willingness to use all possible means against his own people and his neighbours.[94] Commenting on North Korea, Tony Blair argued 'there will be different ways of dealing with different countries'.[95]

Again, the British leadership placed problem solving and action before community. Instead of recalling the UN's importance as a symbol of togetherness, the British focused on the realpolitik of keeping the UN powerful to enable it to act vigorously as a 'problem solver' in the face of serious threats. If the UN failed to deal with the Iraq crisis it would be more difficult to negotiate with other actors in the future.[96] They argued that to avoid it facing the same fate as the League of Nations,[97] it was necessary for the UN to solve the Iraqi problem to preserve its power and authority.[98]

Russia: a defining moment for the international community

Russia, in contrast, described the French-German-Russian view on Iraq as the most rational, since it would preserve the unity of the international community.[99] Putin explained the three states' suggestions for solving the Iraq crisis as stemming from common interests, particularly of a geopolitical nature.[100]

Russia characterised the Iraq crisis as a highly salient issue that would decide the future of international relations in the long term – and fix the foundations of future global relations.[101] A success would signify a precedent for political settlement of other conflicts, reinforce global stability and strengthen the path towards a just world order.[102] Use of force, in contrast, could destabilise the global situation, for example, by stirring up radicalism and causing economic problems.[103] The unilateral use of force would not only make solving the Iraq crisis more complicated, but also have a negative influence on international cooperation against common threats.[104]

Like the French, the Russian leaders described the common stance on Iraq with France and Germany as forming part of a progression in international politics towards multipolarity.[105] In the Russian version, Russia and France's common stance was an historic attempt to solve a serious crisis outside of 'bloc-politics', and it constituted the first brick in the construction of a multipolar world.[106] Multipolarity was labelled a prerequisite for a predictable and stable world.[107] Ivanov described multipolarity as beneficial for global development and as providing equal security for all states.[108] The summit of the Russian, French and German leaders in St Petersburg on 11 April 2003 evidenced, in Putin's view, a search for a functioning world structure and architecture of international security that would be acceptable to all states.[109]

Solution

The European Council, the Presidency and other central EU actors placed the UN 'at the centre of the international order' and the primary responsibility for dealing with Iraqi disarmament with the UN Security Council.[110] Yet, the EU's failure to find a common solution to the Iraq crisis is an outcome that is well known. The main source of conflict was the means to be used to disarm Saddam Hussein. A vestige of unity was discernible in the European Council's attempt to summarise a few common standpoints on 17 February 2003.[111] This attempt to exhibit a united front was fairly futile. An obvious frame conflict was visible between the member states.

Britain: time to act

The British recalled the twelve-year history of trying to make Iraq comply with the demands of the international community. The message was clear: it was no use giving the Iraqi regime more time.[112] The aim of the planned operation was defined as to 'remove Saddam Hussein from power and ensure

Iraq is disarmed of all chemical, biological and nuclear weapon programmes'.[113] Tony Blair urged Europe to unite with the USA in order to
ensure global security.[114]

The Continentals: use of force a last resort

France, Germany and Russia defined the use of force as a last resort.[115]
Nothing justified interrupting the inspections or resorting to the use of
force.[116]

Legitimacy and efficiency stand out as two guiding principles from the
French standpoint. The French leaders defined intervention as legitimate
only if founded on a decision taken by the UN Security Council.[117] The
leaders portrayed collective action as the most efficient way of handling the
Iraqi crisis, as well as other international crises.[118] They also warned that after
any war, a stable peace must be established, and that this would be a difficult
process requiring a multilateral effort.[119] De Villepin described the habit of
acting together as a particular French and European 'diplomatic spirit',
springing from its heritage and the values of sharing, exchanging and appre-
ciating a diversity of cultures.[120] 'Collective security constitutes the principle
on which we must be based at every stage, to adapt and coordinate our
actions efficiently. United, the international community is stronger and better
able to obtain respect for the law.'[121]

It is apparent that while the French described war as an ineffectual
method, the Germans defined it as inappropriate and unacceptable for a
variety of reasons. The German Chancellor, Gerhard Schröder, had categor-
ically opposed an intervention in his election campaign of August and
September 2002. He had reacted negatively to US Vice President Dick
Cheney's call for pre-emptive action in Iraq on 26 August.[122] Schröder's firm
anti-war stance probably contributed to the SPD-green coalition's narrow
victory on 22 September. Fischer called the coalition's stance the 'politics of
peace in an unstable world'.[123] The Germans emphasised that the UN resolution allowed for disarmament and nothing else.[124] They explicitly refused to
accept wars of disarmament.[125] According to Schröder, war is not a normal
political means, but occurs when politics is in stalemate.[126] He argued that the
international community cannot react by resorting to war each time it
suspects that a dictator has produced weapons of mass destruction.[127]

In addition, an intervention would only be acceptable if the German
population supported it.[128] Schröder explained the German unwillingness to
resort to warfare with reference to the population's experience of war, which
is deeply rooted in the collective memory.[129] The German leaders recalled the
experience of European history, arguing that the Europeans were not from
Venus but could be characterised 'survivors of March'. This experience had
taught them that war is a great tragedy and ought to be the very last resort
– only to be used when all peaceful alternatives have been exhausted.[130]

The Russians in turn rejected a unilateral solution to the crisis and promoted multilateralism.[131] Multilateral action through the UN was the only efficient way to solve global problems, including the Iraq crisis.[132] The Russian leaders tried to build up the UN by describing resolution 1441 as a sign of cohesion and of 'moral and psychological support for the UN'.[133] They also conveyed the logic that Russia's significance in world affairs would increase if the UN Security Council's authority was boosted.[134]

The Russian leaders placed great emphasis on the legal aspect, arguing that a global system of counterproliferation had to rely on international law.[135] Putin stated that the world would become more predictable and more understandable if states followed international law – and above all the UN Charter.[136] Ivanov argued that two options were conceivable: to expand international legal cooperation, or to 'divide the world into opposing blocs on whatever principle'.[137]

The Russian leadership argued that an armed intervention could complicate the settlement of the Middle East conflict and radicalise the Islamic world.[138] Putin also warned that Iraq could disintegrate.[139]

Clashing norms and interests, and the implications

The Iraq crisis appeared salient to all the actors because it pertained to the issues of the future world order and the future of Europe. Once again, the UK and Russia focused more on the global level than the other actors. The EU, France and Germany concentrated more on regional implications and solutions, with regard to both Europe and the Middle East.

What can the framing analysis tell us about converging and diverging norms and interests among the leaderships?

Rival interests: problem solving versus structuralism

The framing analysis reveals substantial differences between the main interests of the UK and those of the other actors. The interests pervading the framing of the Iraq crisis centred on the tension between chaos and stability in world affairs, and how to achieve global stability – through either immediate problem-solving action or a global system based on lawful behaviour according to the statutes of the UN.

The British endorsed a more goal-oriented way of acting than the other actors. Their major concern was not who acted, but that the threat was dealt with. Global order was the chief referent object of security. The British message was clear – this order had to be maintained whatever it took. Although the British did not openly promote unipolarity, they did not hesitate in their approval of US command as long as this served their overarching interest – a solution to the crisis and an alleviation of the threat of chaos.

After 11 September 2001, the British line of argument had focused on recapturing a sense of stability in world affairs, a stability that had been unsettled by the terrorist acts. The leadership favoured an international order that could guarantee and endorse the British way of life, economy, and security. The other states had presented an image of an unstable world. Rather than trying to reinstate a world order that had collapsed, they had argued in favour of transforming it in order to achieve greater stability.

In the Iraq crisis, the British again focused on the preservation of the global system. Saddam Hussein threatened the pillars – the welfare, well-being, peace and norms – that the civilised world rested on. Some of the key words that pieced together the British reasoning in terms of interests: 'stability', 'order', 'confidence' and 'prosperity', were placed in opposition to 'chaos' as well as 'weapons of mass destruction', 'terrorism' and 'Saddam Hussein'. According to this logic, there were two 'begetters of chaos' in the international system: terrorists and rogue states possessing weapons of mass destruction. Saddam Hussein was the lethal link between these two. The British thus turned him into a global symbol of evil, in essence the prime symbol of the worst threats in the modern world. If he was removed, it would be easier to make other would-be terrorists and rogue states comply with the demands of the global community. If he was not punished, other would-be troublemakers would step up their activities and disrupt global peace and stability.

In contrast, the French, Russian and German leaders' central interests included the preservation of cooperative structures – primarily the UN. They aimed to increase multilateralism and ultimately to create more efficient cooperative mechanisms suitable for dealing with such crises. France, Germany and Russia described multilateralism as a more efficient method for dealing with new threats.

The Russians – and the French – used the same arguments they had applied during the Kosovo crises. They warned that the rules of conduct in international relations were at stake. The Russians focused on the legal aspect of this problem. They wished to construct a new global legal system so that similar situations would not recur. Only then would the world become more predictable and more stable. The Russian leaders did not conceal that this was in the Russia's interest: Russia's power in world affairs would increase if the Security Council was strengthened.

The EU promoted the same interests as France, Germany and Russia. Multilateralism was defined as the best way to make the world safer and the UN occupied the central role in this endeavour. However, the EU also furthered its particular interests by virtue of being an organisation, promoting its own role as a contributor to global peace. EU officials argued that the Iraq crisis would contribute to making the EU stronger. A step in this process would be the creation of a European Strategic Concept that would explain

the EU's policies. The EU was portrayed as a counterweight to US unilateralism and as a way to strengthen a multipolar world.

France, Germany and Russia actively supported this logic. France and
Russia even endorsed the EU as a pole in a multipolar world. The British,
in contrast, did not elaborate on the EU's potential in the security sphere to
the same extent as the other actors. They conveyed that the best way to
ensure global security was to endorse good relations between the USA
and the EU.

How could Russia, France and Germany oppose the British definition of
Saddam Hussein as an existential threat to the entire civilised world, and
instead focus on the preservation of institutions and multilateral behaviour?
Above all, they questioned the connection between international terrorism,
11 September 2001 and al-Qaida, on the one hand, and Iraq, on the other.
While France, Russia and Germany agreed that *if* Saddam Hussein possessed
weapons of mass destruction, he had to get rid of them, they presented a
counterargument to that of the British by suggesting that evil intent did not
form sufficient grounds for invading Iraq. The international community
ought not to act if there were no evidence of capabilities. The general logic
was that if there were no concrete evidence of a threat, there could be no
countermeasures – at least not in terms of an armed intervention.

The three states also questioned Iraq's place at the top of the international
agenda. If anything, an intervention would destabilise the international
system and risk radicalising the Islamic world, thereby inspiring terrorism all
over the world. It would also weaken the actor that could confront these
forces most efficiently: the anti-terrorist coalition.

Finally, France, Germany and Russia questioned the Iraq's place at the top
of the regional agenda. An armed intervention in Iraq would make it more
difficult for the international community to unite to solve regional problems,
particularly the Israeli-Palestinian conflict. Iraq might also disintegrate as a
result of a war.

Different approaches to norms: common behavioural rules versus absolute norms

The framing analysis exposes that a central difference between the British
favoured norms and those of the other actors was the former's emphasis on
norms, compared with the other actors' focus on institutions and law.
While the British centred on adherence to a set of fixed norms, the other
actors supported a normative logic that endorsed certain common rules of
behaviour.

A central trait of the British normative standpoint was its conviction of
the appropriateness of protecting and promoting certain basic uninfringeable
norms. According to the British normative framework, Western states had a
moral obligation to spread universal values across the globe for the sake of
stability, prosperity and peace. Resolute action, including the use of force, was

permissible in order to advance the aim of protecting or promoting such basic norms.

In contrast, the other leaderships placed greater emphasis on states' duties to perform according to appropriate collective rules of behaviour. A moral, just and ordered world could not be achieved without righteous behaviour that has collectively been agreed on.

The British stance clashed most obviously with Russia's. A central Russian line of argument was the inappropriateness of enforcing norms on a population from outside. The Russians defined interference in the affairs of a sovereign state with the aim of imposing democracy or a change of regime as breaking with the principles and norms of conduct set out in international law and the UN Charter. In addition, the Russian leaders argued that attempts to impose democratic norms by force were futile.

The EU normative stance placed itself somewhere between those of the British and the Russians. EU officials argued that their 'union of values' was particularly well suited for dealing with certain security problems. As is stated above, the EU had experience of democratising former dictatorships and creating peaceful regions. The EU thus endorsed precisely the kind of 'export of values' for the sake of security that the Russians so vigorously argued against. However, in accordance with Russia, the EU stressed that all action had to be legitimised by international law and given UN approval.

> Today we face the consequences in three of the world's more worrying trouble spots North Korea, Kashmir and the Gulf. How can we deal with these problems? Clearly we have to mobilise the greatest international commitment and the broadest authority for what we want to do. That is why it is sensible to base our approach to dealing with these problems on the moral and legal authority of the UN.[140]

The EU thus promoted norms involving confidence building measures aimed at global governance of security problems directed by the UN. Chris Patten opposed a system constructed from the viewpoint of a balance of power and national sovereignty. By ensuring that the UN always had the primary role in global affairs it would be possible to construct a different system based on global governance of security problems. The EU leadership envisaged an active part for themselves in such a reformed system.

The member states and Russia were also concerned about the UN. They endorsed the UN by arguing that it ought to direct multilateral efforts in the security sphere, and that it ought not to be sidestepped. Collective action was defined as the only appropriate behaviour. The British defined their behaviour as appropriate in that it was necessary to act in order to preserve the UN. Recycling an argument used during the Kosovo crisis – although at that time to promote NATO – they argued that if the Iraq crisis was not solved, the UN risked facing the same fate as the League of Nations, becoming insignificant as an actor in world affairs.

In contrast, Russia, France and Germany argued that in order to be appropriate an armed intervention had to be legitimate. Germany emphasised that UN resolution 1441 allowed for the disarmament of Iraq and nothing else. The French and Russians argued that an intervention would be legitimate only if based on a further resolution by the Security Council. The French normative standpoint was summarised as 'the primacy of law and morality over force'. It is noteworthy that the Russians had used this argument during the Kosovo crisis.

The French normative argument was based on three major principles. First, its leaders promoted an active policy of collective security, rejecting unilateralism as a method of solving crises. Second, according to international law and morals, only collective action was legitimate. Unilateral armed intervention was interpreted as an attack on international law and morality. Third, solidarity and justice must guide behaviour in the security sphere. The French Foreign Minister traced collective action to a particular French and European 'diplomatic spirit', founded on the values of sharing, exchanging and appreciation of a diversity of cultures.

While the French regularly referred to community in terms of history and culture, the British instead described the EU as a polity, which would function for as long as its components remained committed and determined to sort out their differences.[141] Tony Blair took an unemotional approach, admitting that there were problems inside the EU, but maintaining that the UK remained engaged in Europe and would try to overcome existing differences.[142]

Like the French, the Russians argued that the appropriate rules of conduct in international society ought to spring from the principle of the 'force of right', not from that of the 'right of force'. They promoted Russia as a state behaving appropriately, according to norms based on international law, UN resolutions and the solution of conflicts by peaceful means.

Finally, the Russians defined the Iraq crisis as salient because if the crisis was solved according to the appropriate rules of behaviour – in accordance with international law and based on UN security resolutions – this would signify a step towards a new and fairer world order. Such a success would set a precedent for settling conflicts using political means and strengthen progress towards a just world order.

Consequences for the EU

In a situation as difficult as the one that preceded the Iraq war, when the member states took starkly opposed positions, the EU Commissioner and its spokespeople on foreign policy issues were almost as constrained as a constitutional monarch in modern times.[143] They had the choice of either saying nothing, or making a statement and thereby inevitably providing support for one of the main political camps.

The latter situation occurred when Chris Patten hinted that an armed intervention would become necessary. He replicated the British argument exactly by stating that 'the alternative would be the sort of humiliation that would make it more difficult to assert the authority of the UN in future cases'. This could be interpreted as a situation where an EU official did not manage to stay loyal to the 'EU-line' but instead sided with his national politicians. It might also be taken as a sign of the lack of a clear EU policy before the outbreak of the war, which made EU officials unsure of what to say on the subject. Patten might not even have been fully conscious that his way of defining the problem coincided exactly with the British framing. Even so, the result is obvious; the EU spokesman articulated the British standpoint, rather than those put forward by the other EU 'internal greats'.

The Iraq crisis was an acute reminder of the EU's limits when it comes to leadership in the security sphere. In the end, the central leadership was powerless. Only the national governments could formulate policy when the issue of national sovereignty was the centre of attention. Patten acknowledged and regretted the EU's shortcoming in the middle of the crisis:

> The Commission is not a member state. We of course contribute to the development of the EU's Common Foreign Policy and we are deploying the instruments within our competence to make it more effective. But many of the issues we are discussing go to the heart of national sovereignty.[144]

The only plausible 'EU solution' was not to take a stand for or against an intervention, but instead to focus entirely on the EU's role in the security sphere in the longer term.

The EU was able to show some progress at the time, although not in the case of Iraq. In spite of the differences over Iraq, the EU managed to settle relations with NATO through the Berlin Plus agreement on 17 March.[145] The European Council meeting on 18–19 March then decided to take over NATO's tasks in Macedonia by 31 March, thereby launching the EU's first military operation – Operation Concordia. Moreover, on 4 July the same year the EU decided to implement its first military rapid reaction operation outside Europe by sending a joint peacekeeping force called 'Operation Artemis' to the Democratic Republic of the Congo (DRC) to contain ethnic violence. The operation was also unique in that it was carried out without resources provided by NATO and signified a new step towards powerful EU actorness in the international arena.

In addition, in 2004 a European Defence Agency, intended to improve crisis-management capacity and support European Security and Defence Policy (ESDP) development, was created to assist member states with developing their defence capabilities for crisis-management operations.[146] A civil-military planning cell within the EU Military Staff in Brussels (EUMS) was also set up. Furthermore, the member states decided that in order to make the EU's armed forces more efficient, thirteen battle groups, deployable within ten days, should be created by 2010 – some from only one country, the majority multinational.[147]

In December 2004 the EU also took over responsibility for the NATO mission in Bosnia Herzegovina, launching a military operation named 'Althea', intended to maintain a secure environment for the implementation of the Dayton/Paris Peace Agreement and to ensure a stable region in the longer term.[148] The EU also became involved in other missions, for example, its first mission in Asia on 15 August 2005 – a joint mission in Aceh, Indonesia, intended to monitor the implementation of the peace agreement between the Indonesian government and the Free Aceh Movement (GAM). Javier Solana described the mission as a sign of the EU's commitment to stability not just in Aceh, but in the entire region.[149]

Finally, the EU's most striking achievement was agreeing a European Security Strategy (ESS) in December 2003, only seven months after the Iraq war was declared to be at an end. The evolution of the strategy was a direct result of the diverging norms and interests exposed during the build-up to the Iraq conflict – differences that revealed an urgent need to formulate a common general framework in the security sphere.

The EU thus expanded its cooperation in the security field at an unusual speed in 2003 not in spite of, but because of the internal differences linked to diverging norms and interests. The EU security integration thus seems to have been driven by a shared understanding that the EU should be a key player in the sphere of security, no matter what internal divergences emerge from time to time. In other words, it is not primarily the EU's role that is in dispute among the internal greats, but the content of its policies.

The Iraq crisis is a reminder of the severe difficulties the EU faces when its member states differ precisely with regard to policy, in this case a dispute that involves the issues of national sovereignty and the ideal framework for global security. The analysis exposes diverging official interpretations of the present global situation and irreconcilable standpoints on how to handle security problems.

Consequences for EU–Russia relations

At one level, the Iraq crisis gave rise to encouraging developments in EU–Russia relations. As a direct consequence of 11 September 2001, Russia finally entered the European discursive space in the security realm. Over Iraq, it also joined forces with a large part of Europe 'in practice'. The Russians were obviously pleased to be operating jointly with other European great powers. This was a significant step towards what the Russian leaders had been trying to achieve since the end of the Cold War: a place in the European security community or architecture. Ivanov concluded that Russia had not stood alone, as it had during the Kosovo crisis, but had operated in solidarity with a wide circle of states.[150] Moreover, he noted that in spite of the serious debates on certain issues, Russia and 'the Europeans' 'understood each other better and better and, as a rule, spoke the same language'. Ivanov's explanation for this progress was that Russian and the EU interests coincided on a range of common problems such as the struggle against international terrorism, crime and drug trafficking, Iraq, the Middle East, Afghanistan and the Balkans. He also identified future opportunities such as common peace-keeping operations, and humanitarian and search-and-rescue missions.[151]

That said, the Iraq war was not followed by any major breakthroughs in practical cooperation. The EU and Russia failed to agree on an EU crisis-management operation in Moldova. The EU operation was intended to substitute for Russian troops in Trans-Dniester on the eastern Moldovan border. The industrialised Trans-Dniester region in eastern Moldova claimed independence from Moldova in 1990 but has no internationally recognised status. By gaining a presence and leverage in Moldova, the EU wished to help regulate this 'frozen conflict', which would serve the EU's goal of stabilising its close neighbourhood.[152] Moldova is seen as a source of human trafficking from eastern Europe. The country has also been identified as a source of money laundering, organised crime, corruption and smuggling.[153] The suggestion for an EU force came out of talks supervised by the Organisation for Security and Co-operation in Europe (OSCE), but no such force materialised. The EU had to continue to deal with Moldova primarily through its European Neighbourhood policy, which is discussed further in Chapter 5.

Moreover, the EU remained critical of the Chechen campaign and a variety of other concrete issues. Ivanov implicitly called for greater understanding on the part of the EU for Russia's handling of terrorism in Chechnya.[154]

It became quite obvious that the EU and Russia were stuck in a summit structure that did not serve to deepen cooperation. The EU–Russia summit in St Petersburg on 30 May 2003 resulted in calls for stronger institutions and streamlined structures for political dialogue, but did not make any substantial progress in the security field. The Cooperation Council was upgraded to the status of a Permanent Partnership Council.[155] The next summit, in Rome in November the same year, resulted in a joint statement highlighting Russia and the EU's shared views on the central role of the UN and on the necessity of fighting terrorism, but it also did not yield many practical results.[156] In 2003, there were no changes to the political reality that necessitated an intensified cooperation. The only visible sign of an intensified partnership was the Russian contribution – of five officers – to the European Union Police

Mission in Bosnia and Herzegovina, which began on 1 January. Bobo Lo argues that the Russian establishment regarded the EU as inefficient.[157]

Perhaps the chances of a truly deepened partnership would have been greater if the EU member states had taken a united stand against the USA over Iraq. In such a case, the EU and Russia could have joined forces – acting as the 'pole' in international affairs that Russia and France had wished to create. However, even if the EU had been able to unite, the member states would not have accepted such an interpretation of a partnership with Russia. The Russian President was probably right when he stated that only France dared to take the initiative to act outside of bloc politics on an international security problem such as Iraq – an initiative that, in the Russian interpretation, signified a first step towards a multipolar world.[158]

Conclusions

Although the EU advanced its formal integration in the realm of security as a consequence of the Iraq war, its internal differences appeared more severe than ever. In a longer perspective, the divergences linked to different views on norms and interests in regional and global security risk impeding concerted action, particularly where the issue of sovereignty is at stake. Russia, on the other hand, seemed to be in step with the EU, France and Germany with regard to basic norms and interests in the international arena, while there were substantial divergences between the UK and Russia. In practice, little was achieved to deepen the cooperation between Russia and the EU. Integration in the security sphere lacked the right stimuli, and progressed slowly but steadily and without major breakthroughs.

Notes

1   The coalition was made up of Australian, British, Polish and US troops.
2   Bush declared the three states 'an axis of evil' in January 2002 and adopted the National Security Strategy in September the same year. 'National Security Strategy of the United States of America', 17 September 2002.
3   Hallenberg, J., 'The Bush administration's goals in invading Iraq', in J. Hallenberg and H. Karlsson (eds), *The Iraq War: European Perspectives on Politics, Strategy and Operations* (New York: Routledge, 2006), p. 22.
4   Aznar, J. et al., 'United we stand: Eight European leaders are as one with President Bush', Opinion Journal.com, 30 January 2003.
5   The Vilnius 10 was formed in 2000 by ten states seeking NATO membership: Albania, Bulgaria, Croatia, Estonia, Latvia, Lithuania, Macedonia, Slovakia, Slovenia and Romania.
6   Radio Free Europe/Radio Liberty, Newsline, 3 October 2001.
7   Schröder, G., 'Joint press conference with Jacques Chirac with France-2 and ARD', 22 January 2003.
8   Analysts argue that Schröder's move might to a significant degree be explained as

part of his strategy to win the election. Howorth, J., 'Discourse, ideas and epistemic communities in European security and defence policy', *West European Politics* 27:2 (2004), pp. 227–228; Pond, E., *Friendly Fire: The Near-death of the Transatlantic Alliance* (Pittsburg: European Union Studies Association, 2004), pp. 56–60.

9 Cook, R., 'Statement in the House of Commons', Hansard Debates, 17 March 2003.

10 'Material breach' indicates a right held by the party affected in a treaty relationship to suspend its obligations under the treaty. The practice is described in the 1969 Vienna Convention on the Law of Treaties, Article 60. Bring, O. and Broström, P., 'The Iraq war and international law: from Hugo Grotius to George W. Bush', in J. Hallenberg and H. Karlsson (eds) *The Iraq War: European Perspectives on Politics, Strategy and Operations* (London: Routledge, 2005), pp. 120–121.

11 Patten, C., 'Address to the European Parliament', 29 January 2003.

12 Ibid.

13 Patten, C., 'Address to the European Parliament', 29 January 2003; de Villepin, D., 'Interview with RTL', 9 December 2002; Blair, T., 'Prime Minister's statement to Parliament following his meeting with President Bush', 3 February 2003.

14 Putin, V., 'Statement at joint press conference with Silvio Berlusconi', 3 February 2003, in *Diplomaticheskii Vestnik* 3 (2003).

15 Blair, T., 'Press conference: Prime Minister Tony Blair and Syrian President Al-Asad', 16 December 2002, 'Speech at the Foreign Office conference', 7 January 2003, 'Press conference: Prime Minister Tony Blair and President Bush at the White House', 31 January 2003, 'Prime Minister's statement to Parliament following his meeting with President Bush', 3 February 2003; Straw, J., 'Written ministerial answer to the House of Commons', 7 January 2003.

16 Straw, J., 'Speech at the FCO Leadership conference', 6 January 2003.

17 Blair, T., 'Prime Minister's statement to Parliament following his meeting with President Bush', 3 February 2003.

18 Blair, T., 'Press conference: Prime Minister Tony Blair and President Bush at the White House', 31 January 2003, 'Joint press conference with Spanish Prime Minister Maria Aznar', 28 February 2003; Straw, J., 'Speech at the meeting of the Transatlantic Partnership', 2 December 2002, 'Speech in Jakarta', 9 January 2003, 'Statement at the UN Security Council Foreign Ministers' meeting on counter-terrorism', 20 January 2003, 'Statement in House of Commons', Hansard Debates, 21 January 2003, 'Speech to the International Institute of Strategic Studies', 11 February 2003.

19 Blair, T., 'Speech at the Foreign Office conference', 7 January 2003, 'PM statement opening Iraq debate', 18 March 2003, 'Address to the nation', 20 March 2003; Straw, J., 'Speech in Jakarta', 9 January 2003, 'Statement in House of Commons', Hansard Debates, 26 February 2003.

20 Blair, T., 'PM statement opening Iraq debate', 18 March 2003.

21 Blair, T., 'Prime Minister's statement on Iraq', 25 February 2003.

22 Blair, T., 'Address to the nation', 20 March 2003.

23 In his address to the nation on 20 March, Tony Blair clearly stated that the mission of the British servicemen and women was to remove Saddam Hussein from power and to disarm Iraq of its weapons of mass destruction. Blair, T., 'Address to the nation', 20 March 2003, 'Statement on European Council meeting 20–21 March 2003', 'PM monthly Downing Street press conference', 25 March 2003, 'Interview with the BBC World Service', 4 April 2003.

24 Straw, J., 'Statement at the UN Security Council Foreign Ministers' meeting on counter-terrorism', 20 January 2003, 'Statement in House of Commons', Hansard Debates, 21 January 2003, 'Speech at the Royal Institute of International Affairs', 21 February 2003; Blair, T., 'Prime Minister's statement on Iraq', 25 February 2003,

'Joint press conference with Spanish Prime Minister Maria Aznar', 28 February 2003, 'PM Statement opening Iraq debate', 18 March 2003, 'Address to the nation', 20 March 2003.

25 Schröder, G., 'Speech on the occasion of the German Steinkohle-Betriebsrätevollversammlung', 29 January 2003; Fischer, J., 'Address to the UN Security Council', 7 March 2003, 'Address to the UN', 19 March 2003; Chirac, J., 'Press Conference', Algeria, 3 March 2003; Putin, V., 'Interview with Bulgarian television and the newspaper *Trud*', 27 February 2003; Ivanov, I., 'Replies to questions from the Greek newspaper *Katimerini*', 24 January 2003.

26 Ivanov, I., 'Replies to questions from the Greek newspaper *Katimerini*', 24 January 2003.

27 Fischer, J., 'Interview with *Der Spiegel*', 30 December 2002, 'Address to the German Bundestag', 13 March 2003; de Villepin, D., 'Press conference after UN Security Council meeting', 7 March 2003; Putin, V., 'Press conference at Elysee Palace', Paris, 11 February 2003, 'Statement on Iraq at a Kremlin meeting', 20 March 2003; Ivanov, I., 'Remarks at joint press conference following talks with Bulgarian Minister of Foreign Affairs Solomon Pasi', Sofia, 30 January 2003, 'Replies after speech at Federation Council Meeting', 26 March 2003.

28 Putin, V., 'Interview with Bulgarian television and the newspaper Trud', 27 February 2003, 'Address at the St Petersburg Summit', 11 April 2003, in *Dipomaticheskii Vestnik* 5 (2003); Ivanov, I., 'Interview with NBC', 27 January 2003, 'Replies after speech at Federation Council meeting', 26 March 2003.

29 'Vy znaete, govoriat, chto Irak predstavliaiet ugrozu. V to zhe vremia sosednie gosudarstva zaiavliaiot o tom, chto Irak ugrozhaiut bezopasnosti SShA. Nikakikh sereznykh veskikh argumentov, kotorye demonstrirovali by, chto Irak segodnia predstavliaet realnuiu ugrozu SShA my tozhe ne vidim. Poetomy segodnia my ne mozhem govorit uverenno o tom, chto Irak predstavliaiet ugrozy regionalnoi i mezhdunarodnoi bezopasnosti.' Ivanov, I., 'Interview with NBC', 27 January 2003.

30 Fischer, J., 'Interview with *Der Spiegel*', 30 December 2002, 'Address to the UN Security Council', 7 March 2003, 'Address to the German Bundestag', 13 March 2003; Ivanov, I., 'Replies to questions from the Greek newspaper *Katimerini*', 24 January 2003, 'Address at UN Security Council meeting', 14 February 2003, 'Replies by Russian Minister of Foreign Affairs Igor Ivanov to questions from Hamshahri and Iranian newspapers', Teheran, 11 March 2003, 'Replies by Minister of Foreign Affairs of the Russian Federation Igor Ivanov to questions from Russian and foreign media', Moscow, 18 March 2003; de Villepin, D., 'Interview with French media on the occasion of the UN Security Council ministerial meeting', 14 February 2003; Chirac, J., 'Interview with *Time Magazine*', 16 February 2003.

31 Fischer, J., 'Interview with *Der Spiegel*', 30 December 2002.

32 Fischer, J., 'Address to the German Bundestag', 13 February 2003, 'Address to the German Bundestag', 13 March 2003.

33 Fischer, J., 'Address to the UN Security Council', 7 March 2003.

34 Fischer, J., 'Address to the German Bundestag', 13 March 2003.

35 Fischer, J., 'Interview in ARD', 24 January 2003, 'Address to the German Bundestag', 13 February 2003, 'Interview with *Der Stern*', 5 March 2003, 'Address to the UN Security Council', 7 March 2003, 'Address to the German Bundestag', 13 March 2003.

36 Fischer, J., 'Address to the German Bundestag', 13 March 2003; Ivanov, I., 'Interview with Kommersant', 5 March 2003.

37 Fischer, J., 'Address to the German Bundestag', 13 March 2003.

38 Ivanov, I., 'Transcript of replies by Minister of Foreign Affairs of the Russian

Federation Igor Ivanov to media questions after his remarks to the State Duma of the Federal Assembly of the Russian Federation', Moscow, 21 March 2003.

39 Ivanov, I., 'Interview with *Trud*', 23 January 2003.

40 Blair, T., 'Joint press conference with President Bush at Camp David', 27 March 2003, 'Message broadcast to Iraqi people', 8 April 2003.

41 Blair, T., 'Statement on European Council meeting 20–21 March 2003''Interview with the BBC World Service', 4 April 2003, 'Message broadcast to Iraqi people', 8 April 2003.

42 Blair, T., 'Prime Minister's statement on Iraq', 25 February 2003, 'Press conference: Prime Minister and Portuguese Prime Minister Barroso', 11 March 2003, 'PM statement opening Iraq debate', 18 March 2003; Straw, J., 'Speech to the International Institute of Strategic Studies', 11 February 2003, 'Speech at the Royal Institute of International Affairs', 21 February 2003.

43 Straw, J., 'Speech at the meeting of the Transatlantic Partnership', 2 December 2002; Blair, T., 'Speech at the Foreign Office conference', 7 January 2003, 'Address to the nation', 20 March 2003.

44 Blair, T., 'Address to the nation', 20 March 2003.

45 Patten, C., 'Address to the European Parliament', 20 March 2003.

46 de Villepin, D., 'Answer to a question in the National Assembly', 14 January 2003, 'Statement at UN Security Council ministerial meeting', 20 January 2003.

47 de Villepin, D., 'Statement in the French Senate', 26 February 2003'.

48 de Villepin, D., 'Interview with *Paris Match*', 16 January 2003, 'Interview with RTL-*Le Monde*-LCI', 16 February 2003.

49 de Villepin, D., 'Statement at UN Security Council ministerial meeting', 20 January 2003.

50 Ivanov, I., 'Transcript of replies by Minister of Foreign Affairs of the Russian Federation Igor Ivanov to media questions after his remarks to the State Duma of the Federal Assembly of the Russian Federation', Moscow, 21 March 2003.

51 Putin, V., 'Interview with Bulgarian television and the newspaper *Trud*', 27 February 2003.

52 Ivanov, I., 'Replies by Russian Minister of Foreign Affairs Igor Ivanov to questions from Hamshahri and Iranian newspapers', Teheran, 11 March 2003.

53 Ivanov, I., 'Transcript of replies by Minister of Foreign Affairs of the Russian Federation Igor Ivanov to media questions after his remarks to the State Duma of the Federal Assembly of the Russian Federation', Moscow, 21 March 2003.

54 Putin, V., 'Interview with France-3', 9 February 2003, 'Interview with Bulgarian television and the newspaper *Trud*', 27 February 2003, 'Statement on Iraq at a Kremlin meeting', 20 March 2003.

55 Ivanov, I., 'Interview with Kommersant', 5 March 2003.

56 Putin, V., 'Address at the St Petersburg Summit', 11 April 2003, in *Dipomaticheskii Vestnik* 5 (2003); Ivanov, I., 'Interview with Kommersant', 5 March 2003.

57 Schröder, G., 'Address to the nation on the situation in Iraq', 18 March 2003, 'Address on the beginning of the war in Iraq', 20 March 2003; Fischer, J., 'Address to the German Bundestag', 13 February 2003, 'Address to the German Bundestag', 13 March 2003, 'Address to the UN Security Council', 7 March 2003, 'Address to the UN', 19 March 2003. The Russians also warned of innocent victims caught up in an armed intervention. Putin, V., 'Statement on Iraq at a Kremlin meeting', 20 March 2003; Ivanov, I., 'Address at UN Security Council meeting', 14 February 2003.

58 Fischer, J., 'Interview with *Der Spiegel*', 30 December 2002, 'Address to the German Bundestag', 13 February 2003.

59 Schröder, G., 'Speech on the occasion of the opening of the CeBIT', 11 March 2003.

60 Schröder, G., ' Interview with *Die Zeit*', 27 March 2003, 'Interview with Sender Phoenix,' 28 March 2003, 'Interview in 3SAT', 3 April 2003.

61 Blair, T., 'Press conference: Prime Minister and Portuguese Prime Minister Barroso', 11 March 2003.

62 Fischer, J., 'Interview with *Der Spiegel*', 30 December 2002, 17 January, 5 February 2003.

63 de Villepin, D., 'Interview with *Le Figaro*', 24 February 2003, 'Interview with ABC News', 2 March 2003.

64 Patten, C., 'Address to the European Parliament', 20 March 2003.

65 Patten, C., 'Address to the European Parliament', 12 March 2003.

66 Patten, C., 'Address to the European Parliament', 29 January 2003.

67 Patten, C., 'Address to the European Parliament', 12 March 2003, 'Address to the European Parliament', 20 March 2003.

68 Solana, J., 'Remarks on the occasion of the Manfred Woerner Award', 24 March 2003.

69 Prodi, R., 'Report on the Spring European Council to the European Parliament', 26 March, 2003.

70 Patten, C., 'Speech at the Westdeutscher Rundfunk ARD Europa Forum', 3 December 2002; Papandreo, G. A., 'Lecture delivered at St Antony's College by the EU Presidency', University of Oxford, 6 May 2003.

71 Papandreo, G. A., 'Lecture delivered at St. Antony's College by the EU Presidency', University of Oxford, 6 May 2003.

72 Solana, J., 'Presidency press conference', 2 May 2003.

73 Fischer, J., 'Interview with Die Zeit', 20 February 2003, 'Interview with Neuen Zürcher Zeitung', 13 April 2003; Chirac, J., 'Interview with Time Magazine', 16 February 2003, 'Interview with TF1 and France-2', 10 March 2003.

74 Fischer, J., 'Address to the European Convent', 3 April 2003.

75 Fischer, J., 'Interview with *Die Zeit*', 20 February 2003.

76 Chirac, J., 'Interview with *Time Magazine*', 16 February 2003, 'Interview with TF1 and France-2', 10 March 2003; de Villepin, D., 'Interview with *Le Soir, El Pais* and *Corriere della Sera*', 27 February 2003.

77 de Villepin, D., 'Address to the National Assembly', 11 December 2002.

78 Chirac, J., 'Statement on the 40th Anniversary of the Elysée Treaty', 22 January 2003.

79 Patten, C., 'Address to the European Parliament', 12 March 2003, 'Address to the European Parliament', 20 March 2003; Papandreo, G. A., 'Lecture delivered at St Antony's College by the EU Presidency', University of Oxford, 6 May 2003; Prodi, R., 'Press conference by the President of the European Commission', Informal Extraordinary European Council, 17 February 2003; Solana, J., 'Speech to the annual dinner of the Foreign Policy Association', 7 May 2003.

80 Simities, C., 'Address to the European Parliament by the Greek Presidency', 26 March 2003.

81 Papandreo, G.A., 'Address to the European Parliament by the EU Presidency', 12 March 2003.

82 Papandreo, G.A., 'Address to the European Parliament by the EU Presidency', 12 March 2003.

83 Fischer, J., 'Address to the German Bundestag', 13 March 2003; de Villepin, D., 'Statement at UN Security Council ministerial meeting', 20 January 2003, 'Interview with the French media on the occasion of the UN Security Council ministerial meeting', 14 February 2003; Ivanov, I., 'Interview with Al-Jazeera', Moscow, 25 January 2003, 'Interview with Kommersant', 5 March 2003, 'Transcript of replies by Minister of Foreign Affairs of the Russian Federation Igor Ivanov to

media questions after his remarks to the State Duma of the Federal Assembly of the Russian Federation', Moscow, 21 March 2003; Putin, V., 'Address at the St Petersburg Summit', 11 April 2003, in *Dipomaticheskii Vestnik* 5 (2003).

84 Chirac, J., 'Interview with *Time Magazine*', 16 February 2003; de Villepin, D., 'Interview with the French media on the occasion of the UN Security Council ministerial meeting', 14 February 2003, 'Interview with *Le Figaro*', 24 February 2003.

85 de Villepin, D., 'Interview with RTL-*Le Monde*-LCI', 16 February 2003, 'Statement in the French Senate', 26 February 2003', 'Press conference after UN Security Council meeting', 7 March 2003.

86 de Villepin, D., 'Interview with ABC News', 2 March 2003, 'Interview with RTL-*Le Monde*-LCI', 16 February 2003, 'Press conference after UN Security Council meeting', 7 March 2003.

87 Putin, V., 'Address at the St Petersburg Summit', 11 April 2003, in *Dipomaticheskii Vestnik* 5 (2003).

88 Fischer, J., 'Interview with Frankfurter Allgemeinen Zeitung', 17 March 2003, 'Address to the German Bundestag', 20 March 2003, 'Interview in ARD', 4 April 2003.

89 Fischer, J., 'Address to the UN', 19 March 2003, 'Interview in ARD', 4 April 2003; Schröder, G., 'Address to the nation on the situation in Iraq', 18 March 2003, 'Address on the beginning of the war in Iraq', 20 March 2003.

90 Fischer, J., 'Address to the German Bundestag', 13 February 2003, 'Address to the UN', 19 March 2003.

91 Blair, T., 'Joint press conference with Spanish Prime Minister Maria Aznar', 28 February 2003, 'PM Statement opening Iraq debate', 18 March 2003; Straw, J., 'Written ministerial aanswer to the House of Commons', 7 January 2003, 'Speech in Jakarta', 9 January 2003, 'Speech to the International Institute of Strategic Studies', 11 February 2003.

92 Straw, J., 'Speech in Jakarta', 9 January 2003.

93 Straw, J., 'Speech to the International Institute of Strategic Studies', 11 February 2003.

94 Straw, J., 'Speech to the International Institute of Strategic Studies', 11 February 2003, 'Speech at the Royal Institute of International Affairs', 21 February 2003, 'Statement in House of Commons', Hansard Debates, 26 February 2003.

95 Blair, T., 'Speech at the Foreign Office conference', 7 January 2003.

96 Blair, T., 'Joint press conference with Spanish Prime Minister Maria Aznar', 28 February 2003.

97 Straw, J., 'Statement to the UN Security Council on Iraq', 5 February 2003, 'Speech at the Royal Institute of International Affairs', 21 February 2003.

98 Blair, T., 'Speech at the Foreign Office conference', 7 January 2003, 'Press conference: Prime Minister Tony Blair and President Bush at the White House', 31 January 2003, 'Prime Minister's statement on Iraq', 25 February 2003, 'Joint press conference with Spanish Prime Minister Maria Aznar', 28 February 2003; Straw, J., 'Speech at the FCO Leadership conference', 6 January 2003, 'Statement in House of Commons', Hansard Debates, 21 January 2003, 'Speech to the International Institute of Strategic Studies', 11 February 2003, 'Speech at Lord Mayor's Easter Banquet', 30 April 2003.

99 Ivanov, I., 'Address at UN Security Council Meeting', 14 February 2003, 'Interview with Kommersant', 5 March 2003.

100 Putin, V., 'Press conference at Elysee Palace', Paris, 11 February 2003.

101 Ivanov, I., 'Article in *Rossiiskaya Gazeta*', 25 March 2003.

102 Ivanov, I., 'Replies by Russian Minister of Foreign Affairs Igor Ivanov to questions from Hamshahri and Iranian newspapers', Teheran, 11 March 2003, 'Replies after speech at Federation Council meeting', 26 March 2003.

103 Ivanov, I., 'Address at UN Security Council Meeting', 14 February 2003, 'Replies by Russian Minister of Foreign Affairs Igor Ivanov to questions from Hamshahri and Iranian newspapers', Teheran, 11 March 2003, 'Replies by Minister of Foreign Affairs of the Russian Federation Igor Ivanov to questions from Russian and foreign media', Moscow, 18 March 2003, 'Replies after speech at Federation Council meeting', 26 March 2003, 'Statement at press conference joint with foreign ministers of France and Germany in Paris', 4 April 2003.

104 Ivanov, I., 'Replies to questions from the Greek newspaper *Katimerini*', 24 January 2003, 'Address at UN Security Council meeting', 14 February 2003, 'Replies by Russian Minister of Foreign Affairs Igor Ivanov to questions from Hamshahri and Iranian newspapers', Teheran, 11 March 2003, 'Transcript of replies by Minister of Foreign Affairs of the Russian Federation Igor Ivanov to media questions after his remarks to the State Duma of the Federal Assembly of the Russian Federation', Moscow, 21 March 2003.

105 Ivanov, I., 'Address at UN Security Council meeting', 14 February 2003, 'Replies by Russian Minister of Foreign Affairs Igor Ivanov to questions from Hamshahri and Iranian newspapers', Teheran, 11 March 2003, 'Transcript of replies by Minister of Foreign Affairs of the Russian Federation Igor Ivanov to media questions after his remarks to the State Duma of the Federal Assembly of the Russian Federation', Moscow, 21 March 2003.

106 Putin, V., 'Press conference at Elysee Palace', Paris, 11 February 2003.

107 Putin, V., 'Interview with France-3', 9 February 2003, 'Press conference at Elysee Palace', Paris, 11 February 2003.

108 Ivanov, I., 'Article in *Rossiiskaya Gazeta*', 25 March 2003.

109 Putin, V., 'Address at the St Petersburg Summit', 11 April 2003, in *Dipomaticheskii Vestnik* 5 (2003).

110 Papandreo, G.A., 'Address to the European Parliament by the EU Presidency', 12 March 2003; Council of the European Union, 'Conclusions', Extraordinary European Council, Brussels, 17 February 2003; Prodi, R., 'Press conference by the President of the European Commission', Informal Extraordinary European Council, 17 February 2003, 'Report on the Spring European Council to the European Parliament', 26 March, 2003.

111 Council of the European Union, 'Conclusions', Extraordinary European Council, Brussels, 17 February 2003; Solana, J., 'Remarks after Colin Powell's report to the United Nations Security Council', 6 February 2003.

112 Blair, T., 'Press conference: Prime Minister Tony Blair and President Bush at the White House', 31 January 2003, 'Prime Minister's statement on Iraq', 25 February 2003, 'Joint press conference with Spanish Prime Minister Maria Aznar', 28 February 2003, 'PM statement opening Iraq debate', 18 March 2003, 'Address to the nation', 20 March 2003.

113 Blair, T., 'Statement on European Council meeting 20–21 March 2003'.

114 Blair, T., 'Speech at the Foreign Office conference', 7 January 2003.

115 Schröder, G., 'Speech on the occasion of the opening of the CeBIT', 11 March 2003; Fischer, J., 'Address to the UN', 14 February 2003, 'Interview with *Der Stern*', 5 March 2003, 'Address to the UN', 19 March 2003, 'Address to the German Bundestag', 20 March 2003; de Villepin, D., 'Interview with the French media on the occasion of the UN Security Council ministerial meeting', 14 February 2003, 'Interview with RTL-*Le Monde*-LCI', 16 February 2003; Chirac, J., 'Interview with

Le Figaro', 20 January 2003, 'Statement on the 40th Anniversary of the Elysée Treaty', 22 January 2003, 'Interview with *Time Magazine*', 16 February 2003; Putin, V., 'Statement at joint press conference with Silvio Berlusconi', 3 February 2003, in *Diplomaticheskii Vestnik* 3 (2003); Ivanov, I., 'Interview with Al-Jazeera', Moscow, 25 January 2003, 'Interview with *Kommersant*', 5 March 2003.

116 'Joint declaration by Russia, Germany and France', Paris, 5 March 2003.

117 Chirac, J., 'Interview with *Le Figaro*', 20 January 2003, 'Statement on the 40th Anniversary of the Elysée Treaty', 22 January 2003.

118 de Villepin, D., 'Interview with RTL', 9 December 2002, 'Speech at the University of Fudan', 10 January 2003, 'Answer to a question in the National Assembly', 14 January 2003, 'Statement at UN Security Council ministerial meeting', 20 January 2003, 'Interview with *Le Figaro*', 24 February 2003; Chirac, J., 'Speech in Paris', 7 January 2003, 'Interview with *Le Figaro*', 20 January 2003.

119 de Villepin, D., 'Interview with the French media on the occasion of the UN Security Council ministerial meeting', 14 February 2003.

120 de Villepin, D., 'Interview with Radio Classique', 12 January 2003.

121 'La sécurité collective constitue le principe sur lequel nous devons nous fonder à chaque étape, pour adapter et coordonner nos actions avec le souci de l'efficacité. Unie, la communauté internationale est plus forte et plus à même d'agir pour faire respecter le droit.' de Villepin, D., 'Speech at the University of Fudan', 10 January 2003,

122 Cheney, D., 'Vice President speaks at VFW 103rd National Convention: Remarks by the Vice President to the veterans of foreign wars 103rd national convention', 26 September 2002.

123 Fischer, J., 'Address to the German Bundestag', 13 February 2003.

124 Schröder, G., 'Speech on the occasion of the German Steinkohle-Betriebsrätevollversammlung', 29 January 2003; Fischer, J., 'Address to the UN Security Council', 7 March 2003, 19 March 2003.

125 Fischer, J., 'Address to the UN', 19 March 2003.

126 Schröder, G., 'Speech on the occasion of the German Steinkohle-Betriebsrätevollversammlung', 29 January 2003.

127 Fischer, J., 'Interview with *Der Spiegel*', 30 December 2002.

128 Fischer, J., 'Interview with Frankfurter Allgemeinen Zeitung', 17 January 2003, 'Address to the UN', 'Address to the German Bundestag', 19 March 2003.

129 Schröder, G., 'Speech on the occasion of the German Steinkohle-Betriebsrätevollversammlung', 29 January 2003, 'Address to the German Bundestag', 19 March 2003.

130 Fischer, J., 'Interview with *Frankfurter Allgemeinen Zeitung*', 17 March 2003, 'Address to the UN', 19 March 2003.

131 Ivanov, I., 'Replies to questions from the Greek newspaper *Katimerini*', 24 January 2003, Ivanov, I., 'Address at UN Security Council Meeting', 14 February 2003.

132 Putin, V., 'Address at the St Petersburg Summit', 11 April 2003, in *Diplomaticheskii Vestnik* 5 (2003); Ivanov, I., 'Interview with *Rossiiskaya Gazeta*', 30 December 2002, 'Remarks at the Presentation of the First Regular Issue of the Journal *Russia in Global Politics*', 20 February 2003, 'Replies by Minister of Foreign Affairs of the Russian Federation Igor Ivanov to questions from Russian and foreign media', Moscow, 18 March 2003, 'Interview with Al-Jazeera', Moscow, 25 January 2003, 'Statement at the UN Security Council meeting', 5 February 2003, 'Transcript of replies by Minister of Foreign Affairs of the Russian Federation Igor Ivanov to media questions after his remarks to the State Duma of the Federal Assembly of the Russian Federation', Moscow, 21 March 2003.

133 Ivanov, I., 'Interview with *Rossiiskaya Gazeta*', 30 December 2002.

134 Ivanov, I., 'Interview with RIA-Novosti, 27 December 2002.

135 Ivanov, I., 'Remarks at the Presentation of the First Regular Issue of the Journal *Russia in Global Politics*', 20 February 2003, 'Article in *Rossiiskaya Gazeta*', 25 March 2003, 'Replies after speech at Federation Council Meeting', 26 March 2003; Putin, V., 'Interview with France-3', 9 February 2003, 'Press conference at Elysee Palace', Paris, 11 February 2003.

136 Putin, V., 'Interview with France-3', 9 February 2003.

137 Ivanov, I., 'Replies after speech at Federation Council Meeting', 26 March 2003.

138 Putin, V., 'Address at the St Petersburg Summit', 11 April 2003, in *Diplomaticheskii Vestnik* 5 (2003); Ivanov, I., 'Interview with *Kommersant*', 5 March 2003.

139 Putin, V., 'Address at the St Petersburg Summit', 11 April 2003, in *Diplomaticheskii Vestnik* 5 (2003).

140 Patten, C., 'Address to the European Parliament', 29 January 2003.

141 Straw, J., 'Statement in House of Commons', Hansard Debates, 25 February 2003.

142 Blair, T., 'Press conference following EU Summit in Brussels', 21 March 2003.

143 For example, King Carl XVI Gustaf is the current Swedish Head of State, but he does not exercise political power and cannot take part in politics. The Swedish monarchy is entirely constitutional.

144 Patten, C., 'Address to the European Parliament', 29 January 2003.

145 The Berlin Plus arrangements include EU access to NATO planning capabilities and to NATO European command options as well as the use of certain NATO assets and capabilities during EU-led operations.

146 Joint Action of the Council of Ministers on 12 July, 2004.

147 A Battle group is a battalion-sized force consisting of 1500 troops.

148 Council of the European Union, 'Council Joint Action 2004/570/CFSP of 12 July 2004 on the European Union military operation in Bosnia and Herzegovina'.

149 Solana, J., 'Statement welcoming launch of Aceh Monitoring Mission', Brussels, 15 September 2005.

150 Ivanov, I., 'Transcript of replies by Minister of Foreign Affairs of the Russian Federation Igor Ivanov to media questions after his remarks to the State Duma of the Federal Assembly of the Russian Federation', Moscow, 21 March 2003.

151 Ivanov, I., 'Article in *Izvestia*', 11 January 2003.

152 European Commission, 'Communication from the Commission to the Council and the European Parliament: Wider Europe – neighbourhood, a new framework for relations with our eastern and southern neighbours'.

153 European Commission, 'Moldova: Country Strategy Paper 2004–2006' and 'National Indicative Programme 2004–2006'.

154 Ivanov, I., 'Article in *Izvestia*', 11 January 2003.

155 EU–Russia summit, 'Joint statement', St Petersburg, 31 May 2003.

156 EU–Russia summit, 'Joint statement', Rome, 6 November 2003.

157 Lo, B., *Vladimir Putin and the Evolution of Russian Foreign Policy* (Oxford: Blackwell Publishing, 2003).

158 Putin, V., 'Press conference at Elysee Palace', Paris, 11 February 2003.

5 The European Union and the major European powers

Introduction

The case studies in this volume reveal that the national leaderships of the three leading EU member states placed different emphases on a number of the referent-objects of security. When issues were discussed at a rudimentary level, it is easy to find unanimity. All the leaders, for example, wanted to protect human rights and enhance regional stability. However, words cannot simply be taken at face value, removed from their context. It is sufficient in this context to recall the rhetoric of the Soviet Union and the USA during the Cold War. Both claimed to stand up for democracy, liberty and other norms that symbolise a 'good' society and a positive world order, but nonetheless diverged sharply on most of the issues of international politics.[1] A closer examination reveals that the EU member states deviated from one another, and none followed completely or agreed totally with the EU-level line.

The fact that the same discrepancies occurred in each of the three cases is particularly striking. The governments had moderate disagreements during the Kosovo crisis but diverged sharply over Iraq, but the framing analysis reveals similar patterns of disagreement during all three crises.

This chapter elaborates on three major differences in the messages given out by the governments, as recorded in the case studies. These 'security gaps' represent analytical devices that aim to clarify basic divergences in reasoning on security. Each gap builds on a central dichotomy.

The first security gap is labelled 'principles vs community' and highlights the role of norms as referent-objects of security. It may seem odd to contrast 'principles' with 'community', but the dichotomy is intended to illustrate how a government can justify sticking to particular principles even when this harms a community of which it forms part. Conversely, it reveals which government tends to place defence of community above laudable principles.

In the latter case, community becomes a strong value per se, which can compete with, and often win over, other kinds of principles. The dichotomy is thus not intended to capture which of the separate leaderships reasoned in terms of norms, and which did not. Such an exercise is less useful, since the case studies envisage that *all* the governments focused on norms as referent-objects of security. Instead, it provides an opportunity to discuss the level of importance that the leaders attached to norms. Did they treat norms as relative or absolute – as negotiable or not?

The second dichotomy, labelled 'the status quo vs reforms', focuses on the governments' visions of an ideal world order. It revolves around their official analysis of whether the current world order must be protected or reformed.

The third dichotomy is labelled 'multipolarity vs unipolarity', and essentially captures whether the governments set out to defend or to reject a unipolar system. While the previous dichotomy focuses on the leaderships' preferred world order – that is, whether they focused on protection of the existing global economic system based on a market economy, the prevailing normative ideals, and so on – this category focuses on the leaderships' favoured *structure* of international system.

The reason for focusing on precisely these gaps is that they evolve from central divergences in the governments' defence of basic norms and interests that are often linked to historical memories, identity and survival. Standpoints related to sovereignty, the use of force, the structure of the international system and the nature of alliances with other actors in the international arena are all examples of the issues in focus. Differences at the rhetorical level over such fundamental issues can hamper coordination and integration in the European security sphere.

In the second part of the chapter, the ways in which the member states frame security are contrasted with the EU's standpoints. This analysis is extended by way of a brief review of recent major EU documents and speeches on security. Does the security framing of any one of the three states correspond better with the EU's official framing than those of the other two, and does the answer depend on what issue-area is in focus? What are the implications of all this for EU 'actorness'?

National divergences over the three major 'security gaps'

First gap: principles vs community

British heroes in an unruly world

The first dichotomy can be illustrated using the metaphor of the United Kingdom as an active, upright but lone wolf facing a cohesive tribe. The case studies indicate that the United Kingdom did not define the norms at stake as appropriate primarily because they symbolised a sort of 'normal', politically correct behaviour that members of the Western community should adhere to. Instead, they were simply righteous, irrespective of the either temporary or permanent standpoints taken by other actors.

This tendency is marked throughout the three crises examined. During the Kosovo crisis, the defence of norms was primary in British reasoning. After the terrorist attacks of 11 September 2001, its leaders again focused on protecting their preferred norms and way of life in the light of attacks by an evil outsider. In essence, they projected the image that the United Kingdom was performing a good deed for the benefit of the rest of the civilised world. The rationale behind this was that they called their favoured norms 'universal', thereby objectively serving the interests of *all* states.

According to the British logic, military force should sometimes be applied in order to protect the universal norms of liberty, democracy, the rule of law and human rights. The leaders displayed a tendency to search for the most efficient means to protect their favoured norms, even if this meant breaking with the established practices of the international community. In the Iraq crisis, they set out to punish a morally irresponsible actor who violated their preferred norms, even if this goal demanded violation of territorial integrity.

Ulf Hedetoft elaborates on historical explanations for the British taste for moral endeavours: 'the almost spine-shivering pleasure of putting your life on the line for a righteous cause.' Writing from the perspective of 1995, he notes that the British war mentality – which includes pride in the moral war successes of the past and the belief that 'the common Brit has genuine grit' – remains an important part of the Anglo-British identity.[2] The findings of the research conducted for this volume confirm that this inclination to consent to warfare for the sake of 'the right principles' remains.

The British Labour Party strengthened the tendency to argue officially in terms of norms when it launched its 'ethical dimension to foreign policy' in May 1997. The 'New Labour' strategy aimed to support the same principles abroad as at home, with a firm conviction that the proliferation of appropriate norms leads to stability and security.[3] Robin Cook argued that: 'Our foreign policy must have an ethical dimension and must support the demands of other peoples for the democratic rights on which we insist for ourselves. The Labour Government will put human rights at the heart of our foreign policy and will publish an annual report on our work in promoting human rights abroad.'[4]

In 2005, the Labour Party remained committed to the idea that principles are a necessary prerequisite for security. According to the 2005 Labour Party Manifesto: 'The UN Charter proclaims the universal principles of human rights and democracy. In an uncertain world they are not only right in principle, they are important guarantees of our national security and prosperity too.'[5] This reasoning echoes the statements made during the three crises examined in this study. Typically, the British depicted the promotion of norms as a guarantee of security, but also of material well-being since the spread of 'the right' norms would generate favourable conditions for free trade. From Kosovo onwards, the British stood in defence of liberal norms that could enhance stability. The leadership thus supported an 'export-of-values' logic – a logic vigorously contested by Russia – in order to secure 'the British way of life'.

France and Germany: 'united we stand'

France and Germany did not rely on a predefined list of uninfringeable norms, but instead defended *common* norms. Above all, they suggested that members of the international community should agree, and then uphold, a shared code of normatively correct conduct that would sustain their community and strength. Ideally, all members of the Western community should adhere to the same appropriate reasoning and behaviour, which would strengthen existing cooperative structures.

An additional dimension to the French and German logic is that the EU states would serve as an 'ethical vanguard' by standing together, and by demonstrating a correct and predictable way of behaving. This would serve as an example to follow for other less law-abiding actors. In the same way that the EU would serve as a model of integration for other regions, the conduct of its constituent parts would serve as a model of good behaviour, and behaviour that was deemed good because it was dictated by common norms negotiated through common institutions (i.e., the EU and the United Nations). This would in turn ensure the long-term and predictable development of a better world governed by fair and democratic processes. In such an ideal world, no government would be left behind, demonised or brought down, but wrongdoers would progressively be reformed and integrated into the community.

France and Germany were already applying a 'community' argument during the Kosovo crisis. They focused intensely on the indivisible nature of the European continent and framed Milosevic's misdeeds as an attack on European civilisation. They referred to a common responsibility, and portrayed the Europeans as fully unified when responding to this threat. After 11 September 2001, the French and German leaders again placed great emphasis on the need to handle the terrorist threat using multilateral efforts. Typical of this kind of reasoning was German Chancellor Gerhard Schröder's argument that multilateral methods were required because security is 'indivisible'. During the Iraq crisis, France and Germany portrayed common resolve as a kind of efficient deterrence. The idea was to make dictators and potential proliferators of weapons of mass destruction realise that they faced a united, and thereby practicably invincible, international front. This logic stood in opposition to the British emphasis on deterrence by the determined and efficient use of force.

The German leaders displayed the strongest inclination to reason in terms of strength by way of community. Whereas the United Kingdom gave priority to a predefined set of norms, ignoring the position of other actors and thereby appearing as a solo flyer, community was foremost in the German rhetoric and multilateralism was presented as the key to stability. Germany signalled a keen ambition to retain and strengthen its position as a key and responsible member of the European security community, demonstrating its willingness to carry its share of the burden with regard to peacekeeping missions.

Yet, the German willingness to stand up for the common good did not lead the leadership to accept easily the idea of military missions. The reluctance of the German leadership to use force in order to impose its favoured norms has a quite specific historical background. Many scholars have elaborated on how Germany's historical experiences have bred a particular unwillingness to use military force.[6] Hedetoft remarks that while the United Kingdom sees itself as a non-military nation forced into military showdowns and taking pride in its heroism and successes, Germany has – since the Second World War – lacked any opportunities to take pride by drawing on memories of heroism during warfare. Moreover, Germany has been affected by the negative memories of a 'plethora of deaths'.[7]

German foreign policy reasoning has evolved since the end of the Cold War. Before the Kosovo conflict, the new red-green coalition government of 1998 had adopted a foreign policy programme that focused on non-military conflict management.[8] However, the Kosovo conflict demanded a reconsideration of past policies. On 16 October 1998 the vast majority of the members of the German Parliament voted in favour of Germany's participation in the North Atlantic Treaty Organisation (NATO) intervention in Kosovo.

The domestic German debate about the Kosovo mission, particularly with regard to the mandate issue, reveals a consciousness about the complexity of the moral and political dilemma.[9] The German Green Party, which had traditionally represented a solid pacifism, underwent a tough internal debate about the moral problems associated with out-of-area operations after its party leader Joshka Fischer argued that the party should support a policy of humanitarian intervention shortly after the Srebrenica massacre in July 1995. In the years that followed, humanitarian arguments received broad domestic support from both the political parties and wider public opinion.[10] At the time of the Kosovo crisis, the opposition parties – the Christian Democrats (CDU) and the Liberal Democrats (FDP) – supported government policy. Only the Socialist Party (PDS) stood out against German involvement in the war. Most of the German editorials – with the exception of, for example, the *Frankfurter Allgemeine*, also accepted the leadership's justifications for an intervention.[11]

Nonetheless, the case studies confirm that the German leadership's framing of security was still informed by an awareness of the potential losses of human life that result from armed action. In the case of Iraq, the leaders focused on the risk to civilians and soldiers that would result from an intervention. Moreover, Schröder explicitly linked the German unwillingness to resort to warfare to the German population's experience of war, which he argued was deeply rooted in the collective memory. The German leaders also deviated a great deal from the British tendency to 'preach' morals. Their pacifism was not of a 'missionary' kind. Schröder explicitly argued that, while Germany maintained its own opinion on the Iraq crisis, it did not wish to criticise other states on moral grounds.

German reluctance to participate in military ventures, coupled with its unwillingness to preach morals and a strong tendency to promote lawful behaviour, result in a cautious approach to out-of-area missions. An example of this caution was the German domestic debate over a potential leadership role in a mission to the Democratic Republic of Congo (DRC) in June 2006, the aim of which was to ensure that the presidential and parliamentary elections were conducted fairly. Germany had agreed in principle to lead the mission, but only if it had a UN mandate and clearly established goals, and other EU states participated. The domestic debate focused on precisely these issues, revealing a strong preoccupation with a normatively justifiable process.[12] To the German leadership, it was not only the goals of a mission, but also the practical process of their fulfilment that had to be morally acceptable and conducted in cooperation with other actors. Germany was particularly wary about the number of lives that might be put at risk during such a mission.

In line with Germany and Russia, France placed a high value on cohesiveness. The French discourse was often coloured by arguments in favour of preserving cohesion and increasing independence and actorness among members of a cultural community that had been forged by a long common history. They stressed the 'European' nature of the norms to be preserved and referred to common European traditions and a common culture. During the Kosovo crisis, they argued that it was necessary to 'cleanse' Europe by pacifying and civilising the 'anomaly' of Serbia – thereby 'Europeanising' the Balkan region. The Balkans had to become European, transforming from 'others' to become 'part of us'. It was not primarily universal norms that were at stake in Kosovo, but a 'certain concept of Europe'. After 11 September 2001, the President of France, Jacques Chirac, referred to France's particular aptitude for grasping cultural divergences and forging cohesion despite differences. Throughout all three crises, the French leaders focused on preserving the global security community that was guaranteed by the UN.

Conclusion: norms in their own right or as resources for community-building

In conclusion, the British message was clear – defence of the right norms, universal rather than European, could contribute to preserving the status quo and sustaining a liberal system that worked for the benefit of the British state and its citizens. France and Germany referred instead to positive norms as particularly 'European', and framed such norms as a means of fortifying community. In addition, the French and the Germans pledged adherence to a moral kind of globalisation and signalled a less ardent commitment to market liberalisation.

The leaderships also diverged with regard to *how* they related to norms. The British tended to treat norms as valuable per se. However, they did not focus as much as the others on the defence of community. They were far more zealous about preserving their national security and independence. Their endorsement of norms seemed closely linked to the process of promoting the national interest. The French and the German leaderships attributed more what may be called 'secondary value' to norms. A solution that infringed on commonly accepted standards of behaviour was less applicable, even if it aimed to promote the 'right' norms. The 'community argument' was central to German and French reasoning during all three crises. The French and German leaderships also placed a heavier moral responsibility on well-regarded members of the international community than the British did. States in the Western community had a particular responsibility to act as positive examples for less obedient actors, towards which it was necessary to show patience and tolerance in order to not distance them any further. In the end, this logic would also serve the national interests of France and Germany, since it would contribute to the creation of a more just, and therefore more peaceful, world.

The second gap: competing world views

British problem solving in defence of the status quo

The United Kingdom applied a status-quo approach throughout the three crises. The leaders framed the crisis in Kosovo as a problem that sprang from the tension between chaos and order. The British Prime Minister, Tony Blair, warned of the disorder that would follow if Serbia was not brought into line. The British leadership extended this argument to a global level of analysis, emphasising that Milosevic had to be stopped in order to stop other dictators from destroying international stability. Similarly, in the aftermath of 11 September, the British focused on demonising those who had upset global stability and caused chaos. Finally, the arguments used against Saddam Hussein in 2003 were remarkably similar to those used against Milosevic during the Kosovo crisis. The object was to avert chaos. The status-quo approach led the British leaders to value global stability at the cost of the national sovereignty of states that either challenged security and the regional or international order, or sheltered non-state actors that did the same. The British leadership took Kosovo as an example of how crises should be handled in the future.

The British did not place as much emphasis as the others on the role of common institutions in achieving international security. The British framed the Kosovo conflict as a threat not to the EU, but to regional and global stability and ultimately to the British national interest. Also, rather than launching long-term strategic visions of how to strengthen or reform common institutions, the British treated events on a case-by-case basis. They evaluated the crises with regard not primarily to institutional consid- erations, but to what had to be done according to basic British principles. In the aftermath of the Kosovo crisis, Blair was clear on this point, stressing that attached importance to norms rather than to institutions.

The British followed this problem-solving logic quite strictly. The leaders appeared to analyse the case, apply their moral principles – endorsing the status quo – in order to decide what had to be done, and then promote almost any vehicle that could solve the crisis effectively. The leadership, for example, focused more on reaching an efficient solution to the Kosovo crisis, and less on the fact that the EU states should unite in order to show their strength and protect their shared norms. After 11 September, the British did not advocate reform to the same degree as the other two states, but instead focused more on the need to deal resolutely with the 'hot spots' generating instability around the world. The leadership identified the opponent, and focused on tracing and eliminating this enemy. In the case of Iraq, the leaders identified what was threatening – weapons of mass destruction and, later, Saddam Hussein as an individual – and set as their goal to get rid of these threats. As a consequence, the British approach to global security politics may best be characterised as a continuing process in which each problem is treated as a unique event for which an effective solution must be found as quickly as possible to ensure that it does as little harm as possible to interna- tional stability and security.

This predisposition to focus intensively on the actual threat to or crisis within the Western security order, and to search energetically for a clear-cut resolution to the problem, leaves little room for nuance in the rhetoric. The British leadership exposed a tendency to define the world as dualistic, and characterised by sharp contrasts between good and evil. Actors with irrecon- cilable policies and principles inhabit this world. The messages during the Kosovo and the Iraq crises were identical: an evil actor had challenged the civilised and ordered world and the only reliable way to re-establish the status quo was to get rid of this deviant actor. The British leadership thus empha- sised the tension between chaos and stability in international relations.[13] Order was juxtaposed to the evil of chaos. If an actor did not fit into the ideal world order, that actor had to be disempowered or deposed. The practice of exclusion loomed large in the British arguments.

The French and Germans: protecting institutionalism and inclusiveness

The French and the German leaders also promoted the cause of greater stability in international affairs, but built up their framing in a different way. As well as highlighting the need for reform, Germany, France (and Russia) showed a clear inclination to treat institutions and structures as referent-objects of security. The message was that a secure world could not be achieved without such cooperative structures.

Above all, the German and French view of order appeared different from that of the British. While the British suggested that the world order at hand was worth defending, the official French and German discourse described the world as unstable and in need of change. Germany and France aimed to reform the world order to enhance stability and justice. They suggested that adherence to common rules of behaviour would guarantee a sense of order in the international system of states, whereas acceptance of the breaking of such rules would generate anarchy.

Germany placed great emphasis on the need to use multilateral, preventive and preferably non-military means in the face of the terrorist threat, arguing that preventive, non-military policies would contribute to solving problems in the Third World and stimulate peace in an 'indivisible' world. Similarly, the French emphasised that the unilateral use of force was not an efficient way to solve crises.

During a crisis, the French and the German leaders did not portray themselves as efficient problem-solvers seeking a quick and certain solution to the emergency at hand. They undertook a complex calculation of the pros and cons of each potential solution. Their reasoning started not so much from what *had* to be done in accordance with 'righteous' principles, as from what *could* be done without too much risk. They placed particular emphasis on which institutional vehicle should be used to solve which crisis, and paid particular attention to any additional relevant circumstances. Depending on the institutional vehicle identified, they discussed the optimal solution with a strict eye on costs and the hazards involved. While the British displayed a great urgency to restore order in the international system, France and Germany did not necessarily allow this to outweigh the fact that a mission could put the lives of soldiers and civilians at risk, affect a region as a whole, and have negative effects at the global level.

The German framing in particular was informed by such a systematic and comprehensive way of reasoning. Of all the actors analysed, the German reasoning was most coloured by this method of logical calculation. The German leaders undertook a sober cost-benefit analysis. They certainly condemned the circumstances prevailing in Iraq, but did not judge the suffering of the Iraqi people to be sufficient cause to risk the lives of soldiers and civilians, regional instability and a weakening of the global cooperative structures for dealing effectively with security problems. The tendency to dwell on every case and to make an official judgement with reference to a wide range of available facts – in essence arguing in accordance with Allison's 'rational actor model' – led the Germans to different conclusions in the crises examined. In Kosovo, this line of argument resulted in the conclusion that the benefits of an intervention outweighed the costs, while in Iraq the opposite result emerged from the same kind of logical calculation.

The French reasoned somewhat differently. Their calculation seemed slightly less informed by unbiased reasoning, taking as many facts as possible into account, and slightly more focused on preserving a sense of community among actors. They appeared reluctant to distance other actors in the international arena, and made particular efforts to emphasise that the international community had to make every possible effort to avoid a clash of civilisations. There was a tendency for the French to seek to include as many actors as possible in the French and the European community. France mostly refrained from contrasting opposing parties' viewpoints and from describing the world in sharp contrasts – as divided into one 'good' camp and one 'evil' camp. Here, the French leaders lived up to the image of fully fledged diplomats in the international arena. They appeared conscious of their role as diplomats, for example, when placing emphasis during the Kosovo conflict on the fact that the French had pursued a 'particularly active and intelligent diplomacy' towards Milosevic.

The French and the Germans argued that although other actors were immoral, they could be tolerated and should be given a second chance. They signalled a greater tolerance inside existing global structures; even though not all nation states lived up to their moral standards, they were still nation states and should be respected as legitimate entities that were entitled to their place in the UN state system. To a larger degree than the British, the French and Germans projected an image of an indivisible world where imperfect actors had to learn to coexist, and where multilateral action was crucial to strengthening the international community and international security.

France and Germany started from a vision of a world that should be managed by means of a common ethical code of conduct that was guaranteed by a few central, shared institutions – the EU and the UN – and by international law. The underlying logic was that, in the longer run, more and more actors would be incorporated in these joint structures. They promoted a world order that was at the same time more flexible and less flexible than the British variant. The inflexibility lay in their understanding of institutions as primary, and their view that actors must adapt to the common rules of behaviour guaranteed by these institutions. A solution could certainly not take any shape. A kind of flexibility may be found in the somewhat more benign vision of other actors than that applied by the United Kingdom.

France and Germany transmitted the message that actors can change, and that reforms that would, for example, increase the benefits of globalisation for the poor could facilitate the transformation of certain states into 'good' members of the international community.

Conclusion: divergent standpoints on norms and the national interest
This gap has something important to say about different views on norms and interests, and about the links between them. The United Kingdom placed greater emphasis on liberal norms that would benefit the status quo in world affairs, and sustain British security and its lifestyle. The British discourse on an ideal world order thus *relied* on the framing of certain norms as central to the achievement of this order, and it aimed to satisfy the national interest. France and Germany placed more emphasis on human rights, solidarity and community. Their zeal for common rules of behaviour and for multilateral structures evolved in parallel with their strong support for norms on human rights and global solidarity. The norm of community, it seems, did not only apply to members of the Western world; ideally, every actor should be trans- formed into a full member of the international community. Such an aim could also be interpreted in terms of national interest, since the ultimate consequence of reform would be to enhance international stability, which in turn would benefit the German and the French states. However, in the official discourse on an ideal world order, significantly more emphasis was placed on solidarity and human rights, and much less on the survival of the economy and normative mores of their respective states. Therefore, the link to the national interest is perhaps as strong as in the British case, but it is significantly less blunt – it is of a different kind – starting from a collective perspective, which at first glance makes it appear slightly less egoistic.

The third gap: multipolarity vs unipolarity

The Anglo-Saxon defence of unipolarity
The British leaders again deviated from the joint approach taken by France and Germany by standing by an 'Anglo-Saxon' view of polarity. Both directly and indirectly, the United Kingdom called attention to the positive aspects of a unipolar system based on the authority of the United States and NATO. Their message was that the world needed these powerful actors in order to reduce the risk of 'spillover' from unreliable states, and to stop dictators such as Saddam Hussein. They described the USA in a positive manner as a non- expansionist and peace-loving actor that loyally takes on the burdens of and responsibilities for global security that automatically come with superpower status. Throughout, they expressed gratitude for the US role in the three conflicts and emphasise the need to keep the USA engaged in Europe. Unlike the other leaderships, the British used the maintenance of NATO's credibility as an argument in favour of bombing Kosovo. They focused much

more on keeping NATO and the USA engaged in European and global security, and on keeping these actors strong. The British did not portray the strengthening of the EU as a security actor as a goal per se. Instead, they argued that the EU should take on a greater responsibility primarily in order to keep the USA engaged in Europe.

Blair projected the image of the United Kingdom as a mediator – a bridge between Europe and the United States. The British argued that the EU should take on a larger responsibility with regard to peacekeeping, but justified this stance not with reference to the need to strengthen the EU, but to satisfy the US demand that the EU should take on a larger share of the burden of peacekeeping in Europe. Moreover, the British did not refer to Europe in terms of an organiser for multipolarity. The EU should increase in importance for practical reasons,, but not at the cost of NATO and the USA – and certainly not in opposition to these actors.

France and Germany: defending multilateralism and multipolarity

France and Germany reacted against a British vision that would allow intervention in sovereign states in order to protect human rights and democracy. They stood firmly by the UN multilateral system and discussed multipolarity in positive terms. Multipolarity and multilateralism were indirectly posed as mutually reinforcing; the world would function more easily according to a multilateral logic if the major actors were organised in a multipolar structure, and vice versa. The French stated that a cooperative and multipolar approach was essential to a successful approach to global problems.

France and Germany argued in favour of containing NATO while simultaneously enhancing the importance of the UN and the EU. Collective security, in their view, was the most efficient way to achieve international stability. Fischer enthusiastically described reaction to the events of 11 September 2001 as a new beginning for multilateralism and for a cooperative approach to international relations.

Germany and France also agreed that the EU should stay independent from the USA. France even articulated a will to realise multipolarity. From Kosovo onwards, the French leadership portrayed its vision of Europe as a central pole in a multipolar world, and as an 'organiser of multipolarity'. The French warned that unipolarity could result in the reign of 'the law of the strongest' in world affairs. They downplayed the significance of NATO in the Kosovo crisis. Like the Germans, they argued that NATO should not be allowed to intervene in international conflicts without the consent of the UN Security Council.

Conclusion: divergent standpoints on polarity

The third gap pertains to tensions emerging from the governments' varying understandings of polarity. This dimension turned out to be quite central to the leaderships' reasoning on issues related to security. Many of the political leaders described their ideal version of the international structure, sometimes in an indirect way but on other occasions in a more direct fashion. Some of the leaders frequently elaborated on their ideal vision of an international order, while others only occasionally spoke in terms of polarity.

In the British version, unipolarity was a normatively favourable order. In a unipolar world, a benign hegemon – the USA – would lead the international community in a favourable way. It would take on a special responsibility to protect members of the international system from attacks by wrongdoers, and unselfishly oversee the best of the system. In contrast, in the French and German framing, multipolarity was portrayed not only as an order that could create stability and peace and thus sustain national interests, but also as a normatively just order. Multipolarity was framed as 'good' per se because it would serve as a guarantee that the 'law of the strongest', that is, brute force, would not rule in international relations. Moreover, in contrast to unipolarity, multipolarity would help to bring more states towards common goals. The working of the system would not only depend on the hegemon. Therefore, multipolarity would strengthen multilateralism, which in turn was considered a normatively good way to address international problems.

The EU and the great powers: splits and convergences

It is a conclusion of this study that the EU is more liable to harmonise with France and Germany than with the British on what primarily ought to be protected in times of crisis. The EU's tendency to emphasise the protection of human rights, institutionalism and multilateralism; its pursuit of an enhanced actorness that can contribute to the evolution of multipolarity; its tendency to defend the UN rather than the USA; and its tendency to express reservations with regard to how security threats should be handled chime better with the analytical and rule-based approach of Germany and France than with the more unconditional, passionate and problem-solving approach of the United Kingdom. The tendency of the French and German leaders to defend institutionalism, multilateralism and international society makes their political messages more compatible with the EU policy line.[14]

There are, however, as is demonstrated below, exceptions to these tendencies. In this section the EU's standpoints are contrasted with those of the three member state governments in order to deepen the understanding of the nature of the rifts between member-state level and the EU level. This section draws on the results of the framing analysis and revisits the major standpoints taken by the EU in the security sphere.

The three gaps between the member states that are highlighted above are closely interconnected. Views on polarity are naturally linked to visions of an ideal global order. There are also links between polarity and community in terms of alliances, which are a central component of discussions of polarity. The shadow of the USA looms large in all three dichotomies.

Support for *multilateralism* and *institutionalism* is a highly significant characteristic of EU security policy. The EU placed great emphasis on the need for multilateralism during the crises examined, in particular after 11 September 2001 and during the Iraq crisis. One natural consequence of this was that it prioritised the UN, while appearing hesitant about US domination of world affairs. Moreover, the framing analysis demonstrates the EU's intention to confirm itself as an actor in the international arena, and to act as a counterweight to the USA.

The EU's approaches to polarity, institutionalism and the nature of international cooperation converge with the French and German standpoints. Although Germany officially held to its Cold War pro-US stance, its leadership's priorities on institutions, common rules of behaviour, multilateralism and international law reveal a substantial rift in relation to the USA. This estrangement became more evident when the administration of President George W. Bush adopted an increasingly unilateralist stance on security issues. In addition, although Germany promoted NATO's continued engagement with European security, it did not give NATO a mandate to intervene in crises similar to that of Kosovo in the future. France also converged with the EU's views on polarity and multilateralism. Its steadfast promotion of the UN, and its emphasis on international community, multilateralism and multipolarity, were coupled with a strong desire for EU Europe to stay independent of the USA. Unlike the British, the French supported the EU's ambition to become a pole in a multipolar world, thus avoiding a unipolar world steered by a single superpower.

The United Kingdom stood closer to the USA, anxious to ensure that the US government remained engaged in European and global security policies. The framing analysis reveals that whether arguing in favour of new principles of intervention, deterring dictators, capturing bin Laden, preserving liberal norms or ousting Saddam Hussein, preserving the NATO alliance with the USA was central to the British arguments. The British wished to remain a primary partner of the USA, and to keep the superpower engaged in international and European security.

These standpoints correlated with the British government's unwavering support for the norms of liberty and democracy, their defence of the status quo in international affairs and their approval of unipolarity. During the Kosovo crisis, Blair linked the United Kingdom's support for a range of favoured norms to the idea of a 'third way' in international affairs, marked by a kind of active internationalism. This third way would provide globalised solutions to globalised problems. Blair hinted that he and the US President, Bill Clinton, agreed on the need to pursue such a path:

This speech has been dedicated to the cause of internationalism and against isolationism. On Sunday, along with other nation's leaders, including President Clinton, I shall take part in a discussion of political ideas. It is loosely based around the notion of the Third Way, an attempt by centre and centre-left Governments to redefine a political programme that is neither old left nor 1980s right. In the field of politics, too, ideas are becoming globalised. As problems become global – competitiveness, changes in technology, crime, drugs, family breakdown – so the search for solutions becomes global too.[15]

Blair finished his speech with an appeal to the US public never to fall again for the doctrine of isolationism, since 'the world cannot afford it'. He promised that 'in Britain you have a friend and an ally that will stand with you, work with you, fashion with you the design of a future built on peace and prosperity for all, which is the only dream that makes humanity worth preserving'.[16]

It is evident that as well as loyalty to the USA, the idea of global market liberalisation was central to the British framing. In this logic, liberal norms would more or less mechanically solve global problems and ensure success and stability. This approach does not fit easily with the EU's passion for forging a more just world order. France and Germany, in contrast, harmonised with the EU's ambitions to reform the world order, and to work preventively by harnessing globalisation in order to boost security.

Moreover, the EU's focus on prevention and its hesitance to use force – as well as its ambition to harness globalisation to create a more just world – also match the official French and German approaches to security better than the British approach. The French inclination to promote prevention is compatible with the EU's overall security aims. The German scepticism about the use of military means also converges with the EU's standpoint. The EU's 'broad toolkit' and its belief in diplomacy as a tool correspond with the typical French inclination to emphasise the force of diplomacy, and with the German approach to security as 'indivisible', requiring a comprehensive approach. While the EU, and France and Germany focused on root causes, non-military means and long-term strategies to address security problems, the British rhetoric dealt much more with immediate and visible threats. The British used less energy to promote prevention and more zeal to target the direct causes of disorder.

The framing analysis also demonstrates that the EU focused extensively on *human rights* as a referent-object of security, particularly in its response to 11 September. Ever since the adoption of the Amsterdam Treaty in 1997, the EU has developed its commitments in the human rights area with particular passion. The Cologne European Council in 1999 decided to draw up a Charter of Fundamental Rights.[17] The focus on human rights is slightly more pronounced in the German and French statements examined during the crises. The United Kingdom placed somewhat more emphasis on promoting democracy.

However, the EU does not converge best with France and Germany in all areas. There are instances in which the official documents and statements correspond better with British reasoning. The framing analysis shows that in the run-up to the Iraq war, the EU Commissioner for External Relations, Chris Patten, reflected the more uncompromising British problem-solving approach when arguing that an intervention might become necessary. In line with the United Kingdom, the EU also displayed a far-reaching missionary zeal, displaying a readiness to impose objectively 'just' norms on non-EU actors – by way of force if necessary – as a condition for membership or as a condition for enhanced cooperation with the EU.

Tendencies for continuity and change: gaps sustained

A review of some of the major EU documents and statements made in the years following the three crises might help to discern whether the EU has evolved more in the direction of the United Kingdom's view on security, or remains more in line with France and Germany. The exercise provides an indication of which of the competing national ways of framing security corresponds best with the EU level, and in which ways. Causal links cannot be established – even if the EU has usurped an idea originally voiced by a specific member state it is likely to have been translated into an 'EU discourse', which diverges somewhat from that of its 'source' at the member-state level. Yet, it *is* possible to establish whether in recent years the EU's major message on central issues in the security sphere has moved closer to the corresponding message of one member state than to that of the others.

The content of major EU documents and statements in 2003–06 indicates that the EU's preferences as explored in the case studies were reinforced rather than weakened. The EU appears to have continued to evolve in a way that converges more with French and German views on security than with those of the United Kingdom.

First, the EU continues to prioritise prevention over immediate problem solving. It has maintained and strengthened its focus on the root causes of terrorism and on forging a better and more just world. The EU Security Strategy confirms the EU's commitment to and responsibility for building a better – a fairer, safer and more united – world.[18] In her introductory address to the European Parliament, Benita Ferrero-Waldner, the new Commissioner for External Relations and European Neighbourhood Policy, defined conflict prevention, crisis management, human rights and effective multilateralism as 'priority issues' for the EU. She also introduced a new concept – that of 'human security'.[19] Two years later, she called human security a 'philosophy underlying the EU's approach to security'. The approach entails that security can only be achieved through development and development only through security. Ferrero-Waldner brought yet another aspect of prevention to the fore – the issue of security sector reform, which aims to create effective armed forces, police services and justice institutions as a prerequisite for the security of a state and its people.[20]

Successive EU Neighbourhood Policies (ENPs) are another example of the EU's approach to security using preventive means. In relation to its close neighbourhood, the EU backs an enduring strategy based on a functionalist logic according to which long-term cooperation will produce more common norms that will enhance security. The message is that the EU will promote shared prosperity and values in its close neighbourhood. The ENPs trace the root causes of political instability in the EU's neighbourhoods to economic vulnerability, institutional deficiencies, conflict, poverty and social exclusion.[21] For example, in The European Neighbourhood Policy of May 2004, the EU reiterates that the countries bordering both the EU and Russia should commit to shared (EU) values, such as 'respect for human dignity, liberty, democracy, equality, the rule of law and respect for human rights'.[22] The significance of the ENPs is marked by the fact that Ferrero-Waldner was also given the title 'Commissioner for Neighbourhood Policy'. She often begins her addresses by envisaging the ENP as a central part of the EU's security policy.[23]

The EU remained focused on mitigating the negative effects of globalisation.[24] This ambition also converges better with the French/German standpoint on globalisation than with that of the British. Moreover, the EU also continues to exhibit a degree of caution with regard to the use of force, a policy stance that corresponds better with the German/French line than with the British stance. For example, the EU counterterrorism strategy mentions military means only as a resource when handling the aftermath of terrorist attacks, or to protect military forces active in international missions.[25] The Security Strategy also emphasises other means, such as stronger diplomatic capabilities that can improve communication between actors and teach them to understand 'the foreign' better, thus minimising the risk of open confrontation and the use of force.[26]

Finally, the EU strengthened its support for effective multilateralism in its 2003 Security Strategy, claiming that 'no single country is able to tackle today's complex problems on its own'. The strategy reflects the EU's strong focus on institutionalism and abidance by rules supporting the 'development of a stronger international society, well functioning international institutions and a rule-based international order'. The document commits the EU to international law and to strengthening the UN.[27] The counterterrorism strategy also clearly reflects a commitment to institutionalism and multilateralism. It aims to construct an international consensus and international standards on the fight against terrorism, particularly through the UN and other international and regional organisations. Cooperation with the USA is not primary but only secondary, behind action through the UN.[28] Ferrero-Waldner emphasises the importance of securing a rules-based, multilateral international order for the future.[29] The 2006 EU White Paper 'Europe in the World' confirms that the EU member states are 'committed supporters of multilateralism'.[30]

Nonetheless, the British have left some important imprints on the Security Strategy. The strategy states that the EU can punish states that refuse to abide by international law. This leaves an opening for the EU to follow the British path towards violating sovereignty in order to impose 'correct' norms on other actors, coming closer to realising its goal of a good international society:

> A number of countries have placed themselves outside the bounds of international society. Some have sought isolation; others persistently violate international norms. It is desirable that such countries should rejoin the international community, and the EU should be ready to provide assistance. Those who are unwilling to do so should understand that there is a price to be paid, including in their relationship with the European Union.[31]

Moreover, while the particular French and German passion for human rights is reflected in the EU documents,[32] so also is the British prioritisation of democracy. In addition to the human rights dimension, the significance of arguments referring explicitly to democracy is visible throughout the major EU documents. In her introductory address to the European Parliament, Ferrero-Waldner particularly emphasised the EU's commitment to human rights and fundamental freedoms, but she also mentioned democracy.[33] Ferrero-Waldner also argued in 2006 in favour of endorsing the 'right' values internationally: 'If we are to preserve an international order based on the rule of law and respect for those values we hold dear – human rights, democracy, good governance – we need to be using all means at our disposal to persuade emerging powers to sign up to it now.'[34]

Finally, in line with the British, the EU Security Strategy deals not only with long-term prevention, but also with the direct causes of disorder, for example, regional conflicts, failed states and the threat posed by weapons of mass destruction. Furthermore, even though the strategy does not exactly extol the USA and NATO, it does refer to their significance in the security sphere.

Normative issues as obstacles to cooperation

Recalling the essence of the three 'security gaps' outlined above, it is reasonable to conclude with regard to the third gap that the EU's standpoints are more in line with those of France and Germany than those of the United

Kingdom. The EU strongly supports multilateralism as the best form of governance of international relations, a stance that is not compatible with an acceptance of US unilateralism and unipolarity. It also demonstrates more affinity with France and Germany with regard to the second gap. It is somewhat less suited to accommodate the British taste for resolute problem solving, and more able to accommodate the French and German preference for far-reaching reform of the world into a more 'just' order, using preventive strategies and, if possible, by non-military means. The European Commission's methods of working, in terms of long-term neighbourhood strategies and ambitious development schemes, are typical examples of preventive activities aiming to create a more just world.[35] Yet, with regard to the first gap – 'principles vs community' – the EU is torn between its ambition to promote law-abiding, common and multilateral behaviour, on the one hand, and its taste for normative missions on the other. The EU's inclination to promote 'objectively' good norms corresponds with the United Kingdom's passionate missionary stance with regard to the export of norms.

These diverging government standpoints on the role of norms in international security are perhaps the most central obstacle to the pursuit of greater unity in the EU. Among the three member states, the United Kingdom placed most emphasis on the endorsement and extension of democracy, the principles of the market economy and liberal norms. France and Germany used more zeal to promote human rights and the observance of rules in the international arena, such as, for example, respect for the UN and for national sovereignty. They were also less impatient with actors that did not live up to their normative standards. Norms appeared somewhat more negotiable for France and Germany than for the United Kingdom. France and Germany focused less on the contrasts between the good and the bad, but argued that the world was an imperfect place that many actors must try to cohabit in relative peace. Some ill-behaved actors had to improve, but this would take time and would also require effort on the part of the Western governments, by way of reforming the entire global system into a more just world order. Norms were important, but only of secondary importance; the main priority was to preserve functional relations between actors.

The EU is situated somewhere between these two different philosophies, while leaning towards the Franco–German position. In line with the United Kingdom, the EU projects a far-reaching missionary profile, and displays a readiness to impose 'objectively just' norms on non-EU actors. Yet, it is important to note that although the EU's inclination to promote norms corresponds with the British focus on norms, the latter promotes intervention primarily for the sake of spreading democracy and order, and for humanitarian reasons. In contrast, Lucarelli and Manners note that the EU appears to favour intervention on humanitarian grounds, rather than to spread democracy.[36] This observation corresponds to the findings of the framing analysis. The EU placed more emphasis on prevention and humanitarian action than on 'spreading democracy by force'. The EU strategy for spreading democracy is more based on long-term schemes aimed at encouraging democratic movements, in particular in its nearest neighbourhoods.

A clue to the reasons behind this difference might be that the British leadership emphasises the *export* of norms as a successful method, while the EU places even more emphasis on *being* a normative example. The EU displays a strong tendency to portray itself as a good example of successful regional integration for the benefit of peace, democracy and other positive values. The plan is not just to accomplish a direct export of 'good' norms to non-members, it is also to a significant extent a strategy to project itself as an attractive model for other, less developed, regions and actors. This logic chimes better with the French and German tendency to place responsibility on members of the Western community to act as role models for less well-behaved actors, than with the United Kingdom's readiness to go to war for the sake of the right norms.

Overall then, the EU's official message seems to converge somewhat better with that of France and Germany, but the tendency is mitigated by a small number of affinities with the United Kingdom, in particular with regard to its passionate belief in the positive effects of 'good norms' on international relations.

Implications for the EU's actorness

The multilevel divergences uncovered and outlined above imply that the EU cannot be characterised as a united actor in the security sphere. The EU's official policy deviates from that of some of its key member states in a variety of ways, and the member states differ from one another. The 2006 White Paper 'Europe in the World' highlights the importance, but also the difficulties, of forging a single EU voice in the realm of security. The paper makes a range of suggestions in order to make the Common Foreign and Security Policy (CFSP) and the European Security and Defence Policy (ESDP) more effective and coherent. It directs special attention to the importance of convergence at the rhetorical level, arguing that the member states must make increased efforts to bring their official messages on security into line:

> Even when the EU has clear objectives and an agreed course of action, the impact and effectiveness of our action is often hampered by mixed messages as well as slow and complex implementing procedures. The EU therefore needs to consider action in the following areas:
>
> Ensuring that, once a policy decision has been taken by the EU, all actors integrate this into their diplomatic and public messages as well as in their own policy development.[37]

As this study demonstrates, this ambition is not so easy to achieve. Even the Security Strategy contains evidence of the insoluble tensions between the preferences of the major member states. The strategy is by itself evidence of the difficult problems ahead with regard to the diverging security standpoints of EU member states. In addition to the tensions discussed above, the strategy does not take a clear stand with regard to the difficult issue of inclusion vs exclusion. The framing analysis indicates that the British more easily fell prey to exclusion, while the other two states focused more on inclusion. The strategy tries to accommodate both stances, suggesting, as is noted above, that states that have placed themselves outside the bounds of international society should rejoin, but if they do not 'there is a price to be paid'.[38]

The Security Strategy also mirrors the tension between the British promotion of liberal market values and the German and French preference for harnessing globalisation, and does not take a clear stand in favour of either. It simply notes that 'Flows of trade and investment, the development of technology and the spread of democracy have brought freedom and prosperity to many people. Others have perceived globalisation as a cause of frustration and injustice.'[39] These words bear witness to the fact that the EU cannot solve the underlying tensions. At most, it can make formal compromises.

Despite all the tensions exposed in this chapter, the EU has developed its actor capacity since the Kosovo crisis in 1999. An EU military force has been created, new political and military bodies established in Brussels and, by 2010, thirteen Battle Groups, deployable within ten days, are to be created in order to make interventions more efficient.[40] The EU also acted in the field, for example, by sending its first military operation outside Europe in 2004, in a mission, carried out without assistance from NATO, to the DRC to attempt to contain ethnic violence.[41] One year later, it sent its first mission to Asia – a monitoring mission intended to monitor the implementation of the peace agreement between the Indonesian government and the Free Aceh Movement (GAM).[42]

The concrete process of strengthening the EU's actorness has been accompanied by visionary statements portraying an actor with a truly global perspective in the security sphere. The High Representative for the Common Foreign and Security Policy, Javier Solana, argues that the EU has a moral obligation to play a global role:

> It is my belief that in this global age a Union of our size, with our interests, history and values, has an obligation to assume its share of responsibilities. We could, in theory, walk away from these responsibilities – but we could not escape the consequences of doing so. However, I am convinced that the same reasons that give the European Union responsibilities – our size and interests, our history and values – also equip us to take responsibilities. The question, therefore, is not whether we play a global role, but how we play that role.[43]

Moreover, official statements, the Security Strategy and a range of other official documents bear witness to the fact that the EU has developed something of an identity independent of the member states. The EU projects its identity by means of its claim to function as a role model for other actors. The 'role-model discourse' indicates a tendency to think of the EU as an actor similar to traditional nation states, in the sense that it possesses something that can be compared with national pride. It has a history of successful institution building that has served to strengthen peace, human rights and other positive values in its neighbourhood. This is portrayed as something unique to be proud of, and as something distinctively European that can be exported to other regions of the world.

Another characteristic trait is the EU's particular way of combining the export of values with enthusiastic law-abiding institutionalism. The EU does approve of exporting values, but it places great emphasis on correct procedures; all out-of-territory action has to be legitimised by international law and given UN consent. Another particular feature is the EU's focus on long-term structural reforms in other regions, with the aim of stabilising and reforming areas outside its own territory.

The EU also stands out by its tendency to treat security from a 'moral' perspective. The case studies revealed a focus on the root causes of security problems, and an inclination to attempt to make the processes of globalisation more 'moral'. The EU's taste for moral endeavours is combined with a strong drive for multilateralism and institutionalism that also contribute to the forging of a distinctive 'EU identity'.

The emerging EU identity – the institutional reforms, the new tasks in the security sphere and the high-flying ambitions for the future – are clear achievements for the EU in its capacity as an actor in the international security arena. They bear witness that not only France and Germany, but also the United Kingdom welcome the EU taking a more active role in the security sphere. Work to strengthen and give more substance to the CFSP and the ESDP has therefore progressed, even in spite of the diverging views on a major issue in international affairs – Iraq. Cooperation in the field of security was not directly damaged by the Iraq crisis, but actually deepened.

This conclusion is supported by Maria Strömvik's research findings, which reveal that the EU's foreign policy cooperation has intensified during or soon after transatlantic disagreements over international security issues. However, these new achievements have not been linked to the controversial issue itself. It seems that when experiencing difficulties in one field, in order to compensate for its shortcomings, the EU tends to advance cooperation in a related foreign policy area where progress is still feasible.[44] Strömvik concludes that: 'the EU's collective foreign policy is successively pushed to new levels when some or all EU members disagree with the US on issues related to international security management, and the new levels are subsequently locked in by new or improved institutional agreements.'[45]

Competition with the USA for global power in the security sphere thus seems to be a major driving force for the EU. The EU's organisation has grown stronger out of every crisis, deepening and widening cooperation in the security sphere, and expanding its institutional structure. Even after 11 September, when the EU was in a way bypassed by the USA's unilateral handling of the war in Afghanistan, it was strengthened as an actor *and* it improved its relations with Russia.

Howorth even argues that the differences between British 'Atlanticism', French 'exceptionalism' and German 'pacifism' have faded, turning into 'a common acceptance of integrated European interventionism, based not solely on the classical stakes of national interest, but also on far more ideal-istic motivations such as humanitarianism and ethics'.[46] This study does not wholly support such a suggestion. Differences have diminished somewhat in the sense that German 'pacifism' is now negotiable, the French and British are more firmly committed to the common European integration project, and all three proclaim adherence to intervention on the basis of humanitar-ianism and ethics.

Hence, the major problem is not a lack of will on the part of the major member states to maintain the EU as a central player in European security, but that they do not agree on in which direction the EU should develop. There are substantial differences of emphasis between the three states, made obvious with utmost clarity by their inability to face the Iraq war united. The case studies confirm strong ongoing differences between the United Kingdom, on the one hand, and Germany and France, on the other.

A pessimist would conclude that the EU's zeal for reform after every crisis or disagreement between the member states that springs from diverging norms does not contribute to finding a solution to the origins of the dispute. In this interpretation, the new initiatives are most of all techniques for diverting attention – both the member states' and the external world's – from the EU's weaknesses in the area of security policy. When confronted with shortcomings in one area, the EU tends to highlight its successes in other areas. By focusing on the implementation of institutional reform, and on new tasks and challenges – such as launching new, groundbreaking military missions – differences are partly concealed.

This method provides officials with the opportunity to continue framing crises as 'wake-up calls', and then boldly to envisage new ways forward. The problem is that there are few indications that the wake-up calls result in a process that will in the end resolve the basic differences. The EU instead appears merely to direct the actors' attention towards a new kind of goal, around which they can unite. Hence, the actors become occupied with new processes and new tasks, and avoid engaging in an open discussion about their basic divergences in the security sphere. During the Iraq crisis, the German Foreign Minister, Joshka Fischer, acknowledged the shortage of honest attempts to converge, warning that the EU member states had not yet united around which world order to promote, and must engage in a discussion of whether it should be cooperative and multilateral, or unilateral.

The rejection of the draft constitutional treaty in the French and Dutch referendums in 2005 signifies another halt to major reforms in the security area, such as the appointment of a foreign minister representing both the Council and the Commission with a Joint External Service, and the agreement of a solidarity clause. These kinds of reforms are crucial if the EU is to function as an effective actor in the security sphere, since it cannot rely on accord among the member states in the face of concrete and controversial security issues. If a new EU constitution had been agreed, the EU might have acquired new tools that could have facilitated the handling of critical situations, similar to the EU's internal divergences over Iraq, in the future.

However, the next time the EU faces a similar crisis, it will most probably become paralysed once again. As long as the member states officially disagree, it will be extremely difficult for the EU to express a consistent, independent line of argument. In this interpretation, the series of 'wake-up calls' from Kosovo onwards make the EU appear as a 'bigger' and more comprehensive actor in the international arena because of its institutional development and practical achievements in terms of missions, but not as a more cohesive or strategically operative actor. While the EU's powers increase, it is somewhat unclear how these powers could or should be used. The EU remains a vehicle in the hands of its most influential member states, and it will be steered by the outcome of disputes arising from differences pertaining to fundamental issues in the security sphere.

In the periods between acute crises, these tensions might not be very visible, and they need not necessarily hinder effective actorness. As long as the EU has the financial means, the EU can promote *both* democracy and human rights, it can 'harness globalisation' *and* target terrorists and proliferators of weapons of mass destruction. In times of sudden crisis, however, such as the Iraq war – where basic interests and values pertaining to sovereignty, the nature of alliances, or basic norms are at stake – the EU risks becoming trapped between the security logics of its major member states. Clashing logics of security among member states will inevitably hamper its activism from time to time.

Yet, in the author's analysis, the implications of the EU's relatively weak actorness for its overall aims in international affairs are not all negative – there can be positive implications as well. Traditional great powers, such as Russia and China and to some extent the USA, appear to be opposed to the EU's further development into a strong, influential, 'ethical power' in world affairs.[47] An EU with a less pronounced profile, emerging from its nature as a multifaceted, divided actor, would probably seem less threatening, or less troublesome, to many traditional states than a powerful actor with far-reaching moral ideals and a capacity to act on them. Indirectly, a 'weaker' EU, with fewer high-flying and unambiguous ambitions, could serve to minimise conflicts with Russia, China and the USA. This might in turn favour the incremental growth of a cooperative and largely multilateral international system, which would clearly be in line with what is perhaps the EU's most central aim in the security sphere.

Notes

1 For example, in 1947 George Kennan accused the Soviet leadership of totalitarian rule and expansionism. Kennan, G., 'The sources of Soviet conduct', *Foreign Affairs* 25 (1947). In the same year, the leading Soviet ideologist Andrei Zhdanov accused the USA of waging an anti-democratic policy, depriving European countries of their independence, and so on. Zhdanov, A., 'Soviet policy and world politics', *The International Situation* (Moscow: Foreign Languages Publishing House, 1947).

2 Hedetoft, U., *Signs of Nations* (Aldershot: Dartmouth Publishing Company, 1995), p. 206

3 Robin Cook said 'In order to achieve our goals for the people of Britain we need a foreign strategy that supports the same goals'. Cook, R., 'Speech on the government's ethical foreign policy', 12 May 1997.

4 Ibid.

5 British Labour Party, *The Labour Party Manifesto 2005: Britain Forward not Back* (London: Labour Party).

6 Howorth, J., 'Discourse, ideas and epistemic communities in European security and defence policy', *West European Politics* 27:2 (2004), pp. 211–234; Berger, T., 'Norms, identity, and national security in Germany and Japan', in P. Katzenstein (ed.), *The Culture of National Security* (New York, Columbia University Press, 1996).

7 Hedetoft (note 2), pp. 207–208.

8 Sozialdemokratischen Partei Deutschlands/Bündnis 90 / Die Grünen 1998, 'Aufbruch und Erneuerung Deutschlands Weg ins 21', Jahrhundert. Koalitionsvereinbarung zwischen (von 1998).

9 Duke, S., et al., 'The major European allies: France, Germany and the United Kingdom', in A. Schnabel and R. Thakur (eds), *Kosovo and the Challenge of Humanitarian Intervention: Selective Indignation, Collective Action, and International Citizenship* (Tokyo: United Nations University Press, 2000), pp. 133–134.

10 Ibid., p.133–134; Takle, M., 'Towards a normalisation of German security and defence policy: German participation in international military operations', *ARENA Working Papers* 2:10 (2002).

11 Eilders, C. and Lüter, A., 'Germany at war: Competing framing strategies in German public discourse', *European Journal of Communication* 15:3 (2000), pp. 415–428.

12 Dempsey, J., 'Merkel under fire over Congo mission', *International Herald Tribune* (20 March 2006).

13 Hellman, M., (2006) *Televisual Representations of France and the United Kingdom Under Globalization* (Stockholm: Department of Political Science, Stockholm University, 1995).

14 The British recognised the need for joint action in view of the terrorist threat, but did not exhibit strong support for multilateralism per se. In the British argument, the

essential issue was not the method or philosophy, but that the threat was dealt with resolutely.

15 Blair, T., 'Doctrine of the international community', Speech at the Economic Club, Chicago, 23 April 1999.

16 Ibid.

17 European Commission, EU Charter of Fundamental Rights.

18 Council of the European Union, 'A secure Europe in a better world: The European security strategy', 12 December 2003, pp. 1, 16.

19 Ferrero-Waldner, B., 'Address to the European Parliament', 5 October 2004.

20 Ferrero-Waldner, B., 'The EU's role in protecting Europe's security', Conference on Protecting Europe: Policies for enhancing security in the European Union, 30 May 2006.

21 Communication from the Commission, 'Wider Europe'.

22 Communication from the Commission, 'European Neighbourhood policy'. Roland Dannreuther's volume summarises a range of EU neighbourhood strategies directed to the south and southeast. Dannreuter, R., *European Union Foreign and Security Policy: Towards a Neighbourhood Strategy* (London: Routledge, 2004).

23 Ferrero-Waldner, B., 'Address to the European Parliament', 5 October 2004, 'The EU in the World', Speech at a European Policy Centre breakfast briefing, 2 February 2006, 'The EU's role in protecting Europe's security', Conference on Protecting Europe: Policies for enhancing security in the European Union, 30 May 2006.

24 Ferrero-Waldner, B., 'The EU in the World', Speech at a European Policy Centre breakfast briefing, 2 February 2006, 'The EU's role in protecting Europe's security', Conference on Protecting Europe: Policies for enhancing security in the European Union, 30 May 2006. The European Security Strategy calls for 'a better distribution of the benefits of globalisation'.

25 Council of the European Union, 'Counter-terrorism strategy', 30 November 2005, pp. 15–16.

26 The European Security Strategy calls for 'Stronger diplomatic capability: we need a system that combines the resources of Member States with those of EU institutions. Dealing with problems that are more distant and more foreign requires better understanding and communication', Council of the European Union (note 18), p. 12.

27 Council of the European Union (note 18), p. 10.

28 'The EU will promote efforts in the UN to develop a global strategy for combating terrorism. Continuing to make counter-terrorism a high priority in dialogue with key partner countries, including the USA, will also be a core part of the European approach', Council of the European Union (note 25).

29 Ferrero-Waldner, B., 'The EU in the World', Speech at a European Policy Centre breakfast briefing, 2 February 2006.

30 European Commission, 'Communication from the Commission to the European Council of June 2006: Europe in the world – Some practical proposals for greater coherence, effectiveness and visibility', 8 June 2006, COM (2006) 278 final.

31 Council of the European Union (note 18), p. 12.

32 The Strategic commitment reads 'To combat terrorism globally while respecting human rights, and make Europe safer, allowing its citizens to live in an area of freedom, security and justice', Council of the European Union (note 25).

33 Ferrero-Waldner, B., 'Address to the European Parliament', 5 October 2004.

34 Ferrero-Waldner, B., 'The EU in the World', Speech at a European Policy Centre breakfast briefing, 2 February 2006.

35 For a review of the EU as a 'development and humanitarian actor' see Bretherton C.

and Vogler, J., *The European Union as a Global Actor* (London: Routledge, 2006), Chapter 5.

36 Lucarelli, S. and Manners, I. (eds), *Values and Principles in European Union Foreign Policy* (London: Routledge, 2006), p. 204.

37 European Commission (note 30).

38 Council of the European Union (note 18), p. 12.

39 Council of the European Union (note 18), p. 3.

40 A Battle Group is a battalion-sized force consisting of 1500 troops.

41 Council of the European Union, 'Council Joint Action 2004/570/CFSP of 12 July 2004 on the European Union military operation in Bosnia and Herzegovina'.

42 Solana, J.,' Statement welcoming launch of Aceh Monitoring Mission', Brussels, 15 September 2005.

43 Solana, J., 'Intervention at the inaugural session of the 2002 conference of ambassadors', Palazzo della Farnesina, Rome', 24 July 2002.

44 Strömvik, M., *To Act as a Union: Explaining the Development of the EU's Collective Foreign Policy* (Lund: Department of Political Science, 2005), p.180.

45 Ibid., p. 182.

46 Howorth (note 6), p. 213.

47 Wagnsson, C., 'The EU as strategic actor, "re-actor" or passive pole', in Jan Hallenberg and Kjell Engelbrekt (eds), *European Union and Strategy: An Emerging Actor* (London: Routledge, 2007).

6 Russia and the EU: the need for pragmatism

Introduction

This chapter analyses how rhetorical divergences, referred to as 'security gaps', hamper cooperation between Russia and the EU. It is a major problem for both entities that these divergences, derived from the official messages taken from the case studies, apparently mirror deep policy controversies linked to existential issues and consequently to the two parties' identities. Ironically, scholars and politicians tend to perceive the EU as an actor that lacks identity, even though it seems more inclined than most nation states to base its foreign policy on a fairly specific conception of its role, namely, that of a morally superior entity. The results of this study envisage that the major member states do not agree on the exact meaning of this role. Nonetheless, the EU still claims, and acts on, an identity as a 'normative power'. This identity is reflected in both gaps.

The first gap – labelled 'export of norms vs national self-determination'– mirrors the tension between the EU's ambition to export norms and Russia's focus on the right of every state to forge its own political destiny without interference. The second gap is more specifically about how the actors focus on different referent-objects of security. Here, the EU – although certainly not ignoring the security of its member states – appears to claim the role of a particularly 'moral' power that sets as its major goal the amelioration of the security situation of non-traditional referent-objects such as individuals and the environment, thus contributing to progress towards a better world. Russia, in contrast, primarily gives its support to the traditional cornerstone of the international system: the sovereign state.

The EU's self-perception and ambitions to be a moral actor constitute a major source of unease for Russia's leaders. The problem is ultimately related to a clash between two actors that have each built their self-esteem on the belief that they have the correct answer to normative dilemmas in the contemporary world.

Russia is burdened by a long legacy of claiming world leadership not only in concrete terms, but also by providing the morally correct answer to the world's problems. In the tsarist period it acted as 'the third Rome', one of the leaders of Christianity, and in Soviet times it acted as the self-proclaimed moral leader of the socialist world. In the post-Soviet era the case studies indicate that Russian leaders strongly refute the idea of exporting norms in the international arena. Yet, in practice, Russia's leaders cannot entirely give up their longstanding performance as morally superior actors in the international arena. The leadership refrains from openly spreading a particular ideology, but it continually conveys the impression that it holds principles that are capable of providing an answer to most of the important issues in international relations. The uninfringeable principle of sovereignty is presented as a necessary condition for stability, Russia's longstanding opposition to separatism and terrorism is portrayed as an ideal example of how to counter terrorism and Russia's resistance to efforts by the United States to bypass the UN Security Council is presented as a righteous struggle against immoral and hegemonic attempts to rule the world. All these are examples of Russia's refusal to give up its role as a leading moral power in world affairs. The fact that a major challenge to this leadership comes from the geographically less significant – and traditionally divided – Western Europe makes the EU's ambitions appear all the more disturbing to Russia.

Russia is also economically inferior to the EU. Although the growing Russian market and Russia's energy assets make Russia by no means unimportant to the EU, Russia clearly depends more on the EU than vice versa.

Nevertheless, despite its economic superiority, the EU cannot remain indifferent to Russia's opposition to its normative ambitions. Even if the EU were to manage to make itself less economically dependent on Russia, for example, by reducing its dependence on Russian energy, it could not escape its dependence on Russia in the security sphere. For example, according to the European Commission, in 2004, 'The EU and Russia have every reason to cooperate on environmental issues, migration, public health, crime, research and other fields affecting the security, stability and well-being of Europe as a whole'.[1] The EU also needs Russia's cooperation to counter drug trafficking to Europe from Central Asia. Benita Ferrero-Waldner, the EU Commissioner for External Relations, acknowledged in 2006 the importance of collaborating against a wide range of serious threats in the 'common neighbourhood'.[2]

In sum, the EU cannot ignore Russia's demand for equal treatment because of the security situation – Russia is potentially a major source of instability that has to be dealt with. That said, in order wholly to appease Russia, the EU would have to refrain from criticising abuses of human rights and other misconduct in Russia. This, in turn, would force the EU to compromise seriously its own emerging identity as a normative power.

This leads to the conclusion that what is really at stake, and what leads to deadlock in emerging cooperation time and again, is the parties' respective identities in the global arena. Furthermore, both actors are particularly vulnerable in this respect. Russia has experienced an enormous and sometimes humiliating transformation of its regional and global role in the past twenty years. The Russian leadership has continually demonstrated that, despite all the changes, it places great emphasis on preserving and strengthening its identity and dignity as a global power. The EU, in turn, is still seeking a role as an actor, and badly needs to cultivate an image that can gain both increased legitimacy in the eyes of EU citizens, and acceptance by major partners in the international arena of the EU as a major actor in international affairs.

The two gaps must be tackled because they are detrimental to practical cooperation. The differences emerging from the gaps, to give one illuminating example, tend to complicate joint efforts to stabilise the so-called shared neighbourhood (the countries that border both Russia and the EU). The EU's attempts to stabilise this region are summarised in its May 2004 Neighbourhood Policy, one of many, which targets six states in the former Soviet Union – Armenia, Azerbaijan, Belarus, Georgia, Moldova and Ukraine – from which there is a risk that soft threats might spill over into the EU. The document reiterates that the countries in the shared neighbourhood must commit themselves to shared (EU) values, that is, 'respect for human dignity, liberty, democracy, equality, the rule of law and respect for human rights'.[3] Russia vigorously rejects the project to export norms to this region, but the EU refuses to give up its ambitions. This causes Russia to refuse much needed cooperation with the EU on peacekeeping, peacebuilding and a range of other stabilisation projects in the region.

The EU's normative ambitions towards the 'shared neighbourhood' form part of its long-term strategy, based on functionalist thinking, according to the logic of which cooperation in a range of areas taking a longer term perspective will produce more common norms and stimulate cooperation in the security realm. The EU is concerned that malfunctioning administrations and poverty in the former Soviet space contribute to transnational problems such as communicable diseases, terrorism, organised crime, and nuclear and environmental hazards. In order to gain better control of these threats the EU wishes to take on a greater role in the region, including in the area of conflict resolution.[4]

Further cooperation between the EU and Russia in the shared neighbourhood would increase the opportunities for the EU to counter threats, gather information and potentially to gain increased influence over Russia's conduct in this region. It would also provide the EU with valuable information about conditions in the Commonwealth of Independent States (CIS), thereby increasing transparency, for example, with regard to Russian actions

in Chechnya. The EU has allocated large amounts of aid intended for reconstruction and development assistance in Chechnya, but has great difficulty
distributing the money on the ground because of the low-intensity warfare
and bureaucratic obstacles.

However, because of the gaps referred to above, 'EU input' into the shared
neighbourhood remains limited. The EU cannot deal with the region
without taking Russia into consideration, since Russia observes EU activities
in the area closely. Apart from Chechnya, there have been few open conflicts
in the area thus far,[5] but it is highly likely that future relations will depend
largely on how far the EU moves to develop its normative ambitions.

The sections below draw on the results of the case studies to elaborate
further on the significance of the two gaps presented above. Recent Russian
and EU statements are reviewed to identify whether the divergences found
in the framing analysis remain. The chapter discusses how the diverging
standpoints affect EU–Russia relations, as well as what can be done to
promote cooperation in spite of the existence of the two security gaps.

Divergences over two major security gaps

The first gap: export of norms vs national self-determination

The first security gap evolves primarily not from differing normative preferences, but more fundamentally from diverging standpoints on the *role* of
norms in international relations. From the EU's perspective, the cultivation
of 'EU norms' that favour stability is also of significant importance beyond
the borders of the EU. Russia, on the other hand, places great emphasis on
the right of all nations to self-determination in terms of type of regime,
political system, and so on.

The framing analysis indicates that the EU focused strongly on norms
during all three crises. For example, it linked the EU stand on the Kosovo
crisis to the EU's founding principles and norms. After 11 September 2001
the EU called for a more just world order and a more moral face to globalisation. In the light of the Iraq crisis, EU officials focused on human rights
and on global governance as a way to overcome amoral political rivalries
rooted in balance-of-power thinking.

Nonetheless, it would still be an oversimplification to suggest that the EU
frames cooperation through the prism of soft threats and norms, while Russia
frames it in terms of interests.[6] Russia has depicted itself as a leading nation
in the virtuous struggle against terrorism, and as a righteous advocate of a fair
world order that is not based on inequality in the shape of unipolarity. For
example, during the Kosovo crisis the Russian leaders portrayed Russia as
setting a good example by promoting norms that safeguarded sovereignty
and a normatively favourable, UN-based, global order. They took the events

of 11 September 2001 as evidence of Russia's identity as a reliable and morally righteous state that focuses firmly on fighting humanity's worst enemy – international terrorism. Russian leaders therefore also express normative standpoints, although in a different way to EU spokespeople. Similarly, the EU defends its economic and security interests, although EU spokespeople do not always express their political priorities in terms of interests.

The dilemma that arises is thus not primarily that Russia is completely preoccupied with interests while the EU is excessively focused on norms. It is rather that the EU has started down a road that aims to realise its foreign policy by using the same methods that have been used during its expansion; that is, states have been incorporated after having become more 'like' the rest of the EU. The EU's country strategy paper on Russia also conveys an obvious 'missionary' stance, stating that 'The EU's cooperation objectives with the Russian Federation are to foster respect for democratic principles and human rights, as well as transition towards market economy'.[7] Another example is the European Initiative for Democracy and Human Rights in Russia, which aims to finance projects pertaining, for example, to human rights, democratisation and conflict prevention. Chris Patten, then EU Commissioner for External Relations, argued in 2000 that the EU should use the money set aside for the European Initiative for Democracy and Human Rights in the external arena to back up its political message.[8] The unmistakeable message was that the EU is waging a kind of 'politics of identity', demanding that its neighbours adopt similar norms and values, gradually becoming more 'like us', and thereby less threatening to the EU.

For their part, the Russian leaders tend to perceive their country as a 'unique' great power, by virtue of its culture, size and history, and cannot easily tolerate the fact that the EU is pursuing an official policy of transforming norms beyond its borders and in Russia. Russian leaders have long been sensitive to issues linked to national pride and equal treatment. In an interview in 1994, the then Russian President, Boris Yeltsin, expressed what would become typical sentiments, signifying that Russia would remain a great power even without nuclear weapons, since its greatness is primarily based on traditions, history and culture.

The Russian leadership still make similar claims not only for great power status, but also for recognition as a significant European power. Russia's demand to be recognised by other European great powers as a European state, fully part of Europe, has remained a characteristic trait of the post-Cold War decades.

The Kosovo case clearly illustrates this point. The Russian leaders displayed a desire to become 'one of the gang' which influenced their handling of the Kosovo crisis. In the end, the desire for a role in a community became more important than relations with Serbia and the wish to play the role of a critical bystander. Most importantly, the leadership did not wish to be left with no influence and no status in European affairs.

Russian leaders typically include references to the need for 'equal treatment' in key speeches and documents. Russia's Medium-Term Strategy for the Development of Relations between the Russian Federation and the EU illustrates Russia's desire for autonomy and respect as a central power in the European sphere of security.

As a world power situated on two continents, Russia should retain its freedom to determine and implement its domestic and foreign policies, the status and advantages of a Euro-Asian state and the largest country in the CIS, and independence in its position and activities within international organisations. From this point of view, partnership with the EU can manifest itself in joint efforts to establish an effective system of collective security in Europe on the basis of equality without dividing lines, including through the development and implementation of the Charter on European Security, in progress towards the creation of the Russia–EU free trade zone, as well as in a high level of mutual confidence and cooperation in politics and economics.[10]

Russia has, as is argued above, a long legacy of presenting itself as not only a great power to be reckoned with, but also a righteous saviour of the world; first, by virtue of its position in the Christian community, and later as a leader of the communist world. This makes it all the more offensive, in the eyes of the Russian leadership, for it to be regarded as a target for missionary efforts originating from outside the country.

As a consequence of these Russian sensitivities, the EU's 'norm project' is easily interpreted as an implicit rejection of Russia as a natural part of Western civilisation. The case studies illustrate vividly how the Russian leadership has reacted by harshly criticising all kinds of normative missions targeted at sovereign states, for example, by equating attempts to export democracy to Che Guevara's attempt to export socialism. Any attempt by the EU to interfere in Russian domestic politics tends to be interpreted extremely negatively by Russian leaders who strongly desire their state to be treated with respect and as an 'equal' in the international arena.

This first gap clearly causes strained relations – an obvious case in point, which is far from the only example, being the EU's criticism of Russia's conduct in Chechnya and Russia's resentment of this critique. Moreover, Russia is reluctant to lose control over its sphere of influence in the former-Soviet space. The CIS has continually been defined as Russia's foremost foreign policy priority.[11] The Russian President, Vladimir Putin, describes Russia's policies towards its closest neighbourhood in a similar manner to the EU's portrayal of its policy – by referring to Russia's interests in stability and economic progress in the area. A major difference is that he does not suggest the export of norms as a way to foster stability.[12]

All the states in the shared neighbourhood – apart from Belarus, which in practice has become a Russian protectorate – remain contested ground over which the EU and Russia might clash. Russia has been particularly concerned about Ukraine's and Moldova's open orientation to Europe. The EU has also maintained a positive stance on the regime change in Georgia, while Russia has not welcomed the change of regime.

Finally, as Chapter 4 on the Iraq crisis vividly illustrates, Russia is negative about the spread of norms not only in its own neighbourhood, but also in the global arena in general. Hence, if the EU chooses to base its foreign policy increasingly on its basic ambition to export norms, the two parties also risk clashing on this point at the global level.

The second gap: 'the individual vs the state'

The case studies clearly show that Russia and the EU provide different answers to the questions of what is primarily *threatened* and how best to *counter threats*. These tensions also result from the two parties' pursuit of identity.

Russia attempts to uphold its customary self-perception as a leading great power in a competitive global situation. It acts as a power that must vigorously stand up for and defend its traditional, state-based role-conceptions in a transforming world. The second gap demonstrates this precisely. It demonstrates how Russia clings to its traditional focus on the state as the main referent-object of security, on military threats, and on military means as an important way to meet challenges. This approach is accompanied by a focus on state-to-state relations and a predominantly global level of analysis.

The Russian emphasis on the threats that emanate from inside the Russian Federation's borders, such as separatism and terrorism, should not be interpreted as a shift in focus away from 'high politics' but ought rather to be seen in the context of a process of state building. The break-up of the Soviet Union raised worries about the stability of the Russian Federation. The leadership may have calculated that the cultivation of 'new', internal enemies would be necessary in order to 'glue' the new state together. In this interpretation, the emphasis on internal and 'soft' threats is fully reconcilable with the focus on sovereignty and high politics.

The EU, in turn, defends an emerging identity that builds on the idea of the EU as a defender of normatively good standpoints and practices that can yield much-needed legitimacy for the EU project from its citizens and member states. The second gap reflects the fact that the EU nurtures this identity by placing more emphasis than Russia on 'non-traditional' referent-objects of security such as the individual, as well as on so-called new threats, preventive methods to increase security, and a predominantly regional level of analysis.

The first point here is the relative importance given to the territorial integrity of the state compared with the security of the individual – and the methods that the actors favour to enhance security. The framing analysis indicates that the 'depth' of the security agenda is a source of serious discord between Russia and the EU. While the EU portrays itself as an ethically good promoter of individual rights, Russia maintains its tradition of prioritising the security of the state. Putin's 2003 Address to the Nation is illustrative of the Russian tendency to prioritise the need to preserve territorial integrity as well as high politics, maintaining Russia as a strong power in international relations, and at the centre of national efforts even at the cost of individual citizens:

> I would like to recall that throughout our history Russia and its people have accomplished and continue to accomplish a truly historical feat, a great work performed in the name of our country's integrity and in the name of bringing it peace and a stable life. Maintaining a state spread over such a vast territory and preserving a unique community of peoples while keeping up a strong presence on the international stage is not just an immense labour, it is also a task that has cost our people untold victims and sacrifice. Such has been Russia's historic fate over these thousand and more years. Such has been the way Russia has continuously emerged as a strong nation. It is our duty never to forget this, and we should remember it now, too, as we examine the threats we face today and the main challenges to which we must rise.[13]

The state is also a central referent-object of security in the EU, but subgroups and individuals are considered important objects of reference as well. The 1999 EU Charter of Fundamental Rights was an important step forward in the process of upgrading the individual as a referent-object because it gave individuals increased opportunities to appeal to agencies with the power to compel member states to protect human rights.[14]

The case studies illustrate this tension well. Territorial integrity was the primary referent-object of security for the Russian leaders during the Kosovo crisis, while the EU approached the Kosovo crisis largely from a humanitarian point of view. In contrast with the EU, the Russian leaders focused on the right of all states to self-determination in the light of the Iraqi crisis, again emphasising the value of territorial integrity and state sovereignty. During all three crises, the EU spokespeople did not, as Russia did, equate the problem of terrorism to the issues of separatism, territorial integrity and state security.

The clash ultimately mirrors a basic division between actors in the international system over the direction of travel for international society. Should it focus on state security and territorial integrity, which could serve to legitimise, for example, brutal crackdowns on separatist movements and terrorist groups; or should it focus more on the security of individual non-state actors, for example, individuals or subgroups such as women, ethnic minorities and disadvantaged populations in the Third World. The EU–Russian Road Map testifies to this tension between the security of the state, on the one hand, and individual justice and freedom, on the other.[15]

A second major point of divergence is the two actors' differing interpretations of multilateralism. The EU is committed to multilateralism as a way to promote human rights, while Russia generally opposes humanitarian intervention and is prone to understand multilateralism in terms of power-balancing, primarily seeing it as an antithesis to US unipolarity.[16] The framing analysis identifies that Russian state centrism is linked to a focus on high politics and a global level of analysis, which tend to involve reasoning in terms of the global balance of power. During all three crises the Russian leaders focused on the problem of an unequal distribution of power in the international system, criticising the effects of unipolarity and US 'rule'. In contrast, the EU started from the viewpoint of human values and European politics in the three crises.

In essence, the second gap is about the normative principles that should prevail in international relations. The two parties claim to have the normatively correct solution to key problems in the security sphere – the problem is that they diverge over what this correct answer is. Russian leaders maintain their traditional emphasis on high politics, the inviolability of sovereignty, great power status, state-to-state relations, power politics, spheres of influence and geopolitical balancing as the best way – also in a moral sense – to promote stability and a secure world. This comes up against a new actor in the international arena, to which the nation state is secondary and individual prosperity and well-being are more important than power politics in the traditional military sense.

These differences have repercussions for concrete cooperation in the security field. The EU's policy of preventive engagement using non-military means stands in contrast to Russia's relative readiness to use military means to curb instability in order to safeguard state security and territorial integrity.

One example of how cooperation on low politics in the security sphere may be undermined by high politics is Russia's obstruction of the EU's 'Northern Dimension' cooperation programme. Russia has proved a difficult partner in this programme. This can be partly explained by Russia's emphasis on sovereignty, which is not compatible with cross-border cooperation – a cornerstone of the Northern Dimension.[17]

In addition, the EU has decided to target terrorism largely by using a 'root causes approach'. After the Iraq war, EU officials called for a new strategic concept that would clarify how the EU could contribute to making the world a better place. While Russia officially supported multilateralism and the focus on root causes, in practice it was more prone than the EU to focus on the direct causes of terrorism. Russia joined with efforts to quell terrorist movements in the aftermath of both the Kosovo crisis and 11

September 2001. It called for a principle to be established in international law that would make states responsible for failing to act against terrorists on their territory or a territory under their jurisdiction. In this respect, the Russian leaders came closer to the British problem-solving stance than to the EU's methods aimed at tackling long-term root causes.

The conflict in Chechnya is another example of how the divergences outlined above can hamper cooperation. Russia has worked hard to gain acceptance for its handling of the Chechen conflict, primarily by empha-sising the links between Chechen separatists, the attacks of 11 September 2001 and terrorists based in Afghanistan.[18] The EU has been disinclined to accept Russian methods.[19] In the autumn of 2004, Russian authorities attracted criticism for their handling of the hostage crisis in the North-Ossetian town of Beslan, where hostage-takers seized an entire school and killed dozens of children. The Russian government reacted by rejecting the criticism as an intrusion into Russian internal affairs, and by linking the hostage taking to the issue of international terrorism – arguing that it was organised from abroad, and claiming that al-Qaida was operating on Russian territory.[20] Debating Chechnya with European leaders in 2005, Putin stated 'We are fighting very cruel people, beasts in the guise of human beings who do not and do not want to understand in what time and world they live. Our response must be equal to the threat they present to modern civilization.'[21]

The Russian logic is evident: when dealing with terrorism any method is justified. The European Commission, in turn, 'calls on the Russian author-ities to thoroughly investigate all claims of human rights abuse and to prosecute those found responsible'. It emphasises that 'The EU, as the largest donor of emergency aid, remains concerned about the humanitarian situation as regards the low level of access to Chechnya for humanitarian aid providers, and the treatment of internally displaced persons (IDPs), and the modest pace of reconstruction in the region'.[22]

In sum, as a consequence of the second security gap, Russia and the EU risk 'playing different games' in the security sphere. While Russia places global politics and state security at the centre of attention, the EU focuses more on regional security and on a broader range of referent-objects of security. Russia and the EU have become somewhat incompatible players in the international arena, which hampers cooperation in areas such as peace-keeping in Russia's perceived sphere of interest. Above all, the two parties tend to clash either when Russia promotes both harsh methods that impinge on human rights and individual freedom, and security with reference to the struggle against terrorism; or when the EU 'interferes' in the affairs of sovereign states with reference to human rights.

Tendencies for continuity and change: gaps sustained

This section reviews some of the major Russian and EU documents and statements made in recent years in an attempt to discern whether the two parties have come closer, or continued to diverge in some important respects, in the years following the three crises examined in this book.

The *first gap* stems from the two parties' historically forged identities. The EU has traditionally used a moral code that promotes a self-image as a 'civilian power' on the global scene. The EU has primarily relied on 'commerce and diplomacy' rather than on military strength.[23] François Duchêne coined early on the notion of the European Economic Community (EEC) as a civilian power.[24] More recently, scholars have suggested that the EU has developed into a normative power that attempts to encourage ethical behaviour in international relations.[25] Major EU documents continually reflect this conclusion. The Treaty of Amsterdam, for example, depicts the EU as a morally responsible organisation, given the task of promoting democracy, liberalism, human rights and international cooperation in world politics.[26] Russia in turn is still criticised in connection with each of these principles. For example, the EU believes that Russia's tendency to restrict the activities of certain actors in civil society – on the grounds of national security – threatens the development of democracy and civil society in Russia. The Russian parliamentary and presidential elections of 2003 and 2004 increased worries about the state of Russian democracy. European leaders also expressed concern in 2004 about Putin's reform of the federal system, which, according to his critics, centralises power at the cost of democracy.[27]

The sentencing of one of the so-called Russian oligarchs, Mikhail Khodorkovsky, in May 2005 to nine years in prison for charges including tax evasion and fraud was criticised by some as politically motivated. The adoption of new legislation restraining the freedom of non-governmental organisations (NGOs) in Russia at the end of 2005 is another example of Russian conduct that has provoked EU criticism.[28] Ferrero-Waldner expressed concern early in 2006 about Russian legislation to restrict the activities of these organisations in Russia, which, for example, could restrict the aims of EU Commission programmes on socio-economic recovery and humanitarian assistance in the North Caucasus because they are partly channelled through NGOs.[29] After the murder of the Russian journalist Anna Politkovskaya in the autumn of 2006, Ferrero-Waldner again raised the EU's concerns:

> It is no secret that the EU is worried about some developments in the field of democracy and human rights and media freedom. The murder of Anna Politkovskaya, who for many in Europe was a model of courageous journalistic investigation in the public interest, has shocked us. Guarantees of media freedom

are essential for a healthy society. Independent media play a vital role in holding the executive and others to account. We hope the investigation into the murder of this fearless and respected figure is both thorough and objective, and justice is seen to be done.[30]

Furthermore, a dispute with far-reaching implications occurred in late 2005 when the EU and Russia disagreed on standards of democracy after the presidential election in Ukraine of November that year. The Russian leadership interpreted the EU's support for the 'orange revolution' in the Ukraine quite negatively. Russia subsequently imposed a ban on Polish meat imports. Russia argued that Polish meat products did not meet EU health standards, but some analysts interpreted this move as revenge for the Polish leadership's support of Viktor Yushchenko's pro-Western leadership in the Ukraine.[31] In November 2006, the Polish government blocked the start of EU negotiations with Russia on a Partnership and Cooperation Agreement (PCA). The Polish leadership argued that the Russian ban on Polish agricultural products was politically motivated and that Russia must lift its ban and sign the Energy Charter before Warsaw would agree to talks on a new PCA.[32]

The EU's dissatisfaction over the state of democracy and human rights in Russia continued to mount in 2007. EU leaders expressed concern over the fact that Russian opposition leaders were hindered from travelling to the EU–Russia summit in the Russian city of Samara in May 2007.[33]

Normative considerations and the export of norms remain central parts of EU policy on the entire Eastern region. Numerous examples reflect that the EU maintains its normative zeal. The EU Commission stated in early 2004 that 'Russian convergence with universal and European values will to a large extent determine the nature and quality of our partnership'. The Commission recommends that the EU and its members states raise 'vigorously and coherently' concerns about political developments in Russia, for example, with regard to respect for human rights and Russian practices that run counter to EU values including: 'democracy, human rights in Chechnya, media freedom and some environmental issues.'[34] Javier Solana reiterated in 2006 the need to promote democracy in the new democracies in the shared neighbourhood. Solana framed the EU as 'a model of what societies can achieve for their citizens. A source of inspiration, enticing governments to change the way their countries work.' He described the change of regimes in Georgia and Ukraine as 'inspiring for all the peoples in the region who are seeking democratisation'.[35] The Commission remained determined in 2007 to build a 'strategic partnership, founded on common interests and shared values'. It particularly mentioned 'democracy, human rights, the rule of law, and market economy principles'.[36] Even the European Security Strategy, adopted at the Brussels Summit in December 2003, emphasises the normative aspect in the EU's relations with Russia, stating that 'respect for common values will reinforce progress towards a strategic partnership'.[37] The

EU thus maintains its implicit prerequisite for further cooperation: Russia must adopt 'European' norms and become 'more like us'.

Russian leaders, in turn, are determined that the EU should treat Russia as an equal partner, rather than as a target or a receiver of EU stabilising policies.[38] In his 2005 address to the Federal Assembly, Vladimir Putin stated that Russia is and will remain a major European power. He emphasised Russia's 'sameness', arguing that it shares everything essential with the rest of Europe and does not 'lag behind' the rest of the continent.[39]

The Russian leadership regularly returns to Russia's right to determine its own future, and to the idea that Russia has something to add to European culture. Russia's Minister for Foreign Affairs, Sergei Lavrov, argued in 2006 that Russia was entitled to set its own standards and 'should not be forced to comply with requirements set by others'.[40] In the same year Putin stated that Russia is 'open to the experience of other countries' but argued that 'Russia – a state with a more than one thousand-year old history – has things to share with European partners'. He placed emphasis on Russia's uniqueness, adding 'only we can travel our road, and it is up to us to make it a success'.[41]

The Russian leadership also demonstrates its defensive stance by mirroring EU critiques of human rights abuses in Russia. The leadership, for example, criticises the EU for not safeguarding the rights of Russian-speaking minorities in 'certain Baltic states'.[42] Seldom has Russian criticism of Western interference in Russia's internal affairs been as pointed as in Putin's address to the Federal Assembly of 2007, when he compared democ-ratisation with colonialism and accused 'some' of trying to deprive Russia's of its economic and political independence:

> To be frank, our policy of stable and gradual development is not to everyone's taste. Some, making skilful use of pseudo-democratic rhetoric, would like to return us to the recent past, some in order to once again plunder the nation's resources with impunity and rob the people and the state, and others in order to deprive our country of its economic and political independence. There has been an increasing influx of money from abroad being used to intervene directly in our internal affairs. Looking back at the more distant past, we recall the talk about the civilising role of colonial powers during the colonial era. Today, 'civil-isation' has been replaced by democratisation, but the aim is the same – to ensure unilateral gains and one's own advantage, and to pursue one's own interests.[43]

The EU and Russia thus maintain, and even seem to strengthen, their respective standpoints with regard to the *first gap*, the former maintaining a zeal for the spread of EU norms as a way to stabilise its near abroad, and the latter remaining extremely wary of such efforts.

The EU and Russia also largely maintain their respective standpoints with regard to the *second gap*, which pertains to the referent-object that should be focused on in the sphere of security – the state or the individual – and the methods to be used to enhance security.

The EU Security Strategy does not convey a need for firmness and hardly refers to the use of force.[44] When promoting the strategy, Javier Solana reiterated the emphasis on soft methods such as effective multilateralism, building a stable neighbourhood, and acting early to address the causes of conflict.[45] The strategy adds some new elements to the original Petersberg logic, describing new threats of which the major ones are terrorism, the proliferation of weapons of mass destruction, regional conflicts, failed states and organised crime. However, the European Security Strategy mainly frames security in a broader societal perspective. According to the strategy, the best protection for the security of the EU is a 'world of well-governed democratic states'.[46] The task of 'pre-emptive action', included in a previous draft, was removed from the Security Strategy and replaced by the milder term 'preventive engagement', which is described as: 'acting decisively before events get out of hand; launching diplomatic initiatives and conducting civilian, police or military operations before countries deteriorate, humanitarian emergencies arise, or when signs of proliferation are detected.'[47]

This is a demonstration of the EU's ongoing strategy of keeping broad structural processes in motion, in contrast to the more narrow Russian focus on the concrete protection of borders and sovereignty. The EU's enduring focus on individual security, human rights and low politics in the security sphere is also mirrored in the EU's emphasis on 'human security' and 'security sector reform'.[48]

The Russian leaders, in turn, officially argue the causes of socio-economic reform and social development, human rights and democracy.[49] Yet, this kind of politically correct rhetoric appears to be mainly part of a rhetorical game. Russian leaders still place major emphasis on the protection of borders and on state sovereignty. In his 2006 address to the Federal Assembly Putin referred to the strong defence of state security undertaken by the US, adding 'we also need to build our home and make it strong and well protected'.[50]

Putin resorts easily to calls for hard and immediate measures as the most important way to alleviate terrorism. He describes the counterterrorism task of the national security system as 'destroying criminals in their den and, if the situation requires, reaching them abroad'.[51] In his 2005 address to the Federal Assembly Putin made a typical call for 'firmness' and for 'eradicating' terrorism:

> Eradicating the sources of terrorist aggression on Russian territory is an integral part of ensuring law and order in our country. We have taken many serious steps in the fight against terrorism over recent years. But we cannot allow ourselves to have any illusions – the threat is still very real, we still find ourselves being dealt serious blows and criminals are still committing terrible crimes in the aim of frightening society. We need to summon our courage and continue our work to eradicate terrorism. The moment we show signs of weakness, lack of firmness,

the losses would become immeasurably greater and could result in a national disaster.[52]

In conclusion, the divergences between Russia and the EU distilled from the case-studies have remained in recent years, and they appear difficult to overcome.

The way forward

The EU's support for the orange revolution in Ukraine in 2004 strongly contributed to Putin's and his leadership's aversion to the EU strategy of exporting norms eastwards. The Russian leaders applied a frostier tone towards the EU in the years that followed this conflict. In 2006 and 2007 serious disputes over energy contributed to a further distancing between the EU and Russia. Russia cut gas supplies to neighbouring states – Georgia, Ukraine and Belarus – and this provoked fears in the EU that Russia might increasingly use its oil and gas assets to blackmail other actors. Russia also refused to yield to EU demand that it open access to its gas pipelines for EU energy companies. Russia was singled out as an unreliable partner in energy area, an accusation that the Russian leadership strongly refuted. In early 2007 Putin complained that 'some people look at us through a prism of past prejudices and see a growing threat in Russia's strength. Some are ready to accuse us of rekindling "neo-imperial ambitions" or … "energy blackmail"'.[53] In April the same year, the chief trade negotiator for the EU, Peter Mandelson, warned that both Russia and the EU believed the other to be using the energy weapon as a political instrument. He concluded that 'The relationship between the European Union and Russia has reached a level of misunderstanding not seen since the end of the Cold War and is in danger of going "badly wrong"'.[54]

To the list of disputes in 2007 can be added Russia's unwillingness to endorse an EU-supported agreement granting independence to Kosovo, and the fierce Russian reaction to Estonia's decision to remove a Soviet war memorial from its capital. Russia's relations with the USA also deteriorated, partly as a result of Putin's sharp reaction to US plans to deploy parts of its ballistic missile defence system in Poland and the Czech Republic.

The conflict over energy – together with the other signs of deteriorating relations between Russia and the EU outlined above – bode ill for any breakthrough in relations in the short term. Yet, the experience of previous ups and downs in EU–Russia relations, and in Russia's relations with the West in general, indicates that these problems may be relatively temporary. The only viable way forward is to take an extremely long-term perspective on Russia-EU cooperation. As Hiski Haukkala puts it, 'Changes in world-views are often slow and cannot be forced. They often take years, even generations to emerge.'[55]

Given the difficulties – at least in the short term – with eradicating rhetorical divergences that pertain to differing basic standpoints on the role of norms in world affairs, and to the primary referent-object of security, pragmatism is the most plausible way for Russia and the EU to advance their integration in the security sphere. Increased cooperation on as many issues and levels as possible can promote a kind of neofunctionalism that might, in the long term, contribute to bringing Russia closer to EU norms and values.[56] The same neofunctionalist logic might simultaneously contribute to a greater understanding inside the EU of Russian particularities and strengths as a partner, and gradually make Russia a natural part of the European security system.

The gaps accounted for above will be difficult to overcome but, in order to keep the kind of long-term processes suggested above in motion, the two parties have at least to ensure that their differences do not become wider. For the EU's part, this means refraining from statements or actions that can increase Russia's sensitivity about its exclusion from Europe. Russian leaders appear painfully aware of the negative perceptions of Russia in many other European states. They are weary of the widespread historical perception of Russia as a threat to Europe, and this fuels their concerns about the development of new dividing lines in Europe. Putin argued in 2006 that 'far from everyone in the world has abandoned the old bloc mentality and the prejudices inherited from the era of global confrontation despite the great changes that have taken place. This is also a great hindrance in working together to find suitable responses to the common problems we face'.[57] Putin rejected European thinking in terms of 'friend or foe' that risks creating new divisions in Europe.[58]

Prozorov suggests that Russia and the EU would be better able to approach one another if they did not continually resort to their accustomed ways of describing their counterpart using the static category of 'cultural difference'. The EU uses rhetorical devices that define Russia as Europe's 'eternal other', and Russian leaders tend to argue in terms of geopolitics and to portray Europe as a historical adversary of Russia.[59] Yuri Federov goes even further, arguing that long-term and extensive cooperation between Russia and the EU can only be realised on Russia's terms – that the EU should 'recognize Russia's special role in the post-Soviet space, refrain from competition in the area and also from attempts to influence Russia's domestic development'.[60]

Without going this far, it is easy to conclude that open criticism does not seem to be an efficient method of altering Russia's behaviour. The EU's criticism of the state of Russian democracy and of Russia's human rights record of the past decade may even have been counterproductive. The Russian leadership has largely responded by becoming more assertive and even less prone to dialogue on normative issues.

Both parties ought to adopt a more modest approach. As Oksana Antonenko and Kathryn Pinnick note, the many one-sided strategies that have been put forward have been unsuccessful. These strategies have been based on 'unrealistic assumptions about the extent to which the other side could transform'. Instead, the EU and Russia have agreed on a common agenda that is perceived to be mutually beneficial. Antonenko and Pinnick argue that Russia has to commit to changes in its legislation, further market liberalisation and to improve domestic and border security.[61] The EU ought to generate a more favourable environment for Russian investment and trade in EU member states and to ensure that Russian citizens can travel with fewer restrictions.[62]

Most importantly, if the two parties are to advance cooperation, the EU must refrain from the vocal normative rhetoric it directs at Russia. In Dmitri Trenins words: 'Western leaders must disabuse themselves of the notion that by preaching values one can actually plant them. Russia will continue to change, but at its own pace. The key drivers of that change must be the growth of capitalism at home and openness to the outside world.'[63] A good deal of pragmatism will be needed if the two parties are to move beyond the many declarations of goodwill and rather hollow official agreements of recent years.

That is not to say that the EU must give up its normative objectives in order to satisfy the Russian demand for equal treatment. Instead, it must consider carefully exactly how best it can realise its normative ambitions. The European Commission might continue its relatively discrete 'governance' approach to its eastern neighbourhood, sustaining long-term projects that promote democratisation, human rights and civil society in Russia. The Commission's focus on the encouragement of people-to-people grass-roots contact as a way to spread EU norms to Russian citizens is one example of such a functional long-term approach.[64]

In order to smooth relations further, the EU could do more to satisfy Russia's quest for equal treatment in a formal institutional context. In relation to NATO, Russia has been appreciative of the institutional reform that resulted in the 'NATO–Russia Council', where all meetings take place in working groups and where the NATO members have not synchronised their standpoints beforehand. All participants, including Russia, discuss solutions on an equal basis. A solution in this vein in an EU context could serve to satisfy the Russian desire for equal treatment. Indeed, the Russian side has called for changes to be made to the Permanent Partnership Council (PPC), set up in May 2003, where ministers from both sides meet to discuss current issues. While the EU wants Russian ministers to meet an EU 'troika' – the relevant minister from the country that currently holds the rotating presidency, his or her counterpart from the previous presidency, and his or her counterpart from the next presidency – the Russians wish to meet ministers from all the EU member states at the same time. The EU has not agreed to this reform out of fear that Russia might exploit divisions between EU member states to its own advantage.[65] For example, in 2006 Russia was criticised for trying to cause divisions between some older EU member states and the newer ones, such as Poland and the Baltic States, which tend to be more critical of Russia.[66] Agreeing to such a suggestion, however, might be worth the price for the EU, since it would probably contribute a lot to the development of mutual relations as a confidence-building measure. In 2006, Putin again emphasised the importance of Russia being treated as an equal in the formal sense, arguing that the renegotiation of the PCA, which expired in 2007, should result in a 'politically significant document geared towards the future and stipulating clearly defined goals and mechanisms for equal cooperation'.[67]

A more clearly pragmatic focus on common material goals would also satisfy the Russian leadership, which clearly prioritises the economic dimension of politics. In 2006, Putin argued in favour of pragmatically looking beyond problematic political issues such as the frozen conflicts in the post-Soviet area to focus instead on 'new positive goals and constantly open up new avenues of cooperation for all Europeans, create new opportunities for their joint business and humanitarian initiatives and projects'.[68] Although, as is stated above, the EU–Russia economic relationship is asymmetrical, Russia is not unimportant to the EU as an economic partner. The European Commission refers to Russia as a major supplier of energy products to the EU, and as a large market for EU goods and services with considerable potential for growth.[69] Moreover, deepening economic integration spills over into the area of security cooperation. In 2006 the President of the EU Commission, José Manuel Barroso, acknowledged that 'deep and comprehensive economic integration between the EU and Russia will allow us to fully exploit the potential of our partnership'.[70]

There are additional areas where the two parties could increase their cooperation. The EU could take advantage of Russian efforts in the field of conflict resolution and mediation. Russia is a member of neither NATO nor the EU, and it plays a particular role in the Balkans for historical reasons.[71] In the Middle East, Russia also has the potential to play the role of an impartial negotiator between Israel and the Palestinians, a task that it made a serious attempt to take on in 2006 by receiving Hamas in Russia, thereby becoming one of the few actors with functional relations with both leaderships in the conflict. Moreover, a joint statement of November 2003 highlighted the possibility of further cooperation in the areas of regional conflict resolution, non-proliferation, arms control, crisis management and disarmament.[72] One possible way forward would be to incorporate Russia into EU security structures by giving it an enhanced role in, or integrating it into, the European Security and Defence Policy (ESDP). The conclusions of the December

1999 EU summit and the May 2000 EU–Russia summit suggest that there is some potential for Russian participation in EU-led operations. A consultation framework was outlined at the December 2000 Nice summit, which established that consultations would be held during crisis situations to discuss Russian participation in crisis-management operations.[74]

Above all, the EU and Russia could make more of their compatible visions for the global arena. Analysing the EU security concept from a Russian perspective, the Russian scholar Yuri Federov notes that the global visions of the EU and Russia are to a large degree compatible. The notion of the EU as a global player fits with Russia's aim to forge a multipolar world. The EU's focus on global terrorism corresponds with Russia's vision of terrorism as a global threat. The EU's commitment to upholding and developing international law, and the priority it gives to strengthening the UN, correspond to Russian rhetorical assessments of the United Nations and international law. The EU's commitment to effective multilateralism corresponds to Russia's promotion of a multipolar world.[75]

The Russian leadership's statements reflect these convergences. Putin emphasised in 2006 that the EU and Russia have 'similar approaches to issues of international security', standing for universal international treaty regimes such as the non-proliferation regime, and sharing a desire to solve severe international problems 'such as the Middle East conflict or the issue of the Iranian "nuclear dossier"'.[76] Moreover, Russian leaders have continually referred to a future multipolar world in which the EU would shoulder the role of a major pole. Addressing the German Bundestag on 25 September 2001, Putin argued that Europe can function as a powerful and truly independent centre of world affairs, especially if it unites its capacities with Russia's human, natural and territorial resources and its cultural, economic and defence potential.[77] In 2003, he argued that 'if Europe wants to be independent and a fully fledged global power centre, the shortest route to this goal is good relations with Russia'.[78] Russia's Medium-Term Strategy associates cooperation with the EU with 'the objective need to establish a multipolar world'. The EU also recognises the value of cooperation with Russia in the global arena, for example, in the Quartet of International Mediators and with regard to Iran.[79]

The European Commission, in turn, acknowledges Russia as a key actor in the UN Security Council with significant influence in the shared neighbourhood and in Central Asia.[80] The EU has often converged more with Russia's standpoints than with the Administration of President George W. Bush on issues in the security sphere, for example, with regard to Iraq, the Israeli–Palestinian conflict, the policy on sanctions on Cuba and the issue of US National Missile Defence. In 2006 Ferrero-Waldner acknowledged that:

> The EU and Russia are increasing their cooperation on the international stage: Russia is a valued partner in the Middle East Quartet, and is playing a construc-

tive role in the search for a diplomatic solution on the Iranian nuclear question. We should aim for equally close cooperation on other sources of instability closer to home, and I look forward to discussing developments in the South Caucasus ahead of my visit to the region later in the week.[82]

These central convergences even enabled the EU and Russia to unite on a common definition of the 'key threats of today' in 2005, namely 'terrorism, the proliferation of WMDs [weapons of mass destruction], existing and potential regional and local conflicts'.[83] This definition appears to be a useful, even strikingly functional, basis for cooperation in the security sphere. At the EU–Russia summit of October 2006 the two parties confirmed their commitment to strengthening the role of the United Nations, the Organization for Security and Co-operation in Europe and the Council of Europe in order to build an international order based on effective multilateralism. They described five priority areas for enhancing cooperation: strengthening dialogue and cooperation on the international scene, fighting terrorism, non-proliferation of weapons of mass destruction, crisis management and civil protection.[84]

Paradoxically, the EU and Russia appear to cooperate more easily in the 'far' than in the 'near' abroad, where Russia anxiously guards its perceived sphere of influence. Increased practical cooperation in the global arena would 'strengthen the European voice' in world affairs, which would be to the benefit of both parties, and it would simultaneously satisfy the Russian desire for equal treatment as well as its great power mentality. This would signify one small but important step forward for the long-term neofunctionalist process of integration discussed above.

Notes

1 European Commission, 'Communication from the Commission to the Council and the European Parliament on relations with Russia', COM 106, 9 February 2004.
2 Ferrero-Waldner, B., 'The European Union and Russia: developing our shared European continent', Speech at the European Studies Institute, Moscow State Institute for International Relations, 23 October 2006.
3 European Commission, 'Communication from the Commission: European neighbourhood policy – strategy paper', 12 May 2004.
4 The frozen conflicts in Armenia, Azerbaijan, Georgia and Moldova are a particular area of concern in this complex network of problems. European Commission, 'Communication from the Commission: European neighbourhood policy – strategy paper', 12 May 2004.
5 Lynch, D., 'The new eastern dimension of the enlarged EU', in J. Batt et al., 'Partners and neighbours: A CFSP for a wider Europe', *Chaillot Papers 64* (European Union Institute for Security Studies, 2003), p. 41; Zagorski, A., 'Russia and European institutions', in V. Baranovsky (ed.), *Russia and Europe: The Emerging Security Agenda. Stockholm International Peace Research Institute* (Oxford: Oxford University Press, 1997), pp. 72–73.

6   Forsberg, T., 'Forging the EU–Russia security partnership in the crucible of trans-Atlantic relations', Paper prepared for the joint International Convention of Central Eastern European International Studies Association & International Studies Association, Budapest, 26–28 June 2003, pp. 4, 16–19; Emerson, M., *The Elephant and the Bear: The European Union, Russia and their Near Abroads* (Brussels: Centre for European Policy Studies, 2001), pp. 21–22.

7   European Commission, 'Russia: Country strategy paper, 2002–2006'.

8   Patten, C., 'Address at Council of Europe Conference', Dublin, 4 March 2000.

9   Yeltsin, B., 'Statement', in *Nezavisimaia Gazeta*, 26 April 1999.

10 'Kak mirovaia derzhava, raspolozhennaia na dvukh kontinentakh, Rossiia dolzhna sokhroniat svobodu opredeleniia i provedeniia svoei vnutrennnei i vneshnei politiki, svoi status i preimushestva evroaziatskogo gosudarstva i krupneishei strany SNG, nezavisimost pozitsii i deiatelnosti v mezhdunarodnykh organizatsiiakh. V ukazannoi perspektive partnerstvo c EC mozhet vyrazhatsia v sovmestnykh usiliiakh po sozdaniiu effektivnoi sistemy kollektivnoi bezopasnosti v Evrope na ravnopravnoi osnove bez razdelitelnykh linii, v t.ch. putem razrabotki i realizatsii Khartii evropeiskoi bezopasnosti, v prodvizhenii – pri nalichii neobkhodimykh uslovii – k sozdaniiu zony svobodnoi torgovli Rossiia – Evrosoius, a takzhe v vysokom urovne vzaimnogo doveriia i sotrudnichestva v politike i ekonomike.' 'Russia's Medium-Term Strategy Towards the EU, 2000–2010'.

11 'Foreign Policy Concept of the Russian Federation', 28 June 2000; Putin, V., 'Annual address by the President of the Russian Federation to the Federal Assembly of the Russian Federation', Moscow, 16 May 2003, 'Annual address by the President of the Russian Federation to the Federal Assembly of the Russian Federation', 26 May 2004.

12 Putin, V., 'Annual address by the President of the Russian Federation to the Federal Assembly of the Russian Federation', Moscow, 16 May 2003.

13 'Khotel by napomnit: na vsem protiazhenii nashei istorii Rossiia i ee grazhdane sovershali i sovershaiut poistine istoricheskii podvig. Podvig v imia tselostnosti strany, vo imia mira v nei i stabilnoi zhizni. Uderzhanie gosudarstva na obshirnom prostranstve, sokhranenie unikalnogo soobshchestva narodov pri silnykh pozitsiiakh strany v mire – eto ne tolko ogromny trud. Eta eshche i ogromnye zhertvy, lisheniia nashego naroda. Imenno takov tysiacheletnii istoricheski put Rossii. Takov sposob vosproizvodsvtva ee kak silnoi strany. I my ne imeem prava zabyvat ob etom. Dolzhny eto uchityvat, otsenivaia i nashi segodniashnie opasnosti, i nashi glavnye zadachi.' Putin, V., 'Annual address by the President of the Russian Federation to the Federal Assembly of the Russian Federation', Moscow, 16 May 2003.

14 Matlary, J., 'Human rights', *ARENA Working Paper* 19:3 (2003), p. 3.

15 European Commission. 'Road map for the Common Space of Freedom, Security and Justice'.

16 Marsh, S. and Mackensteins, H., *The International Relations of the European Union* (London: Longman, 2005), p. 194.

17 Light, M., 'Political patterns and trends', Address at the conference 'Russia and the New Europe', Swedish Institute of International Affairs, 22 November 2005.

18 Radio Free Europe/Radio Liberty, Newsline, 18 September 2001, 25 September 2001, 19 September 2003, 25 September 2003.

19 Rontoyanni, C., 'So far, so good: Russia and the ESDP', *International Affairs* 78:4 (2002), p. 826.

20 Radio Free Europe/Radio Liberty, Newsline, 6 October 2004, 10 October 2004.

21 Radio Free Europe/Radio Liberty, Newsline, 3 November 2005.

22 European Commission, The EU's relations with Russia, 'Overview'.

23 Twitchett, K., *Europe and the World: The External Relations of the Common Market* (New York: St Martin's Press, 1976), pp. 1–2.

24 Duchêne, F., 'Europe's role in world peace', in R. Mayne (ed.), *Europe Tomorrow: Sixteen Europeans Look Ahead* (London: Fontana, 1972), p. 43.

25 Manners, I., 'Normative power Europe: A contradiction in terms?', *Journal of Common Market Studies* 40:2 (2002), pp. 240–1.

26 Treaty of Amsterdam, Article F, Paragraph 1.

27 Communication from the Commission (note 1).

28 The bill requires all NGOs to reregister, and increases state supervision over their organisation.

29 Ferrero-Waldner, B., 'Chechnya after the elections and civil society in Russia', Speech to the European Parliament, Strasbourg, 18 January 2006.

30 Ferrero-Waldner, B., 'The European Union and Russia: developing our shared European continent', Speech at the European Studies Institute, Moscow State Institute for International Relations, 23 October 2006.

31 Dempsey, J., 'A united Europe awaits Putin at EU–Russia summit', *International Herald Tribune*, 16 May 2007.

32 Radio Free Europe/Radio Liberty, Newsline, 27 November 2006.

33 Radio Free Europe/Radio Liberty, Newsline, 21 May 2007.

34 Communication from the Commission (note 1).

35 Solana, J., 'A common vision for a common neighbourhood', 4 May 2006.

36 European Commission (note 22).

37 Council of the European Union, 'A secure Europe in a better world: The European Security Strategy', 12 December 2003.

38 European Commission (note 15); Ivanov, I., 'Remarks before representatives of the sociopolitical and business circles of the FRG on the Theme "Russia-European Union: The state of, and prospects for partnership",' Munich, 10 December 2003; Radio Free Europe/Radio Liberty, 19 May 2006.

39 Putin, V., 'Annual Address to the Federal Assembly', 25 April 2005.

40 Radio Free Europe/Radio Liberty, 19 May 2006.

41 Putin, V., 'Written interview for Russkaya Mysl', 23 November 2006.

42 Ibid.

43 'Priamo skazhy: ne vsem nravitsiia stabilnoe postupatelnoe razvitiie nashei strany. Est i te, kto, lovko ispolzuia psevdodemokraticheskuiu frazeologiiu, khotel by vernut nedavnee proshloe: odni – dlia togo chtoby, kak ranshe, beznakazanno razvorovyvat obshchenatsionalnye bogatstva, grabit liodei i gosudarstvo, drugie – chtoby lishit nashu stranu ekonomicheskoi i politicheskoi samostoiatelnosti. Rastet i potok deneg iz-za rubezha, ispolzuemykh dlia priamogo vmeshatelstva v nashi vnutrennie dela. Esli posmotret, chto proiskhodilo v prezhnie, davnie vremena, to uvidim, chto eshche dazhe v epòkhu kolonializma govorili o tak nazyvaemoi tsivilizatorskoi roli gosudarstv-kolonizatorov. Segodnia na vooruzhenie berutsia demokratizatorskie lozungi. No tsel odna – poluchenie odnostoronnikh preimushchestv i sobstvennoi vygody, obespechenie sobstvennykh interesov.' Putin, V., 'Address to the Federal Assembly 2007'.

44 Council of the European Union, 'A secure Europe in a better world: The European Security Strategy', 12 December 2003.

45 Solana, J., 'A European route to security', Press Release, Brussels, 12 December 2003.

46 Council of the European Union, 'A secure Europe in a better world: The European Security Strategy', 12 December 2003.

47 Ibid.

48 Ferrero-Waldner, B., 'Address to the European Parliament', 5 October 2004, 'The EU's role in protecting Europe's security', Conference on Protecting Europe: Policies for enhancing security in the European Union, 30 May 2006.

49 Radio Free Europe/Radio Liberty, Newsline, 14 September 2004; Putin, V., 'Address to the Federal Assembly, 2004', 'Address to the Federal Assembly 2005', 'Annual address to the Federal Assembly 2006', 10 May 2006.

50 Putin, V., 'Annual address to the Federal Assembly 2006', 10 May 2006.

51 Radio Free Europe/Radio Liberty, Newsline 14 September 2004.

52 'Ukreplenie pravoporiadka neotdelimo ot ustraneniia istochnikov terroristicheskoi agressii na territorii Rossii. Za poslednie gody nami bylo sdelano dostatochno mnogo sereznykh shagov v borbe s terrorom. No illiuzii byt ne dolzhno: ugroza eshche ochen silna, my eshche propuskaem ochen chuvstvitelnye udary, prestupniki sovershaiut eshche uzhanye zlodeianiia, tseliu kotorykh iavliaetsiia ustrashenie obshchestva. I nam nuzhno nabratsia muzhestva i prodolzhit raboty po iskoreneniiu terrora. Stoit tolko proiavit slabost, miagkotelost – poter budet neizmerimo bolshe, i oni mogut obernutsiia obshchenatsionalnoi katastrofoi.' Putin, V., 'Address to the Federal Assembly 2005'.

53 Radio Free Europe/Radio Liberty, Newsline, 23 January 2007.

54 Bilefsky, D., 'Senior EU aide issues warning on Russia ties', *International Herald Tribune*, 20 April 2007.

55 Haukkala, H., 'A problematic "strategic partnership",' in D. Lynch (ed.) *EU–Russian Security Dimensions*, WEU Occasional Paper 46 (July 2003), p. 18.

56 Ibid., pp. 18–19.

57 Putin, V., 'Annual address to the Federal Assembly 2006', 10 May 2006.

58 Putin, V., 'Russia–EU partnership crucial for united, prosperous Europe', 23 November 2006.

59 Prozorov, S., *Understanding Conflict between Russia and the EU: The Limits of Integration* (New York: Basingstoke, 2006), p. 181

60 Fedorov, Y., 'European Security and Defence Policy: Russia's reading', in Bo Huldt, et al., *European Security and Defence Policy: A European Challenge* (Stockholm: Swedish National Defence College, 2006), p. 196.

61 Antonenko, O. and Pinnick, K., 'The enlarged EU and Russia: From converging interests to a common agenda', in O. Antonenko and K. Pinnick (eds), *Russia and the European Union* (New York: Routledge, 2005), p. 5.

62 Ibid., p. 6.

63 Trenin, D., 'Russia leaves the West', *Foreign Affairs*, 85:4 (2006).

64 European Commission (note 1).

65 Barysh, K., 'EU–Russia relations: The EU perspective', in D. Johnson and P. Robinson (eds), *Perspectives on EU–Russia Relations* (London: Routledge, 2005), p. 31.

66 Radio Free Europe/Radio Liberty, Newsline,s 29 November 2006, 18 October 2006, 23 October 2006, 8 November 2006.

67 Putin, V., 'Russia–EU partnership crucial for united, prosperous Europe', 23 November 2006.

68 Putin, V., 'Written interview for Russkaya Mysl', 23 November 2006.

69 European Commission (note 22).

70 EU–Russia summit, 'Joint Statement', Helsinki, 24 November 2006.

71 Rontoyanni (note 16), p. 82; Webber, M., 'Third-party inclusion in European Security and Defence Policy: A case study of Russia', *European Foreign Affairs Review* 6 (2001), p. 425.

72 EU–Russia summit, 'Joint Statement', Rome, 6 November 2003.

73 Council of the European Union, Presidency Conclusions, Helsinki European Council meeting, 10–11 December 1999; EU–Russia summit, 'Joint Statement', Moscow, 29 May 2000.

74 Council of the European Union, 'Presidency Conclusions, Nice European Council meeting, 7–9 December 2000'.

75 Fedorov (note 60), p. 194

76 Putin, V., 'Russia–EU partnership crucial for united, prosperous Europe', 23 November 2006.

77 Putin, V., 'Address to the German Bundestag', 25 September 2001.

78 Radio Free Europe/Radio Liberty, Newsline, 28 May 2003.

79 Ferrero-Waldner, B., 'The European Union and Russia: developing our shared European continent', Speech at the European Studies Institute, Moscow State Institute for International Relations, 23 October 2006.

80 European Commission (note 22).

81 Marsh and Mackenstein (note 16), p. 195.

82 Ferrero-Waldner, B., EU–Russia Foreign Ministers Troika Meeting, 14 February 2006.

83 European Commission (note 15).

84 European Commission, 'Fact sheet: EU–Russia, Common Space of External Security'.

7 Will greater Europe unite?

Dividing lines between European leaderships

The purpose of this book is to assess whether the major European players defend similar referent-objects of security and pursue similar objectives, and to suggest implications for greater Europe's chances of emerging as a cohesive global actor. Do Russia, the EU and the three major EU member states pursue reasonably similar agendas in the security sphere – by giving priority to analogous referent-objects of security – and are they able to adopt a unified policy line in the global arena?[1]

My analysis suggests that the entities referred to above are united on a range of specific issues in the security sphere, for example, on the peace process in the Middle East and on the need to prioritise the struggle against terrorism and the spread of weapons of mass destruction. However, and some may regard this as unfortunate, they do not 'speak with one voice' on basic issues of principle since these often tend to involve their security identities. They are divided on issues pertaining to the role of norms in international affairs, and on how to achieve stability. The case studies indicate that the national leaderships did not alter their way of arguing too much during the period of study – the leaderships' standpoints on security are characterised more by continuity than by change.

A number of unexpected dividing lines and convergences have been identified. Two findings are particularly striking: first, paradoxically, even though the EU has undergone remarkable transformations, strengthening its capabilities and its capacity as an actor in the security sphere, the 'big three' member states deviate in some important – even crucial – ways. My analysis suggests that over time their framing of security is characterised by a lack of change rather than by change. There is a substantial difference between the British support for the USA, unilateralism and the status quo in global affairs, and the preference of the EU, France and Germany for multilateralism and reform of the global order.

The European voices on security differ mainly over emphasis rather than substance, but the tendencies of the leaderships to highlight and stand up for their own policy lines cause real problems. This is particularly apparent when core issues related to sovereignty and to rules of behaviour in international relations are at stake, as was the case during the Iraq war.

Second, Russia diverges from the EU on a number of major issues, most importantly on the role of norms, on the use of force and on the primary referent-objects of security. Yet, the analysis suggests that, as long as the EU does not intervene too much in the internal affairs of sovereign states for moral purposes, the EU and Russia should be able to deepen their partnership by drawing on a range of common positions. My study demonstrates that Russia and the EU share some major standpoints in the security sphere, such as the need to combat terrorism and to limit unilateral tendencies in world affairs. They have agreed a definition of the 'key threats of today' – 'terrorism, the proliferation of WMDs [weapons of mass destruction], existing and potential regional and local conflicts'.[2] Moreover, they have demonstrated an ability to converge on a range of current issues in the global arena, such as the Kyoto Protocol and the peace process in the Middle East.

Before elaborating further on the implications and consequences this has for political practice it is necessary briefly to recapitulate the major findings. The constructivist approach enables an analysis in which each actor's expressed conception of security matters – as expressed in their own words – can be studied. Chapters 2–4 'recorded' the reactions of the leaderships to three major crises – the Kosovo crisis of 1999, the aftermath of 11 September 2001 and the Iraq war of 2003 – which resulted in five distinctive 'stories on security'. The analytical Chapters 5 and 6 interpreted the findings by elaborating the major divergences found in the 'five stories', which are labelled 'security gaps'.

The security gaps, which emerge from the empirical findings on how the actors express themselves, are used as analytical devices that expose the major dividing lines in the European security sphere. My analysis shows that two major security gaps create tensions in EU–Russia relations, whereas three quite different security gaps complicate political relations inside the EU. Each gap builds on a central dichotomy.

The first security gap in EU–Russia relations is labelled 'export of norms vs national self-determination'. From the time of the Kosovo crisis in 1999, the EU has waged a 'politics of identity', demanding that other states adopt EU norms in order to become more stable and therefore less threatening. Moscow in turn refuses to be treated as a target for the export of norms. As a consequence of this gap, the EU and Russia are effectively hampered in their efforts to make progress with integration.

The second security gap is labelled 'the individual vs the state' and is partly intertwined with the first. It reflects the fact that the EU nurtures its emerging identity as a 'normative power' by placing emphasis on 'non-traditional' referent-objects of security. Russia by contrast sticks to its identity as a centralised state, the primary concern of which is to safeguard the central attributes of the sovereign state – if necessary using military means.

Both security gaps are essential to the identities of the two actors, which make them particularly difficult to overcome. The EU's focus on the export of norms and non-traditional referent-objects of security is to a large extent tied to its self-perception as a normative power. In its role as a proud great power confident in its approach to dealing with issues in the international arena, and determined to decide its political destiny without interference from the outside, Russia is also reluctant to compromise its identity. A parallel can be drawn between Russia and the United Kingdom in this respect. Their global focus and strong belief in their own political preferences during the three cases studied appear to be linked to their respective imperial pasts, during which they grew accustomed to projecting their own image and to playing significant roles in the international arena. France and Germany, by contrast, display a tendency to stand close to the EU, making use of it in order to boost their self-image. The EU's extensive 'tool-kit' and its focus on preventive means complement Germany's post-war tradition as a civic nation. The case studies indicate that the French government has made use of the EU in order to boost its own role in international affairs; it has been the official French view that the EU should become a pole in a multipolar world, thereby also providing France with a more central role in global politics.

This means that diverging self-perceptions have left imprints not only on EU–Russia relations, but also on relations between EU member states. The most central differences within the EU have been presented in terms of three security gaps, which are primarily sustained by deviating standpoints on the role of the USA, on the role of norms and institutions, and on the solutions to security problems.

The first security gap is labelled 'principles vs community' and shows how the EU, French and German leaderships prioritised enhancing the sense of community in the international system by ensuring that everyone abides by the same rules of behaviour. The British appeared torn between this European ambition and US practice, according to which being 'morally appropriate' above all meant acting loyally in defence of a fixed set of liberal democratic norms, even if this required treating the rules of behaviour in the United Nations system as negotiable.

The second security gap, 'competing world views', highlights that even though all the leaderships aimed to achieve greater stability in world affairs, they envisaged different methods to reach this end. The British government primarily aimed to achieve stability through the practice of exclusion; by eliminating unwanted elements whenever it was confronted by them. The

French and German leaders promoted a vision of a stable international society that included all states and could be achieved through reforms implemented by international institutions. The British leaders did not ignore the idea of international community, but were less accepting in their attitude towards those actors that did not live up to the standards of such a community. This suggests that the British demonstrated a problem-solving approach to international relations; that is, they promoted the solution that could restore order and the status quo most effectively and as quickly as possible.

The third security gap, 'multipolarity vs unipolarity', revolves around the tension between two visions of international relations as either multipolar or unilateral/unipolar in nature. The UK expressed satisfaction with a unipolar system in which a benign hegemon shoulders a large burden of responsibility for international peace and security. In contrast, the French and German leaderships promoted multilateralism and multipolarity.

These serious divergences between European leaderships indicate how greater Europe's ability to act as a united power on the global scene is being undermined. The political consequences of the gaps are considered below and the chapter discusses the prospects for Europe being able to function as a central player in the global arena, as well as the consequences this might have as a result for the USA.

The nature of divergences on security in greater Europe

The constructivist analysis did not prejudge what constitutes security for the European leaderships, but instead 'listened in' to each unique 'story on security'. By remaining receptive to the politicians' own constructions of reality, the empirical analysis revealed intricate patterns of divergence and convergence that could not have been predicted. Because of the constructivist research design, for instance, the convergences between Russia, France and Germany became an important finding – one that would have been likely to be overlooked if a realist approach, for example, had been used.

The results of the empirical enquiry indicate that further EU integration in the sphere of security is a highly delicate issue, not primarily because of diverging interests among member states, but because member states are unwilling to negotiate on their favoured norms and identities which are tightly intertwined with their respective nation states and historical backgrounds. The constructivist research design, which took norms and identities seriously, did not draw the conclusion that the EU's strength lies in its capacity as a strong 'normative power' – as Ian Manners argues – but on the contrary, concluded that the EU is seriously divided on some central points on its normative agenda.[3]

My conclusion is not quite as pessimistic as that of the neorealist scholar

Adrian Hyde-Price, who strongly doubts the EU's chances of becoming a cohesive global security actor.[4] Yet, my findings do call EU cohesiveness into question. The interesting point here is that neorealists disregard the EU as a security actor because they disregard EU integration, which in turn stems from their conviction that norms do not play any significant role in the sphere of security. My conclusion is that EU integration in the sphere of security is difficult – although not impossible – to achieve primarily because of the power of norms over the decision making of nation states.

Furthermore, scholars focusing on EU–Russia relations usually apply a non-theoretical approach, but nevertheless tend to be constrained by preconceptions that emerge from conventional knowledge of what has historically separated Russia from Europe. Such traditional ways of approaching EU–Russia relations risk missing facts that run counter to conventional wisdom, for example, the unexpected finding that, in some important ways, Russia converges better with France, Germany and the EU than does the UK. In the three cases studies, the British primarily focused on the protection of stability and order, a set of predefined norms, the economy and a world order where the USA plays a central role; whereas all the other actors, including Russia, focused more on the protection of multilateral working methods, international law and institutions, and community between international actors. Conventional analyses of EU–Russia relations could easily have rationalised the divergences over Kosovo by simple reference to Russia's historical affiliation with the Serbs, or to its resentment of the North Atlantic Treaty Organisation (NATO) in general. In contrast, the constructivist approach applied in this volume serves to deepen the understanding of the nature of differences – Russia's opposition was targeted at an emerging unilateral world order and aimed at securitising the terrorist threat while simultaneously demonstrating the illegitimacy of separatism as a movement.

That is not to say that the constructivist research design that guides this study has yielded an all-encompassing analysis that provides all the important answers to issues in the realm of European security. Yet, by conducting an inductive empirical analysis, the study has provided some new answers to whether European leaderships defend analogous referent-objects of security.

The constructivist design also assumes that state identities and interests are not given, but remain open to the possibility that leaderships change their standpoints over time. This starting point allowed us to reveal that Russia, France and Germany did not agree from the outset, but converged only gradually. During the Kosovo crisis, the Russian leadership chose to stick to an independent line of reasoning, according to which its primary concern was to protect the world from terrorism and unipolarity. This position left the Russian leadership isolated and without influence. The terrorist attacks of 11 September 2001 acted as a catalyst that revealed the importance of the terrorist threat. After 11 September it became easier for Russian leaders to communicate with their European counterparts, both because they shared a central official goal in the security sphere, to protect themselves from terrorist attacks, and because it became evident that Russia shared its scepticism about unilateral behaviour with both Germany and France. These central points of convergence enabled Russia to escape its exclusion from the European community of discourse on security, which it had experienced since the Kosovo crisis.

Another advantage of the time aspect is that it reveals the gradual convergence between French and Russian standpoints; that France's framing of the Iraqi conflict as a manifestation of unilateralism and the 'law of the strongest' in international relations was almost a replication of the Russian framing of the Kosovo conflict, which it presented as being about US unilateral rule and the enforcement of US interests on the rest of the world.

Furthermore, a more narrow research design prone to take certain circumstances as given could easily have ignored the fact that the Western states did not ally with the USA after 11 September to the extent that is commonly assumed. Immediately after the attacks all actors readily proclaimed loyalty to the USA, largely according to the idiom 'we are all Americans', but this was no more than an initial reaction. Quite soon, both France and Germany adopted a more hesitant posture towards the USA and its handling of the situation. Both parties were clearly disturbed by the new unilateral behaviour of the USA, largely based on the idea of self-sufficiency and reliance on 'coalitions of the willing' rather than on its traditional NATO allies. My analysis exposes French and German disenchantment with the US way of doing things as early as the autumn of 2001, when they were given fairly insignificant roles in the war in Afghanistan. This disappointment left imprints on France and Germany's interpretation of the Iraq crisis, and ultimately led to open divisions over the war in Iraq.

It is now time to place the empirical findings in the context of the theories on international relations such as realism, liberalism and international society. These theories were not used as points of departure driving and influencing the design of the empirical study, but are applied afterwards in order to derive meaning from the empirical results. Realist and liberal explanations for divergences are consequently not contrasted against constructivist explanations. Constructivism has been used as the analytical design, while liberalism and realism are detailed theories that can help to bring clarity to the empirical findings.

The results of the empirical examination confirm the validity of a central conviction inherent in its constructivist point of departure – that politicians' reasoning on security matters is never steered by a single logic, that is, by realist or idealist thinking. The analysis did not presuppose that the states studied adopted realist standpoints emerging from their historic legacy as

European great powers, although a small number of such findings could be noted in the case of Russia and the UK. Nor did it presuppose that they reasoned according to an idealist–institutionalist framework by virtue of their affiliation to the postmodern institutionalist logic of the EU. Instead, various logics normally inform the reasoning of political actors. In the view of the British Prime Minister, Tony Blair, the export of the 'correct' norms is a natural part of the national interest since 'the spread of our values makes us safer'. The German Foreign Minister, Joschka Fischer, described Europe as a community of material interests *and* of common norms. The analysis also illustrates that arguments linked to norms and interests may be mutually reinforcing.

My analysis envisages that norms can play into political reasoning in a variety of ways, which can yield quite different political results. In some cases, 'fixed' normative standpoints may serve as the underlying rationale for behaviour, while in other cases leaderships do not act on a set of favoured norms, but express their ambition to realise a new and different normative order. When contrasting the British logic with that of France and Germany, below, we see that while the preservation of prevailing norms served as the basic *rationale for action* in the British case, realisation of a normatively just world order served as the long-term goal in the case of France and Germany. Norms thus formed part of the reasoning of both camps, but in quite different ways.

The case studies reveal that the British conception of order is compatible with a realist zero-sum view of international interaction. My analysis shows that the leadership's rhetoric on order translates into a will to maintain stability in world affairs, preserving the prevailing balance of power and promoting 'hegemonic' norms and interests. The overarching logic of British reasoning entails that the current world order must be preserved in order to ensure the UK's security, prosperity, way of life and specific system of values. The leadership framed promotion of norms as a guarantee of security and material well-being since the spread of 'the right norms' would generate favourable conditions for free trade. The leadership thus supported an 'export-of-values' logic to secure 'the British way of life', which corresponds with the US tendency to argue in terms of spreading US-style democracy and security – also for the sake of world security.

Hence, throughout the crises, the British supported a problem-solving stance on international relations that did not have reforms to bring about a peaceful 'ideal' world as its aim, but aimed first and foremost to preserve the status quo. Blair framed the crisis in Kosovo as emerging from the tension between chaos and order in world affairs, and warned of the disorder that would follow, also on a global level, if Serbia was not brought into line. In the aftermath of 11 September, the British again accused wrongdoers of upsetting global stability and causing chaos. The arguments used against

Saddam Hussein were very similar to those used against Milosevic. The ultimate object was to avert chaos.

This British outlook on international affairs may not be characterised primarily as idealistic/liberal but instead as classical realist, by virtue of its lack of trust in other actors (at least in wrongdoers), its zero-sum view of conflict, its strong emphasis on order and the status quo and its reliance on typically realist concepts such as deterrence. British leaders portrayed the world in a realist manner, according to which actors are inevitably bound to conflict, and such conflict must be resolved effectively.

Paradoxically, this does not signify that the British reasoning was informed solely by interests and rationalistic calculations. On the contrary, the British used their normative preferences to underpin and justify their basically 'realist policy'. The overarching British rationale for action was to preserve hegemonic norms and values such as democracy, the rule of law and liberty. From the perspective of the British, these norms would be best protected by way of a power-maximising, problem-solving, and non-reform-minded realistic logic of action that allowed for the use of force in defence of the status quo.

France's and Germany's conceptions of order were more implicit. They employed the concept less often than the British. Instead, by standing up as an 'ethical vanguard' in international relations, the states would serve as an example of correct, peaceful behaviour that would, in turn, ensure the long-term and predictable development of a better world governed by fair and democratic processes. France and Germany thus demonstrated more of an idealistic belief in long-term transformations that can make the world more peaceful. In such an ideal world, there would be no need to exclude wrong-doers in order to ensure stability and order, since no government would be left behind or brought down – offenders would instead be progressively reformed and integrated into a peaceful international society. This utopian, Kantian logic contrasts with the British emphasis on the need for deterrence through determined and efficient use of force.

The view of order of the French and German leaderships is in line with an institutionalist approach to politics, according to which states are central actors in international relations but where institutions also matter. Interpreting the French and German official statements from an institutionalist point of view is useful, since it clarifies that they largely conceptualise international relations in accordance with an institutionalist basic outlook on the world. According to institutionalists, institutions enhance actors' trust in one another by increasing their opportunities to negotiate and their expectations about the solidity of international agreements, and by boosting the opportunities for supervising one another's adherence to shared commitments.[5] Typical of this kind of reasoning was Chancellor Schröder's argument that security is 'indivisible' and therefore requires multilateral methods.

Moreover, if we add a perspective of 'international society' to this institutionalist outlook on the world, the two states' ultimate aim is exposed – an all-European, or even global, security community. In Bull's definition, a society of states exists 'when a group of states, conscious of certain common interests and common values, form a society in the sense that they conceive themselves to be bound by a common set of rules in their relations with one another, and share in the working of common institutions'.[6] This is precisely what the French and Germans aimed for – that all actors should be included in a world tied together by shared norms and rules of behaviour.

The findings of the three case studies point in the same direction. The standpoints of the German and French governments fit particularly well with the specifics of multilateralism. Not only do they commit to shared values – notably, not just all righteous values, but shared ones – they are also concerned with securing common habits and rules. Their standpoints refer to norms as resources for community building, which is a goal in itself, rather than as being important in their own right. The German preoccupation with 'correct', internationally acceptable processes, and the French stress on common action, prove the extent to which this observation is valid. The 'community argument' was central to the German and French way of arguing during all three crises.

Multilateralism is characterised by three specific traits: diffuse reciprocity; generalised principles of conduct; and, finally, indivisibility, which implies a general belief among the participants in the system that peace is indivisible.[7] John Ruggie argues that multilateralism increases the stability of the international system because states tend to adapt to generalised principles of conduct that stipulate appropriate conduct for a set of actions without regard to the actors' particular interests.[8] In opposition to neorealists, James Caporaso argues that 'cooperation depends on a prior set of unacknowledged claims about the embeddedness of cooperative habits, shared values, and taken-for-granted rules'.[9] This corresponds quite well with the German and French emphasis on process. In the interpretation of the French and German leaderships, it was essential to do the right thing – ensuring stability – but perhaps even more important to act in the right way, adhering to United Nations standards and avoiding hazardous military ventures. Unity of action, in accordance with the ideal of multilateralism, was of primary importance to the French and German leaderships. They went along with the general ambition to export values for the sake of security, but were more cautious than the UK about the implementation of this idea.

Finally, to the Russians, 'being normative' signifies conserving the prevailing rules of conduct in international affairs. The Russian leadership conveyed the impression that the preservation of the United Nations system of rules would guarantee the privileges of the nation state in international relations – in particular, it would ensure the principle of territorial integrity

– and would also function as a guarantee against arbitrary acts conducted by the hegemon. The Russians' way of arguing corresponds to a realistic outlook on the world, in which the state remains the major actor in international affairs. The Russian leaders' support for the UN corresponds to institutionalism as well, but their support appears to originate not primarily from a belief in institutionalism as a way to resolve problems in today's world (as in the German and French case), but from a determination to use every possible means to contain the hegemon.

In sum, whereas the Russian leaders appeared quite 'realistic' and only pledged allegiance to institutionalism when this was suitable for their ends, France and Germany based their approach on a belief in the power of institutions, multilateralism and the viability of international society. This particular combination appears quite natural, given that in the opinion of scholars promoting an international society, multilateralism and strong institutions are a prerequisite for stability. Institutionalism, multilateralism and international society thus go hand in hand.

All this suggests that, to extrapolate, the British came close to a normative standard according to which action in the security sphere can be justified if it deals with a problem in an efficient way. They presented an essentialist view on norms, according to which a set of specific norms was considered 'good' in its own right, and thus worth preserving at almost any cost. They held a perspective on international relations as inherently unstable and on the use of force as an undesirable but unavoidable phenomenon in an imperfect world, all of which makes the British appear 'realistic'. Germany and France, by contrast, stood out as believers in progress by virtue of their standpoint that the world can be, and should be, reformed in order to realise long-term peace and stability, which makes them appear 'liberal/idealistic'.

It should be pointed out that, according to the analysis, France is a special case in this regard. Over the years, France has taken a somewhat ambivalent position on the need for a United Nations mandate. However, French support for the United Nations regulatory framework and for multilateralism appear more important to the overarching official policy than the urge to solve individual conflicts at any price. The French can pragmatically deviate from their rule, but such deviations are not standard procedures but unique events.

The consequences for the European pursuit of security

Rhetorical divergences, as the constructivist research approach asserts, have repercussions for political practice. The differences elaborated above account for the serious problems encountered by the EU in evolving its 'actorness'. My analysis shows that even though France, the UK and Germany support the European Security and Defence Policy (ESDP) in principle, they disagree on the significance and the aims of the project. The fact that the three major member states place varying emphases on the need for order, multilateralism, an institutional (United Nations) mandate for international intervention, and reform of the international system is a central stumbling block for the EU's ability to forge consensus on controversial issues in the security sphere.

What makes this all the more problematic is that the differences between the big three do not appear to have diminished with the passage of time. My empirical results indicate that continuity in reasoning and standpoints in the area of security on the part of the separate governments prevailed even during a most turbulent period of time, when the EU developed itself as an actor in the security sphere, and when 'external shocks' forced member states to take stands on new and serious issues in international affairs. Moreover, the traditional standpoints were demonstrated most clearly at crucial moments when the governments were forced to take a stand, such as during the Iraq war. The British appeared most conservative. The leadership tirelessly voiced its belief in the need to deter dictators, punish wrongdoers, stand by the USA, ensure stability and preserve the 'correct' norms. France and Germany appeared more visionary; they also kept to their major lines of argument, but developed their arguments in line with the EU's evolving emphasis on the need to change the international structure.

It is all the more intriguing, then, that the integration and development of the ESDP progresses by way of institutional reform and joint action. This suggests that great tension remains between stability and change. The EU integration project gains momentum when the major member states are most divided. This may indicate how deeply the EU project has taken root inside the separate governments – there is obviously no turning back. The central message to internal and external audiences from the three leaderships is that no matter what the difficulties are in merging ideas and identities, the EU *is* a security community.

It is, however, a community plagued by severe tensions. It is difficult for governments to speak with one voice on all issues. The EU cannot develop into a coherent 'normative actor' with a clear-cut message when, as the case studies demonstrate, the major member states are divided on the role and status of norms in the international arena. The EU is not solely an 'island-of-peace' and it is unclear how it will develop in the future. France and Germany promote the EU as a positive model for others to follow, while the UK wishes to model the EU after its own preferences, turning it into a more active player in the global arena that can envisage the use of force to spread the correct 'universal' liberal values. This leads to an EU that is far from consolidated and coherent in normative terms. The EU's efforts to integrate in the security sphere could be severely hampered and even spoiled as a result of these divergences.

In a sense, it appears easier for a traditional nation state such as Russia to cultivate its image as a normative actor than it is for the EU. Russia is a highly centralised state, the government of which has been able to present a fairly coherent message over a long period of time. The EU, by contrast, must negotiate between all the separate member states. Moreover, Russia's claim to morality is much more limited. According to the Russian leadership, being normative essentially means to stand against unipolarity and terrorism, and stand up for the rule of law in international relations. In the EU documents, being normative is more than that – in essence it demands an entirely new and just world order.

This suggests that the EU remains divided, which has serious consequences for practical politics. Despite the EU leadership's continual framing of crises as 'wake-up calls', no real and sustainable 'wake up' has occurred. The major member states have not decided to negotiate on their national positions and move towards greater consensus, including on issues related to sovereignty, norms, global order and relations with the USA. The diversities cultivate a sense of uncertainty in the surrounding world about what the EU can or will achieve with its rapid reaction capacity. The EU may best be characterised as an actor with a wide and comprehensive toolbox, but no one knows precisely how these tools will be used. In some less controversial but significant areas, the EU is able to unite in spite of the underlying tensions. The adoption of strategies directed at its 'near abroad', strategies for conflict prevention, engagement as a global actor in the environmental field, and the comprehensive counterterrorism strategies bear witness to the EU's capacity to issue policy documents that have longstanding consequences in the international arena. Such long-term policies can function even when the EU is divided with regard to basic strategic issues.[10]

The EU's failure to generate a coherent policy towards Russia is due partly to the basic divisions discussed above, and partly to the EU's institutional complexity, which has resulted in a multifaceted and sometimes ill-synchronised policy. In 2004, the EU officially conceded that its attempts to handle relations with Russia were ineffective and inconsistent, and lacked an overall strategy. There is a tension between the EU's diverse aims. The Commission depends on functional relations with the Russian leadership to be able to advance reforms in the economic sector, which may restrain EU criticism of human rights violations in Russia. Policy aims in one field may thus serve to hold back aims in another.

Moreover, EU member states traditionally expend much diplomatic effort on bilateral security interplay in the European security sphere. The first chapter asked whether EU institutional constraints push member states to adapt to a common EU foreign policy line, or if the established players still find it easy to join with other states when they think fit, hence bypassing the common EU position. In relation to Russia, the answer is clear: key EU member states – the UK, France, Italy and Germany – have been surprisingly active on their own account in relation to Russia, each attempting to forge a 'special relationship' with Putin for its own benefit. While the Commission has criticised Russian policy in Chechnya, major member states such as Germany and France have been more supportive.[11] Even self-proclaimed institutionalists such as Germany deal with Russia in a largely bilateral fashion, not least in the area of energy policy. Each individual government's desire for a special relationship with Moscow remains a key stepping stone in the evolution of EU–Russia relations.[12] Old habits die hard and forging a good relationship with Moscow has historically been in the interest of each of the European great powers.

The Commission acknowledges this problem. In a communication to the European Parliament and the Council in early 2004, the Commission calls for increased 'policy coherence' in the EU's relations with Russia. This could, for example, be accomplished by drawing 'red lines' for the EU during preparations for each EU–Russia summit or 'positions beyond which the EU will not go'. The Commission calls on all 'EU actors' to be guided by 'agreed EU objectives and positions':

> There is a need for increased EU coordination and coherence across all areas of EU activity – sending clear, unambiguous messages to Russia. It is only via engagement, making full use of our combined negotiating strength, that the EU can promote a fully functioning rules-based system in Russia, to the benefit of both.[13]

Furthermore, Moscow also favours bilateral relations in the security sphere. Despite Russia's mainly positive tone towards the EU, the leadership still appears to regard bilateral relations as the basis for its European policy. Russia has demonstrated an ability to use bilateral relations rather than go through EU institutions when this serves its political ends.[14] In November 2003, Putin remarked that Russia stands closer to individual European states on many important international issues than the EU states do in relation to one another.[15] Typically, Putin argued in 2006 for the development of mutually beneficial economic contacts and other ties as a result of Russia's dialogue with 'the European Union in general and with its leading countries – Germany, France, Italy, Spain and other EU members'.[16] The tendency for bilateral contacts between Russia and a few 'chosen' EU governments is further strengthened by the arrival of a number of new EU member states that are less positive towards Russia – Poland and the Baltic states in particular.[17]

The EU's non-cohesive stance towards Russia may be negative from a short-term perspective, particularly so for smaller member states that cannot draw as much benefit from strong bilateral ties with Russia as the leading member states and would thus need a strong EU policy line towards Russia.[18] Yet, regular bilateral contacts can contribute to Russia's gradual adaptation to

European standards, interests or values and could work to the advantage of EU–Russia rapprochement in the longer term. Bilateral processes on all levels – ranging from cultural exchanges to trade and regular summits – can contribute to the logic of neofunctionalism discussed in Chapter 6. Bilateralism should therefore not be interpreted negatively, but as an important building block in the greater edifice of links between Russia and the remainder of Europe. Intense interaction at all levels can – in a long-term perspective – lead to a better understanding of differences, and fuel further integration between Russia and the EU, including in the security sphere.

From this perspective, Germany and France appear very important in bringing Russia closer to European standards. France and Germany tend to favour closer relations with Russia than most other EU member states. Russia, Germany and France's common opposition to the Iraq war contributed to strengthening relations between Russia and the EU at large. To the French, it is important to cultivate relations with Russia, to a large extent, because of its capacity to function jointly with the EU as a counter-weight to US hegemony. Economic ties and cooperation in the energy sector are other strong driving forces behind the deepening of bilateral relations, even more so from a German perspective. Germany is Russia's most important trading partner in the EU, and Germany is dependent on its imports of Russian oil and gas. The German government launched a regular intergovernmental consultation process with Russia in the spring of 2001, which bears witness to the fact that relations with Russia are important to Germany. The new German Chancellor, Angela Merkel, continued her predecessor's strategy of prioritising relations with Russia. The mutual will to strengthen relations has yielded an array of practical results. Russia has supported Germany's pursuit of a permanent seat on the United Nations Security Council, and Germany supported Russia's ambition to hold the chairmanship of the G8 in 2006. When Germany assumed the rotating EU Presidency in January 2007, it drafted a special plan to promote German and EU ties with Russia.[19]

In this logic, Russia will be drawn closer to West European standards and traditions not because of the oil and gas flowing through pipelines from east to west, but as a result of personal encounters, further institutionalisation and exchanges at all levels. A major difference between the Cold War period and the current situation is that Russians in a wide range of sectors of society now regularly encounter their European neighbours. The logic of function-alism is inevitably at work and is likely – in the longer term perspective – to contribute both to drawing Russia closer to the EU and to alleviating European prejudges about Russia. It has been suggested that Russia might turn its economic interactions away from Europe to China and Asia.[20] Even if this scenario were to prove correct, Russia is nevertheless likely to grow increasingly close to European standards and norms because, in general,

Russians turn to Europe more naturally. Russians tend to travel not to their giant neighbour, China, but to Europe, whether to ski in the Alps or to study in European universities. According to Arkady Moshes, the Russian elite has become 'addicted to the European lifestyle'. Moshes concludes that Russia should be approached at grassroots level so that Russians will come to realise that there is a world out there that welcomes them and that they are a part of, and that they will get something out of Europe.[21]

Andrei Tsygankov warns Western policy makers about focusing excessively on an exclusive relationship with the Kremlin and the ruling elite, since such a policy can alienate the majority of Russians and is likely to fail when the leadership changes. He argues that it is essential to remain attentive to attitudes across Russian society.[22] This chimes well with Antoneko and Pinnick's recommendation that Russia and the EU should focus more on 'bottom-up' convergence based on small, successful practical projects rather than on grand visions and top-level meetings.[23] Similarly, Michael McFaul argues that given the current difficulties, the West should focus on the integration of 'Russians, not Russia, into Western institutions'. He recommends that the strategy must involve 'comprehensive, sustained, and meaningful engagement of all elements of Russian society' and concludes: 'It was common wisdom a decade ago to think that the integration of the Russian state into Western institutions would facilitate changes in Russian society. Now is the time to consider the opposite sequence – that the integration of Russian society into the West may in turn facilitate the Western integration of the Russian state.'[24]

This functionalist logic makes the Russian leadership's opposition to the export of EU norms, as well as their attempts to hold back Westernising 'colour revolutions' in the Commonwealth of Independent States (CIS), appear futile. The real 'threat' is the Russians themselves and their preference for European mores and standards. If this functionalist interpretation of the effects of institutionalisation, bilateralism and grassroots contacts holds true, Russian leaders can hardly prevent a further diversification of Russian society – they have already 'lost the battle over Russian minds'.

Needless to say, this does not signify that Russia is turning into a copy of France or Germany, but that Europe will not remain as 'foreign', and will not endlessly be conceptualised as Russia's 'other', and vice versa. In fact, in a not too distant future, China might become more of an 'other' both to Russia and the EU. China has traditionally been perceived as a potentially serious security challenge to Russia, and the growing economic strength of China and the immense Chinese population of over one billion people is of concern to Russian decision makers.[25]

In sum, my findings suggest that a number of serious hurdles to deeper EU–Russia cooperation remain. In particular, Russia resists the export of norms by the EU in the regional and global arenas, and the EU finds it hard to tolerate abuses of human rights and freedoms in Russia. Also, the state remains the main referent-object of security for Russian politicians, whereas the EU has placed increasing priority on 'new' referent-objects such as the environment and the individual. Moreover, Russia's global interpretative horizon, its focus on military means and its harsh measures to quell terrorism fit better with US standpoints than with the EU's outlook on the world.[26] Yet, Russia and the EU converge on key issues of global politics. Moreover, in a longer perspective, if the logic of functionalism suggested above does its work, both parties might relax their rigid standpoints on issues of principle, which will help to remove current obstacles to further rapprochement in the security sphere.

Some area specialists and scholars with other theoretical points of departure, such as realism or geopolitics, tend to apply a somewhat more gloomy view of the future of EU–Russia relations.[27] The rather optimistic interpretation suggested here can partly be ascribed to the constructivist point of departure that highlights processes, which is helpful when assessing potential for change. The case studies demonstrate that even though the parties' basic standpoints have remained much the same, the EU and Russia have been closer at some points in time – for example after 11 September 2001 – and have had open and serious disagreements on other occasions. This indicates that the prospects for rapprochement should be evaluated in a longer perspective; even though relations were frosty in 2006 and 2007, in the long run the logic of neo-functionalism can contribute to bringing down obstacles to closer cooperation.

There is no determinism in this – events might develop differently – but the Russian leadership's and electorate's weariness of being left isolated from the rest of Europe speaks in favour of incremental rapprochement. It is likely that the fear of exclusion will increase as neighbouring states strengthen their ties with the EU. Hiski Haukkala suggests that the EU is aware of this and that it is 'simply willing to wait out its recalcitrant partner, relying on its immense and slow gravity to pull the laggard into line'.[28] How swiftly this process unfolds is impossible to foresee. Needless to say, much will depend on the positions taken by upcoming Russian administrations, particularly whether they continue to place restraints on processes towards a more open and democratic Russian society. Studies of how the Russian leadership justifies its policies, in the vein of this volume, will be useful in evaluating the potential for EU–Russian rapprochement in the years to come.

The use of force as a dividing line

What, then, is the potential for security cooperation in Europe? Are Russia, the EU and the major EU member states able to unite on similar security agendas, and what are the implications for the USA?

My findings suggest that contemporary Europe is not characterised by self-help and anarchy. The EU has successfully forged a security community and, notably, one that often includes Russia. However, serious divergences have been revealed by the research in this volume. One particularly problematic source of conflict is the difference between the British problem-solving/activist logic and the French-German process-oriented, long-term and reform-minded logic. This tension leaves the EU in an awkward situation. Like the UK, the EU has displayed a missionary stance and a readiness to impose what it sees as 'objectively just' norms on non-EU actors, if necessary by the use of force. At the same time, it has supported the French/German demand for appropriate behaviour according to institutional – primarily United Nations – rules.

The EU is thus torn between two philosophies, which makes it particularly difficult to predict the direction that it will take in the future. Will the EU develop its identity in the direction of an 'appropriate' body that sticks close to the UN rules-based system and the idea of multilateralism? Or will it instead develop its identity in a way that allows breaking with rules of behaviour in order to safeguard, or spread, its favoured values in the world – that is, move closer to the US way of behaving? If this tension is not resolved, the EU risks becoming paralysed, as it was during the Iraq war, when it faces a dilemma in which it is forced to choose between either the British or the French-German logic.

The EU's indecisiveness is a consequence of its position between pro-Atlanticist member states, and member states that tend to reject unilateralism and US hegemony. It is also a result of its ambivalence about how far it should develop its normative ambitions, and its hesitance about the use of force in international relations. If the EU faced only the first dilemma, it would manage by carefully navigating its diplomacy. The latter problem is more complicated. Here, it is not only the standpoints of the member states that the EU must take into account. The problem is also deeply intertwined with the EU's own identity. The EU has developed a particular self-image as an 'island-of-peace', with claims to act in a particularly 'normative' way and therefore to function as a model for other regions and powers.

This issue is essentially about justifiable means in international relations, and whether long-term stability and a just world order can be, and should be, achieved. The British stance has been defined as an essentially realistic one that denies the prospect of a peaceful world in the future. However, from the point of view of the British government, the UK acted in order to bring about a more stable and thus better world during the three crises under scrutiny. Put somewhat differently, the spread of 'universal' norms – even by military means – is a traditional liberal practice. The difference between France and Germany, on the one hand, and the British, on the other, is therefore not primarily that the former displayed good intent and the latter did not, but that their ambitions differed and they envisaged different methods for realising their goals.

France and Germany demonstrated an incremental approach that emphasised 'correct' processes and long-term solutions. It was the British view that a swift war of necessity that removed from power one of the worst criminals in the world would do more to reform the security order than avoidance and long-term reforms targeting underdevelopment. This thinking is efficiently caught by Ian Clarke, who notes that 'A warless world may not only not be a just one, it may in fact prevent the creation of a just one, as the prevention of violence may obstruct desirable change'.[29]

The central question here is whether the use of force – even if the goal is to spread 'peaceful norms' – is reconcilable with the image of an inherently 'peaceful' entity such as the EU, which claims to be a model for other actors. Ian Clarke's distinction between three ways to achieve international order – '(1) international order through the recognition of the role of force and through its utilisation; (2) international order through placing constraints on the use of force; and, finally, (3) international order through the eventual rejection of the special place which force has in international relations' – sheds further light on this dilemma.[30] The EU's dilemma is that it has not decided under which circumstances the use of force is legitimate in international relations. It has not yet fully settled on whether it should act in line with Clarke's point number 2 or point number 3.

Much therefore boils down to different standpoints on the ideal solutions to security problems. Should the EU adopt a problem-solving stance that includes exclusion and the use of force beyond its borders, even in a preemptive fashion, or should it go along with France and Germany's preference for preventive means, inclusion and long-term solutions? The schema in Table 7.1 illustrates the EU's dilemma. It outlines the conditions that should be met before the actors are willing to agree a 'problem-solving intervention', that is, one that aims to solve an immediate conflict by way of military intervention.

The schema should not be interpreted as a forecast of the standpoint of a particular leadership in a future crisis. It serves as a model of the tendencies that dominate the actors' reasoning. Where the USA places itself in this schema is open to debate. My suggestion is not based on empirical observations and should be interpreted as an exercise to stimulate further reflection. Russia, by contrast, can be situated quite easily in the schema. It is obvious from my empirical findings that Moscow refutes the general idea of value-export and emphasises the need for legal processes in world affairs, that is, that action has to be sanctioned by the United Nations. It is also highly negative about the idea of 'humanitarian intervention', but ready to use force in order to quell terrorism.

What is most striking about this schema is that it works reasonably well

Table 7.1   The readiness of leaderships to engage in international problem solving

	Problem solving involving use of force aimed at restoring status quo	*Problem solving involving use of force aimed at humanitarian intervention and/ or spreading values*	*Problem solving involving use of force aimed at quelling terrorism*
USA	Yes	Under specific circumstances, if the stakes are not too high	Yes
UK	Yes	Yes	Yes
France, Germany	No	Under specific circumstances, if the stakes are not too high	Under specific circumstances, if the stakes are not too high
Russia	No	No	Yes
EU	?	?	?

for all the actors except the EU. If viewed from this angle, it is wholly unclear what stand the EU will take on future crises in international affairs. Will it ally with the British, more activist stance, making use of its military means, or hesitate and remain focused on the long-term transformation of international relations, in line with the approach taken by France and Germany? It is genuinely uncertain whether the EU will prioritise making use of the 'correct' means, and only achieve its end of a more 'normative' world in the long term, or if it will side with the British in efficiently combating menaces on the global stage by using coercive means when necessary.

This raises particular concerns about the EU as a normative actor. The European Security Strategy states that 'Europe should be ready to share in the responsibility for global security and in building a better world'. Yet, the text does not provide any clear indication of exactly how the EU wishes to achieve this new world. On the one hand, the strategy states that 'Spreading good governance, supporting social and political reform, dealing with corruption and abuse of power, establishing the rule of law and protecting human rights are the best means of strengthening the international order'. The text indicates, however, that such preventive methods will not be enough: 'We need to develop a strategic culture that fosters early, rapid, and, when necessary, robust intervention.'[31] This illustrates the EU's dilemma – the difficult choice between immediate problem solving and long-term strategies.

It will not be easy for the major member states to give up their individual political visions. It is most likely that they will proceed only very gradually towards greater convergence – if they do so at all. Further research is also required to elucidate the stand that the other EU member states take on this decisive issue. Do they wish the EU to remain a rather inactive island-of-peace – a positive example for other regions and powers – or should it pursue a more activist, problem-solving policy? The latter alternative would signify not that the EU is becoming 'less' normative, but that it is adopting a different view on what it *is* to be normative in the contemporary world.

A triangular diplomatic game between the USA, Russia and the EU

Where does all this leave the USA? The case studies indicate that the relationship between Washington, Brussels and Moscow can be characterised as a kind of triangular diplomatic game. During the Kosovo crisis, EU-Europe and the USA collaborated closely, but Russia was distanced. After 11 September 2001, Russia came close to both parties, initiating practical counterterrorist measures in collaboration with both Washington and Brussels. My analysis suggests that this time, when the USA left the EU behind somewhat, the EU started to act more independently of Washington. It established its own interpretation of the crisis, which was more focused on root causes. Russia also strengthened its relationship with the EU by developing a joint approach against terrorism. The links between the USA and Europe were thus somewhat weakened, but the bonds between Russia and Europe were strengthened. The EU was split during the Iraq war. The UK went with the USA, while the other two major member states, and Russia, distanced themselves from Washington. As a result, the bonds between Russia and the EU were, again, strengthened, while the bonds between Washington and Brussels/Moscow were weakened.

If, in the future, the EU encounters new dilemmas similar to those encountered during the build up to the Iraq war – dilemmas where it finds it hard to unite with the USA – it might instead join Russia in criticising Washington. If this evolves into a pattern, will the EU and Russia then gradually become tied together by identifying a common 'other', that is, by perceiving the USA as something of an antagonist in the realm of security?

It is highly unlikely that the EU would turn away completely from the USA. The economic bonds between the EU and the USA are strong enough to impede any deep divide in the overall relationship. Moreover, the EU and its major member states are still preoccupied with preserving and maintaining a mutual interest in the 'transatlantic link' – ensuring that the USA stays involved in Europe. The EU and its major member states are only likely to challenge Washington on significant issues in global politics occasionally, such as was seen during the Iraq war. Russia in turn has also been slow to give up its long-established focus on the USA as its primary partner in international relations. It traditionally shares a global perspective on security politics with the USA, including, for example, strong emphases on the struggle against international terrorism, on solving regional conflicts and on combating the proliferation of weapons.[30] It is most likely that it will refrain from openly challenging Washington except on issues of great significance for its interests or identity.

Yet, on occasions when the EU – and Russia – perceive that they have to stand up for their respective security identities and interests, in the face of conflicts involving serious issues pertaining to rules of the game in international relations, they might choose to join forces against Washington. A prerequisite for this would be that the EU were capable of taking a joint stand at all, that is, that it were not paralysed as a result of disagreements among its member states emerging from the security gaps.

If the EU finds a way round its internal divisions, it is likely to become more attractive to Russia as a strong and united pole in world affairs. This optimistic interpretation would signify a renewed Europe that becomes ever more integrated and gradually learns to work efficiently with Russia – at least in crucial sub-areas in the security sphere such as the promotion of multilateralism, and the struggle against terrorism, proliferation, transnational crime and drug trafficking.

Indeed, Russia and the EU converge more easily in the global than in the regional arena. A likely rationale for this is that they are unwilling to negotiate over their interests as regional great powers, where each wishes to contribute their own favoured solution to security problems, and each wishes to realise their own favoured version of European security. The major dividing line here is between Russia promoting a security order that sustains territorial integrity and the security of sovereign states, by military means if necessary, and the other actors who – to varying degrees – prioritise individual security, human rights and the adoption of preventive rather than military means.

The difficulties in uniting in the regional arena could be alleviated in a longer term perspective if the neofunctional logic of rapprochement outlined above does its work. Increased contacts at all levels are likely to stimulate a gradual Russian adaptation to European standards and norms. The logic of functionalism can also help both sides to become more tolerant of their remaining differences. The two parties' respective needs to project themselves as unique powers with particular identities might also reduce as they grow more confident with regard to their specific roles in the regional and global arenas. Two former antagonists, or 'others', might then become good, or at least functional, neighbours. They might come to the conclusion that they have too much in common to let fixations over identity ruin their partnership.

In the global arena, the two parties need one another in order to 'strengthen the European voice' in global affairs and are glued together by a range of common positions. They share a range of interests, such as the struggle against transnational threats and the spread of weapons of mass destruction, and a will to make the European voice heard in the global arena. To Russia, Europe is more of an asset than a threat in a potentially multipolar world. Russia is more likely to balance against the USA and, even more likely, China than against the EU. Russia and the EU can also unite on a number of key common normative concerns, most notably a will not to allow a single power to govern world affairs.

All these convergences might induce Russia and the EU to tone down their respective preoccupations with asserting their respective identities in exchange for placing increased priority on pragmatic cooperation. If so, the USA will face a more potent Europe that works against unilateralism and 'the law of the strongest' in global affairs. Scholarly endeavours need to pay close attention to EU–US relations, since the EU will continue to develop its approaches to security in conjunction with US security policy.

A more gloomy future for EU–Russia relations is also possible. Europe might not manage to unite on common security concerns because of the tensions inherent in the 'security gaps' identified in this volume. The EU's internal differences, also exposed in this volume, should not be underesti-mated here. Future research will have to monitor carefully both EU–Russia relations and how the EU resolves its internal tensions between the British 'problem-solving' stance on global affairs and the incremental stance adopted by France and Germany, which aims for a more thorough reform of the international system. Yet, as has been argued above, the future of European security might not primarily hinge on high-level EU–Russia relations. Of greater importance might be grassroots contacts between citizens of greater Europe, and the continuing evolution of bilateral relations.

Notes

1 As is argued in Chapter 1, the EU is represented in this volume by the small number central actors who are given the task of acting as the primary spokespersons for the EU on matters related to the CFSP and the ESDP. The major focus has been on the Secretary-General of the Council and High Representative for the Common Foreign and Security Policy, the Commissioner for External Relations, the President of the Commission and the Presidency. In contrast, 'EU-Europe' is envisaged as the EU plus its major member states.

2 European Commission. 'Road map for the Common Space of Freedom, Security and Justice'.

3 Manners, I., 'Normative power Europe: A contradiction in terms?', *Journal of Common Market Studies* 40:2 (2002).

4 Hyde-Price, A., *European Security in the Twenty-First Century: The Challenge of Multipolarity* (London: Routledge, 2007).

5 Keohane, R., *International Institutions and State Power: Essays in International Relations Theory* (Boulder: Westview Press, 1989), p. 2

6 Bull, H., *The Anarchical Society: A Study of Order in World Politics* (London: Macmillan, 1977), p. 13.

7 Caporaso, J., 'International relations theory and multilateralism: The search for foundations', in J. Ruggie (ed.), *Multilateralism Matters: The Theory and Praxis of an Institutional Form* (New York: Columbia University Press, 1993), p. 53; Ruggie, J., 'The anatomy of an institution', in Ruggie (ed.), *Multilateralism Matters*, p. 11; Waever, O., 'John G. Ruggie: transformation and institutionalization', in Iver Neumann and Ole Waever (eds), *The Future of International Relations Masters in the Making* (London: Routledge, 1997), pp. 184–185.

8 Ruggie (note 7), p. 11.

9 Caporaso (note 7), p. 82.

10 Wagnsson, C., 'The EU as strategic actor, "re-actor" or passive pole', in Jan Hallenberg and Kjell Engelbrekt (eds), *European Union and Strategy: An Emerging Actor* (London: Routledge, 2007).

11 Averre, D., 'Russia and the European Union: Convergence or divergence?', in *European Security* 14:2 (2005), p. 181.

12 Haukkala, H., 'The role of solidarity and coherence in EU's Russia Policy', *Studia Diplomatica* 19:2 (2006)., p. 48; Leijins, A., 'The CFSP and the PCA: Between realpolitik and values', in A. Leijins (ed.), *The EU Common Foreign and Security Policy Toward Russia: The Partnership and Cooperation Agreement as a Test Case* (Riga: Latvian Institute of International Affairs, 2006), p. 7.

13 European Commission, 'Communication from the Commission to the Council and the European Parliament on relations with Russia', COM 106, 9 February 2004.

14 Averre (note 11), p. 181; Haukkala (note 12), p. 48.

15 Putin, V., 'Interview with the ANSA Italian News Agency, *Corriere della Sera* Newspaper and the RAI Television Company', 3 November 2003.

16 Putin, V., 'Address to the Ambassadors of the Russian Federation', 23 August 2006.

17 Chapter 6 demonstrates that Russia has tried to create divisions between older EU states and such newcomers.

18 Haukkala (note 12), pp. 49–50.

19 Radio Free Europe/Radio Liberty, Newsline, 1 December 2006.

20 Moshes, A., 'Prospects for EU–Russia foreign and security policy cooperation', *The EU Russia Review* 2 (2006), p. 23.

21 Moshes, A., Speech at the conference 'What Next for EU–Russia Relations', Stockholm, 13 February 2007.

22 Tsygankov, A., *Russia's Foreign Policy: Change and Continuity in National Identity* (Lanham, MD: Rowman & Littlefield, 2006), p. 187.

23 Antonenko, O. and Pinnick, K., 'The enlarged EU and Russia: From converging interests to a common agenda', in O. Antonenko and K. Pinnick (eds), *Russia and the European Union* (New York: Routledge, 2005), pp. 6–7.

24 McFaul, M., 'Russia and the West: A dangerous drift', *Current History* October (2005).

25 Petersson, B., *National Self-Images and Regional Identities in Russia* (Aldershot: Ashgate, 2001), pp. 95–96, 101–103; Zagorski, A., 'Russia and European institutions', in V. Baranovsky (ed.), *Russia and Europe: The Emerging Security Agenda*, Stockholm International Peace Research Institute, (Oxford: Oxford University Press, 1997), p. 523.

26 Wagnsson, C., 'The alien and the traditional: The EU facing a transforming Russia', in J. Hallenberg and H. Karlsson (eds), *Changing Transatlantic Security Relations: Do the US, the EU and Russia Form a New Strategic Triangle?* (London: Routledge, 2006).

27 Allison, R., 'Russian security engagement with the European Union' and 'Russia in Europe or Russia and Europe?', in Roy Allision, M. Light and S. White (eds), *Putin's*

Russia and the Enlarged Europe (Malden/Oxford: Blackwell Publishing, 2006), pp. 91–93, 175–180; Averre (note 11), pp. 191–195; Roberts, C., *Russia and the European Union: The Sources and Limits of 'Special Relationships'* (Carlisle: Strategic Studies Institute, 2007).

28 Haukkala, H., 'The relevance of norms and values in the EU's Russia policy', UPI Working Papers 52 (2005), p. 19.

29 Clarke, I., *The Hierarchy of States: Reform and Resistance in the International Order* (Cambridge: Cambridge Studies in International Relations, 1989), p. 14.

30 Ibid.

31 European Security Strategy, pp. 1, 11.

32 Wagnsson (note 26), p. 118.

Bibliography

Books and articles

Adler, E., 'Seizing the middle ground: Constructivism in world politics', *European Journal of International Relations*, 3:3 (1997).

Aggestam, L., *A European Foreign Policy? Role Conceptions and the Politics of Identity in Britain, France and Germany* (Stockholm: Stockholm University Department of Political Science, 2004).

Allison, R., 'Russian security engagement with the European Union' and 'Russia in Europe or Russia and Europe?', in Roy Allison, M. Light and S. White (eds), *Putin's Russia and the Enlarged Europe* (Malden/Oxford: Blackwell Publishing, 2006).

Antonenko, O. and Pinnick, K., 'The enlarged EU and Russia: From converging interests to a common agenda', in O. Antonenko and K. Pinnick (eds), *Russia and the European Union* (New York: Routledge, 2005).

Averre, D., 'Russia and the European Union: Convergence or divergence?', *European Security* 14:2 (2005).

Baldwin, D., 'The concept of security', *Review of International Studies* 23 (1997).

Barysh, K., 'EU–Russia relations: The EU perspective', in D. Johnson and P. Robinson (eds), *Perspectives on EU–Russia Relations* (London: Routledge, 2005).

Barysh, K. and Kekic, L., 'Putin should tilt toward the EU: Russia at a crossroads', *International Herald Tribune*, 17 July 2003.

Berger, T., 'Norms, identity, and national security in Germany and Japan', in P. Katzenstein (ed.), *The Culture of National Security* (New York, Columbia University Press, 1996).

Bilefsky, D., 'Senior EU aide issues warning on Russia ties', *International Herald Tribune*, 20 April 2007.

Bloom, W., *Personal Identity, National Identity and International Relations* (Cambridge: Cambridge University Press, 1990).

Bretherton C. and Vogler, J., *The European Union as a Global Actor* (London: Routledge, 2006).

Bring, O. and Broström, P., 'The Iraq war and international law: From Hugo Grotius to George W. Bush', in J. Hallenberg and H. Karlsson (eds), *The Iraq War: European Perspectives on Politics, Strategy and Operations* (London: Routledge, 2005).

Buckley, M., 'Russian perceptions', in M. Buckley and S. Cummings, *Kosovo Perceptions of War and its Aftermath* (London: Continuum, 2001).

Bull, H., *The Anarchical Society: A Study of Order in World Politics* (London: Macmillan, 1977).

Burns, T., 'Rhetoric as a framework for analyzing cultural constraint and change', *Current Perspectives in Social Theory* 19 (1999).

Buzan, B., *Peoples, States and Fear: An Agenda for International Security Studies in the Post-Cold War Era* (Hertfordshire: Harvester Wheatsheaf, 1991).

Bynander, F., *The Rise and Fall of the Submarine Threat: Threat Politics and Submarine Intrusions in Sweden 1980–2002* (Uppsala: Acta Universitatis Upsaliensis, 2003).

Caporaso, J., 'International relations theory and multilateralism: The search for foundations', in J. Ruggie (ed.), *Multilateralism Matters: The Theory and Praxis of an Institutional Form* (New York: Columbia University Press, 1993).

Clarke, I., *The Hierarchy of States: Reform and Resistance in the International Order* (Cambridge: Cambridge Studies in International Relations, 1989).

Clarke, M., 'British perceptions', in M. Buckley and S. Cummings (eds), *Kosovo Perceptions of War and its Aftermath* (London: Continuum, 2001).

Dannreuter, R., *European Union Foreign and Security Policy: Towards a Neighbourhood Strategy* (London: Routledge, 2004).

Dempsey, J., 'Merkel under fire over Congo mission', *International Herald Tribune*, 20 March 2006.

Dempsey, J., 'A united Europe awaits Putin at EU-Russia summit', *International Herald Tribune*, 16 May 2007.

Deutsch, K., *Political Community and the North Atlantic Area: International Organization in the Light of Historical Experience* (Princeton, NJ: University of Princeton Press, 1957).

Dombrowski, P. and Ross, A., 'The "new strategic triangle" and the US grand strategy debate', in J. Hallenberg and H. Karlsson (eds), *Changing Transatlantic Security Relations: Do the US, the EU and Russia Form a New Strategic Triangle?* (London: Routledge, 2006).

Duchêne, F., 'Europe's role in world peace', in R. Mayne (ed.), *Europe Tomorrow: Sixteen Europeans Look Ahead* (London: Fontana, 1972).

Duke, S., et al., 'The major European allies: France, Germany and the United Kingdom', in A. Schnabel and R. Thakur (eds), *Kosovo and the Challenge of Humanitarian Intervention: Selective Indignation, Collective Action, and International Citizenship* (Tokyo: United Nations University Press, 2000).

Edelman, M., *Constructing the Political Spectacle* (Chicago: University of Chicago Press, 1988).

Eilders, C. and Lüter, A., 'Germany at war: Competing framing strategies in German public discourse', *European Journal of Communication* 15:3 (2000).

Emerson, M., *The Elephant and the Bear: The European Union, Russia and their Near Abroads* (Brussels: Centre for European Policy Studies, 2001).

Entman, R., 'Framing: Towards clarification of a fractured paradigm', *Journal of Communication* 43:4 (1993).

Eriksson, J., *Threat Politics: New Perspectives on Security, Risk and Crisis Management* (Aldershot: Ashgate, 2001).

Fedorov, Y., 'Strategic thinking in Putin's Russia', in Y. Fedorov and B. Nygren (eds) *Russian Military Reform and Russia's New Security Environment* (Stockholm: Swedish National Defence College, 2003).

Fedorov, Y., 'European Security and Defence Policy: Russia's reading', in Bo Huldt et al., *European Security and Defence Policy: A European Challenge* (Stockholm: Swedish National Defence College, 2006).

Fierke, K. M. and Wiener, A., 'Constructing institutional interests: EU and NATO enlargement', *Journal of European Public Policy*, 6:5 (1999).

Finnemore, M., 'Constructing norms of humanitarian intervention', in P. Katzenstein (ed.), *The Culture of National Security* (New York: Columbia University Press, 1996).

Fischer, J., 'Address to the German Bundestag', 26 March 1999.

Fischer, J., 'Statement in the Leipziger Volkszeitung', 10 April 1999.

Fischer, J., Statement in *Deutschlandfunk*, 11 April 1999.

Fischer, J., 'Interview with *Die Zeit*', 15 April 1999.

Fischer, J., 'Interview with *Der Spiegel*', 19 April 1999.

Fischer, J., 'Interview with SWR', 23 April 1999.

Fischer, J., 'Interview with *Tagesspiegel*', 23 May 1999.

Fischer, J., 'Statement in *Tagesthemen*', 31 May 1999.

Fischer, J., 'Statement in ZDF', 7 June 1999.

Fischer, J., 'Statement in *Tagesthemen*', 9 June 1999.

Fischer, J., 'Interview with *Frankfurter Allgemeinen Zeitung*', 17 January 2003.

Fischer, J., 'Interview in ARD', 24 January 2003.

Fischer, J., 'Address to the German Bundestag', 13 February 2003.

Fischer, J., 'Interview with *Die Zeit*', 20 February 2003.

Fischer, J., 'Interview with *Der Stern*', 5 March 2003.

Fischer, J., 'Address to the UN Security Council', 7 March 2003.

Fischer, J., 'Interview with *Frankfurter Allgemeinen Zeitung*', 17 March 2003.

Fischer, J., 'Interview in ARD', 4 April 2003.

Fischer, J., 'Interview with Neuen Zürcher Zeitung', 13 April 2003.

Forsberg, T., 'Forging the EU-Russia security partnership in the crucible of trans-Atlantic relations', Paper prepared for the joint International Convention of Central Eastern European International Studies Association & International Studies Association, Budapest, 26–28 June 2003.

Friis, L. and Murphy, A., '"Turbo-charged negotiations:" the EU and the Stability Pact for south-eastern Europe', *Journal of European Public Policy* 7:5 (2000).

Hallenberg, J., 'The Bush administration's goals in invading Iraq', in J. Hallenberg and H. Karlsson (eds), *The Iraq War: European Perspectives on Politics, Strategy and Operations* (New York: Routledge, 2006).

Haukkala, H., 'A problematic "strategic partnership"', in D. Lynch (ed.), *EU–Russian Security Dimensions,* WEU Occasional Paper 46 (July 2003).

Haukkala, H., 'The relevance of norms and values in the EU's Russia policy', UPI Working Papers 52 (2005).

Haukkala, H., 'The role of solidarity and coherence in EU's Russia Policy', *Studia Diplomatica* 19:2 (2006).

Hedetoft, U., 'National identity and mentalities of war in three EC countries', *Journal of Peace Research* 30:3 (1993).

Hedetoft, U., *Signs of Nations* (Aldershot: Dartmouth Publishing Company, 1995).

Hellman, M., *Televisual Representations of France and the United Kingdom Under Globalization* (Stockholm: Department of Political Science, Stockholm University, 2006).

Herring, E., 'Military security', in A. Collins (ed.), *Contemporary Security Studies* (Oxford: Oxford University Press, 2007).

Howorth, J., 'Discourse, ideas and epistemic communities in European security and defence policy', *West European Politics* 27:2 (2004).

Hyde-Price, A., *European Security in the Twenty-First Century: The Challenge of Multipolarity* (London: Routledge, 2007).

Ischinger, W., 'Statement', 13 April 1999, in *Deutschlandfunk*.

Ischinger, W., 'Statement', 7 May 1999, in *Deutschlandfunk*.

Ischinger, W., 'Statement', 17 May 1999, in *ZDF-Morgenmagazin*.

Ivanov, I., 'Joint press conference with Madeleine Albright', 26 January 1999, *Diplomaticheskii Vestnik* 2 (1999).

Ivanov, I., 'Press conference', 25 March 1999, *Diplomaticheskii Vestnik* 4 (1999).

Ivanov, I., 'Press conference', 29 March 1999, *Diplomaticheskii Vestnik* 4 (1999).

Ivanov, I., 'Address to the participants at the first Russian global conference of the Russian media,' 21 June 1999, *Diplomaticheskii Vestnik* 7 (1999).

Ivanov, I., 'Address to the participants at the global conference for former foreign ministers,' 7 July 1999, *Diplomaticheskii Vestnik* 8 (1999).

Ivanov, I., 'Speech at MGIMO', 29 October 1999, *Diplomaticheskii Vestnik* 11 (1999).

Ivanov, I., 'Press conference', 13 June 2000, *Diplomaticheskii Vestnik* 8 (2000).

Ivanov, I., 'Address to the Russian Duma', 27 March 2003, *Diplomaticheskii Vestnik* 4 (2003).

Katzenstein, P. (ed.), *The Culture of National Security: Norms and Identity in World Politics* (New York: Columbia University Press, 1996).

Kennan, G., 'The sources of Soviet conduct', *Foreign Affairs* 25 (1947).

Keohane, R., *International Institutions and State Power: Essays in International Relations Theory* (Boulder: Westview Press, 1989).

Krause, K., 'Critical theory and security studies: The research programme of "critical security studies"', *Cooperation and Conflict* 33 (1998), pp. 298–333.

Krauthammer, C., 'The unipolar moment', *Foreign Affairs* 70:1 (1990/1991).

Kupchan, C., 'The rise of Europe, America's changing internationalism, and the end of US primacy', *Political Science Quarterly* 118:2 (2003).

Kuusisto, R., *Western Definitions of War in the Gulf and in Bosnia*, Commentationes Scientiarum Socialum 54 (Helsinki: Finska Vetenskaps-Societeten, 1999).

Leijins, A., 'The CFSP and the PCA: Between realpolitik and values', in A. Leijins (ed.), *The EU Common Foreign and Security Policy Toward Russia: The Partnership and Cooperation Agreement as a Test Case* (Riga: Latvian Institute of International Affairs, 2006).

Light, M., 'Political patterns and trends', Address at the conference 'Russia and the New Europe', Swedish Institute of International Affairs, 22 November 2005.

Lo, B., *Vladimir Putin and the Evolution of Russian Foreign Policy* (Oxford: Blackwell Publishing, 2003).

Lucarelli, S. and Manners, I. (eds), *Values and Principles in European Union Foreign Policy* (London: Routledge, 2006).

Lynch, D., 'Russia faces Europe', *Chaillot Papers 60* (European Union Institute for Security Studies, 2003).

Lynch, D., 'The new eastern dimension of the enlarged EU', in J. Batt et al., 'Partners and neighbours: A CFSP for a wider Europe', *Chaillot Papers 64* (European Union Institute for Security Studies, 2003).

Manners, I., 'Normative power Europe: A contradiction in terms?', *Journal of Common Market Studies* 40:2 (2002).

Manners, I., 'The constitutive nature of values, images and principles in the European Union', in S. Lucarelli and I. Manners (eds), *Values and Principles in European Union Foreign Policy* (London: Routledge, 2006).

Manners, I., 'Normative power Europe reconsidered: Beyond the crossroads', *Journal of European Public Policy* 13:2 (2006).

Marsh, S. and Mackensteins, H., *The International Relations of the European Union* (London: Longman, 2005).

Matlary, J., 'Human rights', *ARENA Working Paper* 19:3 (2003).

Matz, J., *Constructing a Post-Soviet International Political Reality* (Uppsala: ACTA Universitatis Upsaliensis, Statsvetenskapliga Föreningen, 2000).

McFaul, M., 'Russia and the West: A dangerous drift', *Current History* October (2005).

McSweeney, B., *Security, Identity and Interests: A Sociology of International Relations* (Cambridge: Cambridge University Press, 1999).

Meshkov, A., 'Russia and the European security architecture', *International Affairs* 48 (2002).

Milliken, J., 'The study of discourse in international relations: A critique of research and methods', *European Journal of International Relations* 5:2 (1999).

Morgenthau, H., *Politics Among Nations: The Struggle for Power and Peace*, revised by Keeth W. Thompson (Boston: McGrawHill, 1993/1948).

Moshes, A., 'Prospects for EU-Russia foreign and security policy cooperation', *The EU Russia Review* 2 (2006).

Moshes, A., Speech at the conference 'What next for EU–Russia relations', Stockholm, 13 February 2007.

Papandreo, G. A., 'Address to the European Parliament by the EU Presidency', 12 March 2003.

Papandreo, G. A., 'Lecture delivered at St Antony's College by the EU Presidency', University of Oxford, 6 May 2003.

Perelman, C., *The Realm of Rhetoric* (Notre Dame: University of Notre Dame Press, 1982).

Petersson, B., *National Self-Images and Regional Identities in Russia* (Aldershot: Ashgate, 2001).

Pinder J. and Shishkov, Y., *The EU and Russia: The Promise of Partnership* (London: The Federal Trust, 2002).

Pond, E., *Friendly Fire: The Near-death of the Transatlantic Alliance* (Pittsburg: European Union Studies Association, 2004).

Popescu, N., 'The EU in Moldova: Settling conflicts in the neighbourhood', *EU Institute for Security Studies Occasional Paper* 60 (2005).

Prozorov, S., *Understanding Conflict between Russia and the EU: The Limits of Integration* (New York: Basingstoke, 2006).

Putin, V., 'Interview with the German Newspaper *Welt am Sonntag*', 11 July 2000, *Diplomaticheskii Vestnik* 7 (2000).

Putin, V., 'Interview with CBS, CTV and RTR', 13 December 2000, *Diplomaticheskii Vestnik* 1 (2001).

Putin, V., 'Statement at joint press conference with Silvio Berlusconi', 3 February 2003, *Diplomaticheskii Vestnik* 3 (2003).

Putin, V., 'Address at the St Petersburg Summit', 11 April 2003, *Dipomaticheskii Vestnik* 5 (2003).

Roberts, C., *Russia and the European Union: The Sources and Limits of 'Special Relationships'* (Carlisle: Strategic Studies Institute, 2007).

Rochefort, D. and Cobb R. (eds), *The Politics of Problem Definition: Shaping the Policy Agenda* (Lawrence: University Press of Kansas, 1994).

Rontoyanni, C., 'So far, so good: Russia and the ESDP', *International Affairs* 78:4 (2002).

Ruggie, J., 'The anatomy of an institution', in J. Ruggie (ed.), *Multilateralism Matters: The Theory and Praxis of an Institutional Form* (New York: Columbia University Press, 1993).

Safanov, A., 'The world needs a global antiterrorist system', *International Affairs: A Russian Journal of World Politics, Diplomacy and International Relations* 2003 (49).

Schröder, G., Joint press conference with Jacques Chirac with France-2 and ARD, 22 January 2003.

Schröder, G., 'Speech on the occasion of the German Steinkohle-Betriebsrätevoll-versammlung', 29 January 2003.

Schröder, G., 'Speech on the occasion of the opening of the CeBIT', 11 March 2003.

Schröder, G., 'Address to the nation on the situation in Iraq', 18 March 2003.

Schröder, G., 'Address to the German Bundestag', 19 March 2003.

Schröder, G., 'Address on the beginning of the war in Iraq', 20 March 2003.

Schröder, G., 'Interview with *Die Zeit*', 27 March 2003.

Schröder, G., 'Interview with Sender Phoenix', 28 March 2003.

Schröder, G., 'Interview in 3SAT', 3 April 2003.

Schön, D. and Rein, M., *Frame Reflection: Towards the Resolution of Intractable Policy Controversies* (New York: Basic Books, 1994).

Sergeev, I., 'Press conference', 31 March 1999, *Diplomaticheskii Vestnik* 4 (1999).

Sjursen, H., 'Security and defence', *ARENA Working Papers* 10:3 (2003).

Skak, M., 'Russian security policy after 9/11', Paper prepared for the Joint International Convention of Central Eastern European International Studies Association and International Studies Association, Budapest, 26–28 June 2003.

Smith, M., *Europe's Foreign and Security Policy: The Institutionalization of Cooperation* (Cambridge: Cambridge University Press, 2004).

Snow, D. and Benford, R., 'Master frames and cycles of protest', in A. Morris and C. McClurg Mueller (eds), *Frontiers in Social Movement Theory* (New Haven, Conn.: Yale University Press, 1992)

Solana, J., 'Decision to ensure a more responsible Europe', *International Herald Tribune*, 14 January 2000.

Solana, J., 'A broad consensus against terrorism', *Financial Times*, 13 September 2001.

Strömvik, M., *To Act as a Union: Explaining the Development of the EU's Collective Foreign Policy* (Lund: Department of Political Science, 2005).

Takle, M., 'Towards a normalisation of German security and defence policy: German participation in international military operations', *ARENA Working Papers* 2:10 (2002).

Tonra B. and Christiansen, T. (eds), *Rethinking European Union Foreign Policy* (Manchester: Manchester University Press, 2004).

Trenin, D., 'Russia leaves the West', *Foreign Affairs*, 85:4 (2006).

Tsygankov, A., *Russia's Foreign Policy: Change and Continuity in National Identity* (Lanham, MD: Rowman & Littlefield, 2006).

Twitchett, K., *Europe and the World: The External Relations of the Common Market* (New York: St Martin's Press, 1976).

Vahl, M., 'A privileged partnership: EU–Russian relations in a comparative perspective', *DIIS Working Paper* 3 (2006)

Verheugen, G., Statement on SWR, 23 April 1999.

Verheugen, G., Statement on N-TV, 5 June 1999.

Volmer, L., 'Statement', 14 April 1999, *Deutschlandfunk*.

Volmer, L., 'Statement', 23 April 1999, *ZDF-Morgenmagazin*.

Volmer, L., 'Statement', 7 June 1999, *Deutschlandfunk*.

Waever, O., 'John G. Ruggie: transformation and institutionalization', in Iver Neumann and Ole Waever (eds), *The Future of International Relations Masters in the Making* (London: Routledge, 1997).

Wagnsson, C., *Russian Political Language and Public Opinion on the West, NATO and Chechnya: Securitisation Theory Reconsidered* (Stockholm: Statsvetenskapliga Institutionen, 2000).

Wagnsson, C., 'The alien and the traditional: The EU facing a transforming Russia', in J. Hallenberg and H. Karlsson (eds), *Changing Transatlantic Security Relations: Do the US, the EU and Russia Form a New Strategic Triangle?* (London: Routledge, 2006).

Wagnsson, C., 'The EU as strategic actor, "re-actor" or passive pole', in Jan Hallenberg and Kjell Engelbrekt (eds), *European Union and Strategy: An Emerging Actor* (London: Routledge, 2007).

Waltz, K., 'Structural realism after the Cold War', *International Security* 25:1 (2000).

Webber, M., 'Third-party inclusion in European Security and Defence Policy: A case study of Russia', *European Foreign Affairs Review* 6 (2001).

White, B., *Understanding European Foreign Policy* (Basingstoke: Palgrave, 2001).

Yeltsin, B., 'Statement on Russian Television', 24 March 1999, *Diplomaticheskii Vestnik* 4 (1999).

Yeltsin, B., 'Address to the Russian Federal Assembly', 30 March 1999, *Diplomaticheskii Vestnik* 4 (1999).

Yeltsin, B., 'Statement', *Nezavisimaia Gazeta*, 26 April 1999.

Yeltsin, B., 'Interview with Der Spiegel,' 28 June 1999, *Diplomaticheskii Vestnik* 7 (1999).

Yeltsin, B., 'Statement in the Kremlin', 31 August 1999, *Diplomaticheskii Vestnik* 9 (1999).

Zagorski, A., 'Russia and the shared neighbourhood', in D. Lynch (ed.), 'What Russia sees' *Chaillot Paper 74* (2005).

Zagorski, A., 'Russia and European institutions', in V. Baranovsky (ed.), *Russia and Europe: The Emerging Security Agenda*, Stockholm International Peace Research Institute (Oxford: Oxford University Press, 1997).

Zhdanov, A., 'Soviet policy and world politics', *The International Situation* (Moscow: Foreign Languages Publishing House, 1947).

Zolo, D., *Invoking Humanity: War, Law and Global Order* (London: Continuum, 2002)

Internet sources

The speeches and statements of Tony Blair were accessed from www.pm.gov.uk; www.publications.parliament.uk; and www.number-10.gov.uk.

The speeches and statements of Jacques Chirac were accessed from www.doc.diplomatie.fr.

The speeches and statements of Robin Cook were accessed from www.publications.parliament.uk; and www.fco.gov.uk.

Council of the European Union documents were obtained from www.consilium.europa.eu; and www.europarl.europa.eu.

The speeches and statements of Dominique de Villepin were accessed from www.doc.diplomatie.fr.

European Commission documents were accessed from http://europa.eu.

EU-Russia Summit Joint Statements were accessed from http://europa.eu; and www.delrus.cec.eu.

The speeches and statements of Benita Ferrero-Waldner were accessed from http://europa.eu.

The speeches and statements of Joscher Fischer were accessed from www.auswaertiges-amt.de; and http://213.61.121.230/www/de/index_html.

The speeches and statements of Igor Ivanov were accessed from www.mid.ru.

The speeches and statements of Lionel Jospin were accessed from www.doc.diplomatie.fr.

The speeches and statements of Chris Patten were accessed from http://europa.eu.

Radio Free Europe/Radio Liberty, Newsline, www.rferl.org.

The speeches and statements of Romano Prodi were accessed from http://europa.eu.

The speeches and statements of Vladimir Putin were accessed from www.mid.ru; http://president.kremlin.ru; and www.kremlin.ru.

The speeches and statements of Alain Richard were accessed from www.doc.diplo-matie.gouv.fr.

The speeches and statements of Jacques Santer were accessed from http://ec.europa.eu.

The speeches and statements of Gerhard Schröder were accessed from www.bundeskanzler.de; and www.bundestag.de.

The speeches and statements of Javier Solana were accessed from
www.consilium.europa.eu.

The speeches and statements of Jack Straw were accessed from www.publications.parliament.uk; and www.fco.gov.uk.

The speeches and statements of Hubert Védrine were accessed from www.doc.diplomatie.gouv.fr.

The speeches and statements of Ludger Volmer were accessed from www.auswaertiges-amt.de.

In addition, the following resources were consulted:

www.opinionjournal.com (Aznar et al., 30 January 2003)

www.labour.org.uk (British Labour Party Manifesto 2005)

http://bushlibrary.tamu.edu (Bush, 29 January 1991)

www.nti.org (Bush–Putin summit, 13–15 November 2001)

www.whitehouse.gov (Cheney, 26 September 2002)

www.guardian.co.uk/indonesia/Story/0,2763,190889,00.html (Cook, 12 May 1997)

www.eu2001.be (De Ruyt, 1 October 2001)

www.russiaeurope.mid.ru/concept.html (Foreign Policy Concept of the Russian Federation, 28 June 2000)

www.doc.diplomatie.fr (Joint Declaration by Russia, Germany and France, 5 March 2003)

http://europa.eu (Kastrup, 25 March 1999)

www.eu2001.be (Michel, 2 October 2001)

www.doc.diplomatie.fr (Moscovici, 6 May 1999)

www.russiaeurope.mid.ru (National Security Concept of the Russian Federation, 10 January 2000)

www.whitehouse.gov/nsc/nss.pdf (National Security Strategy of the United States of America, 17 September 2002)

www.fco.gov.uk/Files/kfile/EU_Russia_Summit_PC.pdf (Putin, 5 October 2005)

http://web.ebscohost.com (Putin, 23 August 2006)

www.kremlin.ru (Putin, 10 May 2006)

www.delrus.cec.eu.int/en/p_245.htm (Russia's Medium Term Strategy Towards the EU, 2000–2010)

http://trade-info.cec.eu.int (Russia's Trade With the EU)

www.germany.info (Schröder, 24 March 1999)

www.eu2003.gr (Simities, 26 March 2003)

www.patent-net.de/politik/koalitionsvereinbarung.html (Sozialdemokratischen Partei Deutschlands)

http://daccessdds.un.org/doc/UNDOC (Straw, 5 February 2003)

www.europarl.europa.eu (Treaty of Amsterdam)

Index

EU authorised representative for GPSR:
Easy Access System Europe, Mustamäe tee 50,
10621 Tallinn, Estonia
gpsr.requests@easproject.com